AVENGERS VOL. 3: PRELUDE TO INFINITY. Contains material originally published in magazine form as AVENGERS #12-17. First printing 2014. ISBN# 978-0-7851-6654-2. Published by MARVEL WORLDWIDE, INC., a subsidiary of MARVEL ENTERTAINMENT, LLC. OFFICE OF PUBLICATION: 135 West 50th Street, New York, NY 10020. Copyright © 2013 and 2014 Marvel Characters, Inc. All rights reserved. All characters featured in this issue and the distinctive names and likenesses thereof, and all related indicia are trademarks of Marvel Characters, Inc. No similarity between any of the names, characters, persons, and/or institutions in this magazine with those of any living or dead person or institution is intended, and any such similarity which may exist is purely coincidental. **Printed in the U.S.A.** ALAN FINE, EVP - Office of the President, Marvel Worldwide, Inc. and EVP & CMO Marvel Characters B.V.; DAN BUCKLEY, Publisher & President - Print, Animation & Digital Divisions; JOE QUESADA, Chief Creative Officer; TOM BREVOORT, SVP of Publishing; DAVID BOGART, SVP of Operations & Procurement, Publishing; C.B. CEBULSKI, SVP of Creator & Content Development; DAVID GABRIEL, SVP Print, Sales & Marketing; JIM O'KEEFE, VP of Operations & Logistics; DAN CARR, Executive Director of Publishing Technology; SUSAN CRESPI, Editorial Operations Manager; ALEX MORALES, Publishing Operations Manager; STAN LEE, Chairman Emeritus. For information regarding advertising in Marvel Comics or on Marvel.com, please contact Niza Disla, Director of Marvel Partnerships, at ndisla@marvel.com. For Marvel subscription inquiries, please call 800-217-9158. **Manufactured between 4/18/2014 and 5/26/2014 by R.R. DONNELLEY, INC., SALEM, VA, USA.**

10 9 8 7 6 5 4 3 2 1

AVENGERS

WRITERS: **JONATHAN HICKMAN & NICK SPENCER**

ARTIST, #12-13: **MIKE DEODATO**

ARTIST, #14-17: **STEFANO CASELLI** WITH MARCO RUDY & MARCO CHECCHETTO [#17]

COLOR ARTIST: **FRANK MARTIN** WITH EDGAR DELGADO [#15]

LETTERER: **VC'S CORY PETIT** WITH CLAYTON COWLES [#15]

COVER ART: **DUSTIN WEAVER & JUSTIN PONSOR** [#12]
AND **LEINIL FRANCIS YU & SUNNY GHO** [#13-17]

ASSISTANT EDITOR: **JAKE THOMAS**

EDITORS: **TOM BREVOORT WITH LAUREN SANKOVITCH**

COLLECTION EDITOR: **JENNIFER GRÜNWALD**
ASSISTANT EDITOR: **SARAH BRUNSTAD**
ASSOCIATE MANAGING EDITOR: **ALEX STARBUCK**
EDITOR, SPECIAL PROJECTS: **MARK D. BEAZLEY**
SENIOR EDITOR, SPECIAL PROJECTS: **JEFF YOUNGQUIST**
SVP PRINT, SALES & MARKETING: **DAVID GABRIEL**
BOOK DESIGN: **JEFF POWELL**

EDITOR IN CHIEF: **AXEL ALONSO**
CHIEF CREATIVE OFFICER: **JOE QUESADA**
PUBLISHER: **DAN BUCKLEY**
EXECUTIVE PRODUCER: **ALAN FINE**

"EVOLVE"

PREVIOUSLY IN AVENGERS

I AM AN ARTIST. I'M ATTEMPTING TO MAKE THE WORLD SENTIENT.

EACH BOMB I SENT CARRIED A SPECIFIC CHARGE. A TRAIT THAT ALL LIVING SPECIES POSSESS.

SELF-AWARENESS. REPRODUCTION.

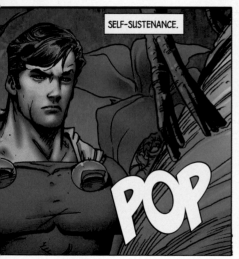

SELF-SUSTENANCE.

POP

POP

POP

POP

ŌŪŪŌ

OKAY...

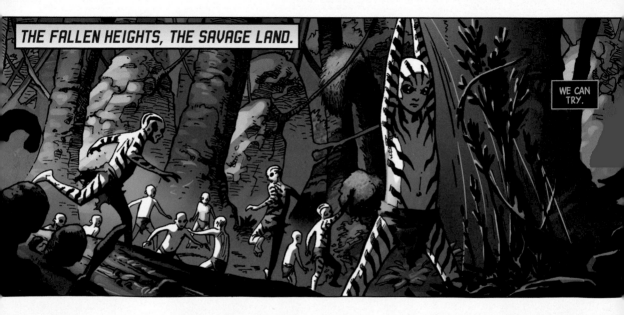

THE FALLEN HEIGHTS, THE SAVAGE LAND.

WE CAN TRY.

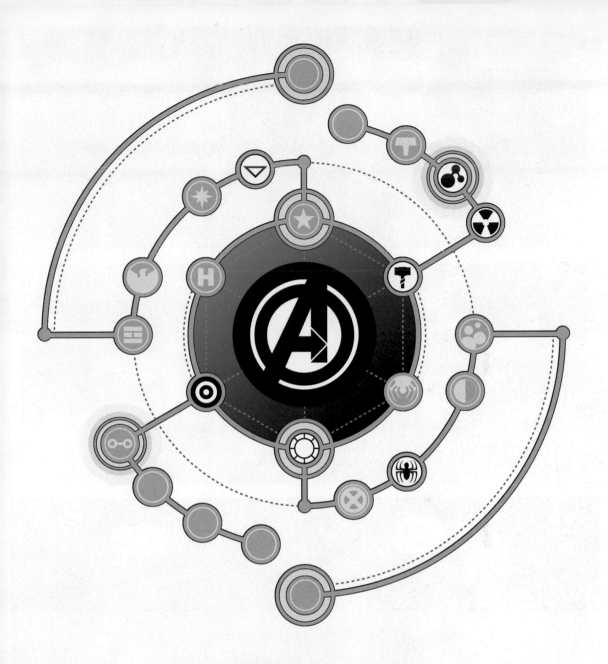

EARTH'S MIGHTIEST HEROES

CAPTAIN AMERICA · IRON MAN · THOR · HAWKEYE · BLACK WIDOW · HULK
WOLVERINE · SPIDER-MAN · CAPTAIN MARVEL · SPIDER-WOMAN
FALCON · SHANG-CHI · SUNSPOT · CANNONBALL · MANIFOLD
SMASHER · CAPTAIN UNIVERSE · HYPERION

"THE LEGEND OF CREATION, LAID BARE AND LAUGHING.

"THE UNIVERSE ITSELF BREAKING APART BEFORE THEIR EYES.

HELP THEM, FATHER--"

THEY ARE ONLY MEN.

THOR--A MOMENT?

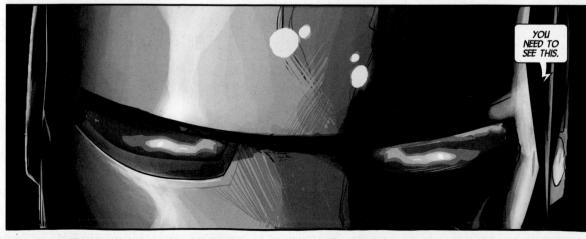

YOU NEED TO SEE THIS.

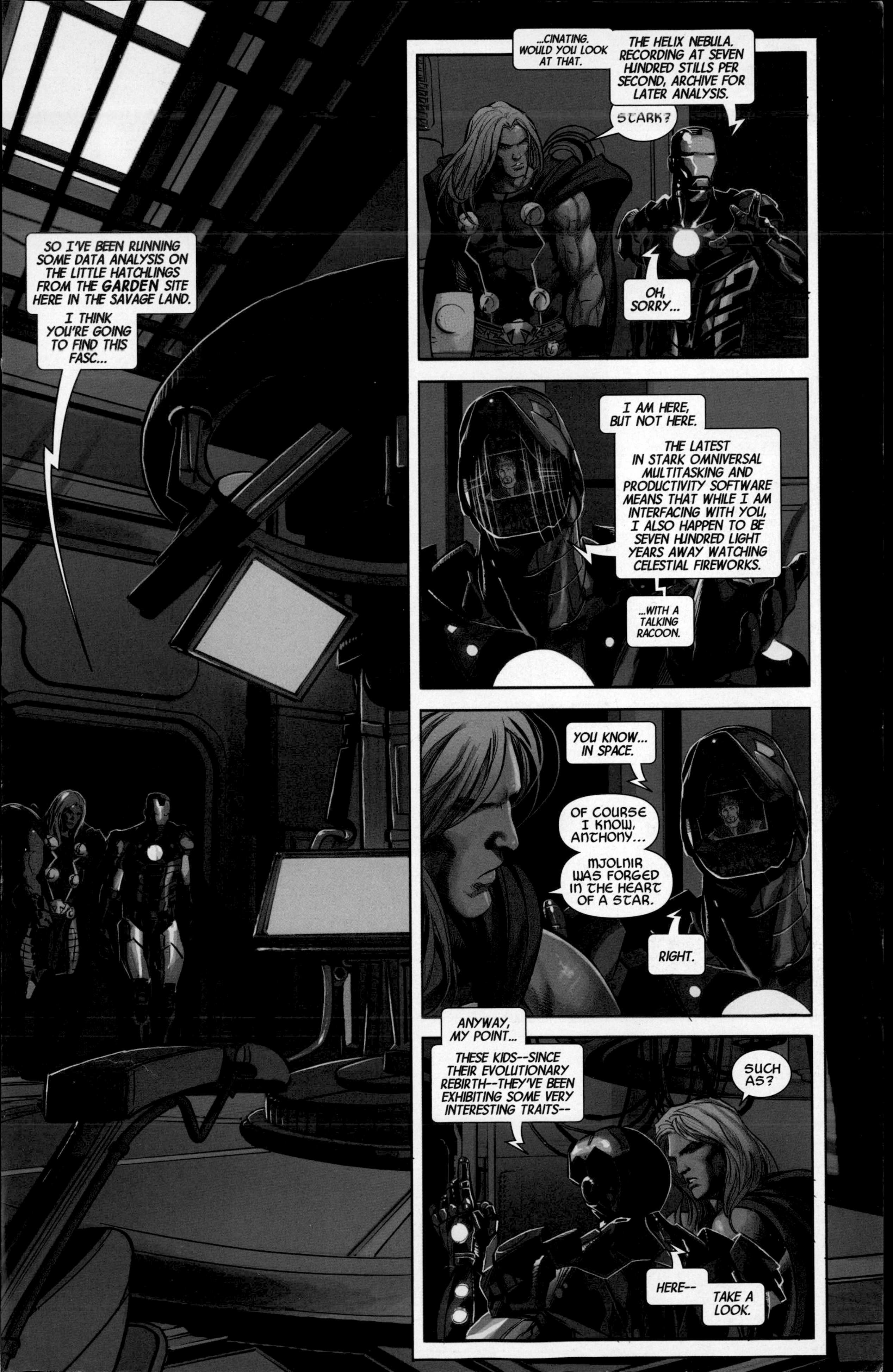
SO I'VE BEEN RUNNING SOME DATA ANALYSIS ON THE LITTLE HATCHLINGS FROM THE GARDEN SITE HERE IN THE SAVAGE LAND.
I THINK YOU'RE GOING TO FIND THIS FASC...
...CINATING. WOULD YOU LOOK AT THAT.
THE HELIX NEBULA. RECORDING AT SEVEN HUNDRED STILLS PER SECOND, ARCHIVE FOR LATER ANALYSIS.
STARK?
OH, SORRY...
I AM HERE, BUT NOT HERE.
THE LATEST IN STARK OMNIVERSAL MULTITASKING AND PRODUCTIVITY SOFTWARE MEANS THAT WHILE I AM INTERFACING WITH YOU, I ALSO HAPPEN TO BE SEVEN HUNDRED LIGHT YEARS AWAY WATCHING CELESTIAL FIREWORKS.
...WITH A TALKING RACOON.
YOU KNOW... IN SPACE.
OF COURSE I KNOW, ANTHONY...
MJOLNIR WAS FORGED IN THE HEART OF A STAR.
RIGHT.
ANYWAY, MY POINT...
THESE KIDS--SINCE THEIR EVOLUTIONARY REBIRTH--THEY'VE BEEN EXHIBITING SOME VERY INTERESTING TRAITS--
SUCH AS?
HERE--
TAKE A LOOK.

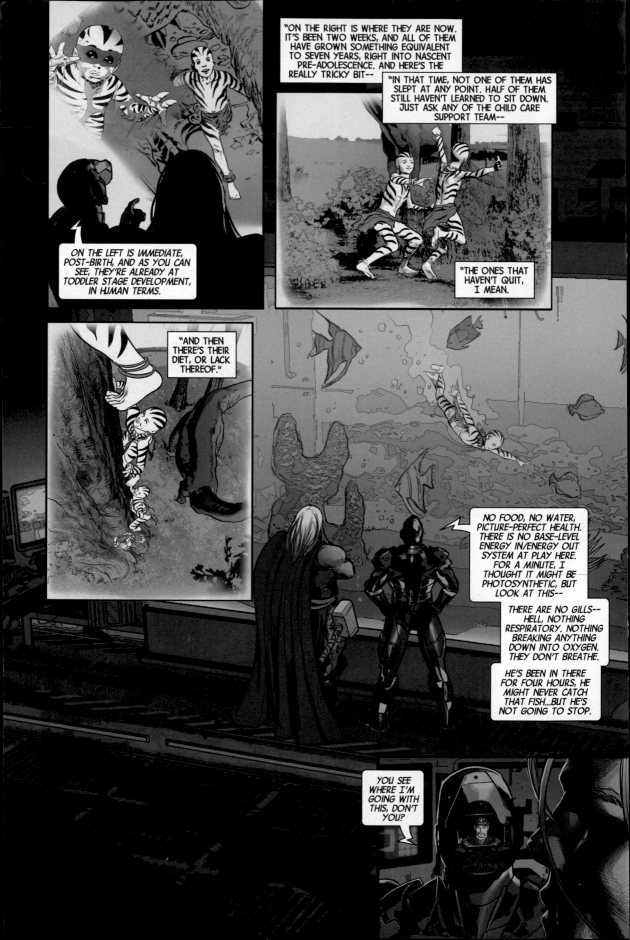

"ON THE RIGHT IS WHERE THEY ARE NOW. IT'S BEEN TWO WEEKS, AND ALL OF THEM HAVE GROWN SOMETHING EQUIVALENT TO SEVEN YEARS, RIGHT INTO NASCENT PRE-ADOLESCENCE. AND HERE'S THE REALLY TRICKY BIT--

"IN THAT TIME, NOT ONE OF THEM HAS SLEPT AT ANY POINT. HALF OF THEM STILL HAVEN'T LEARNED TO SIT DOWN. JUST ASK ANY OF THE CHILD CARE SUPPORT TEAM--

ON THE LEFT IS IMMEDIATE, POST-BIRTH, AND AS YOU CAN SEE, THEY'RE ALREADY AT TODDLER STAGE DEVELOPMENT, IN HUMAN TERMS.

"THE ONES THAT HAVEN'T QUIT, I MEAN.

"AND THEN THERE'S THEIR DIET, OR LACK THEREOF."

NO FOOD, NO WATER, PICTURE-PERFECT HEALTH. THERE IS NO BASE-LEVEL ENERGY IN/ENERGY OUT SYSTEM AT PLAY HERE. FOR A MINUTE, I THOUGHT IT MIGHT BE PHOTOSYNTHETIC, BUT LOOK AT THIS--

THERE ARE NO GILLS-- HELL, NOTHING RESPIRATORY. NOTHING BREAKING ANYTHING DOWN INTO OXYGEN. THEY DON'T BREATHE.

HE'S BEEN IN THERE FOR FOUR HOURS, HE MIGHT NEVER CATCH THAT FISH...BUT HE'S NOT GOING TO STOP.

YOU SEE WHERE I'M GOING WITH THIS, DON'T YOU?

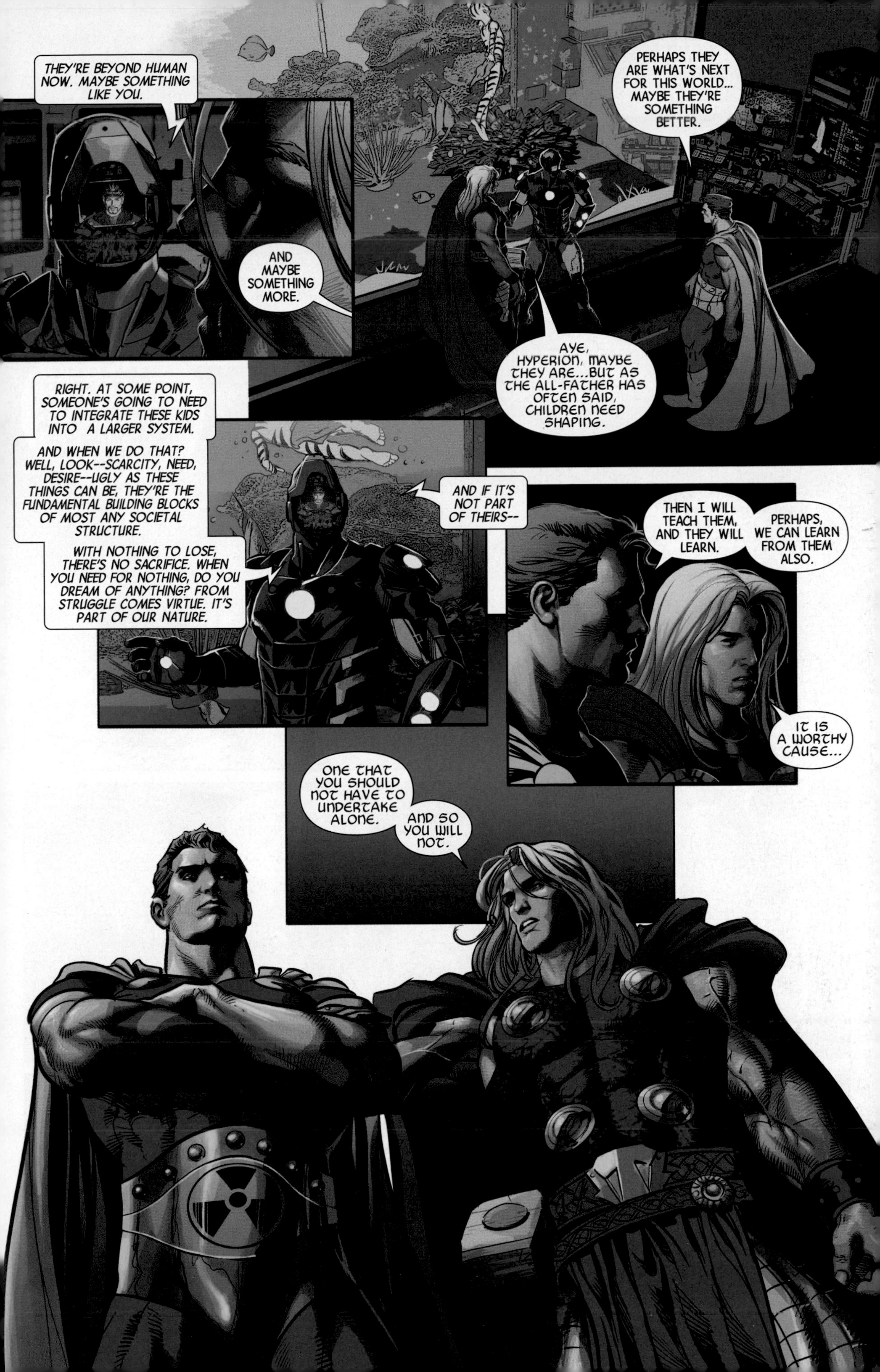
THEY'RE BEYOND HUMAN NOW. MAYBE SOMETHING LIKE YOU.
AND MAYBE SOMETHING MORE.
PERHAPS THEY ARE WHAT'S NEXT FOR THIS WORLD... MAYBE THEY'RE SOMETHING BETTER.
AYE, HYPERION, MAYBE THEY ARE...BUT AS THE ALL-FATHER HAS OFTEN SAID, CHILDREN NEED SHAPING.
RIGHT. AT SOME POINT, SOMEONE'S GOING TO NEED TO INTEGRATE THESE KIDS INTO A LARGER SYSTEM.
AND WHEN WE DO THAT? WELL, LOOK--SCARCITY, NEED, DESIRE--UGLY AS THESE THINGS CAN BE, THEY'RE THE FUNDAMENTAL BUILDING BLOCKS OF MOST ANY SOCIETAL STRUCTURE.
WITH NOTHING TO LOSE, THERE'S NO SACRIFICE. WHEN YOU NEED FOR NOTHING, DO YOU DREAM OF ANYTHING? FROM STRUGGLE COMES VIRTUE. IT'S PART OF OUR NATURE.
AND IF IT'S NOT PART OF THEIRS--
THEN I WILL TEACH THEM, AND THEY WILL LEARN.
PERHAPS, WE CAN LEARN FROM THEM ALSO.
IT IS A WORTHY CAUSE...
ONE THAT YOU SHOULD NOT HAVE TO UNDERTAKE ALONE.
AND SO YOU WILL NOT.

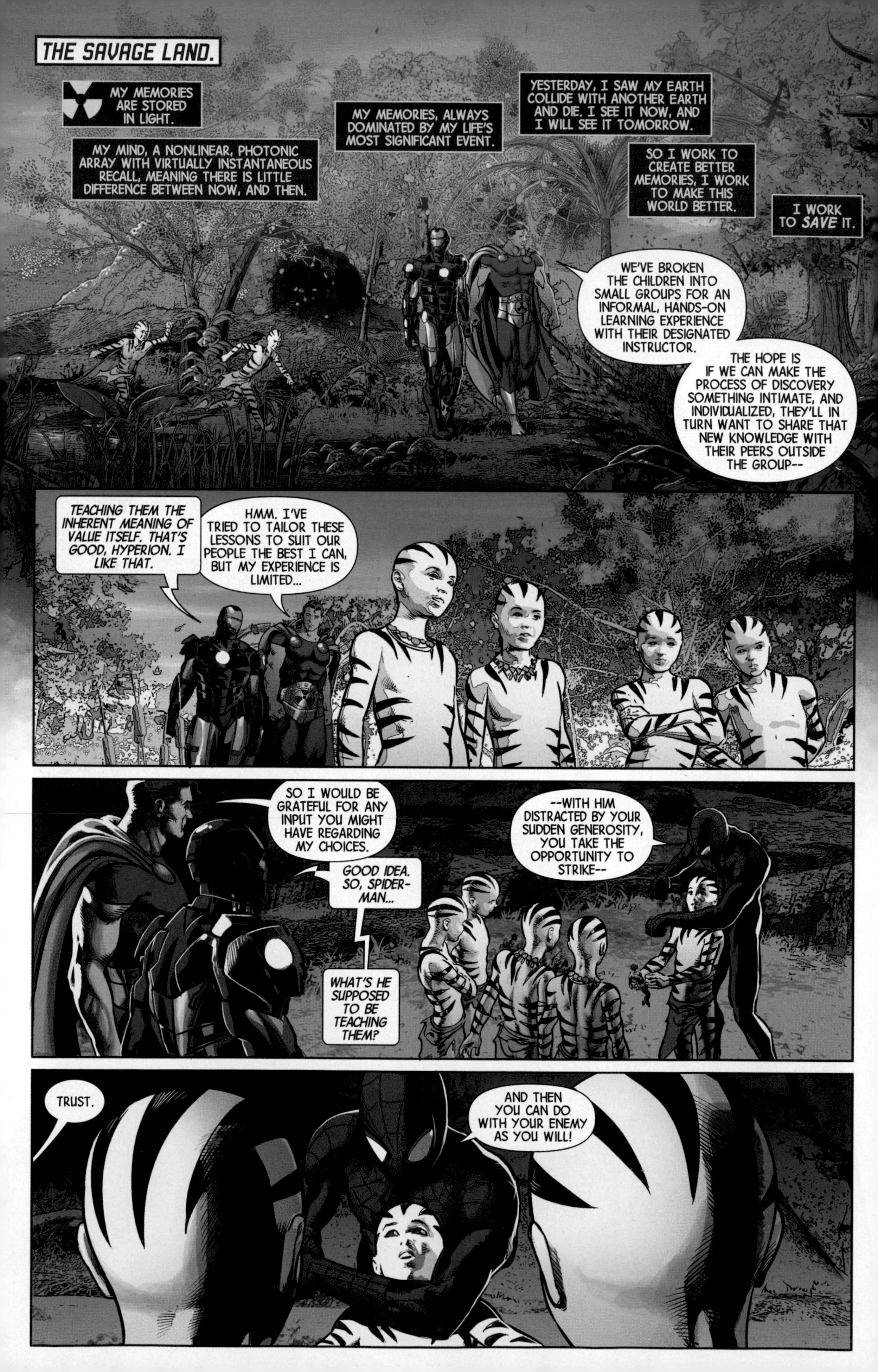
THE SAVAGE LAND.
MY MEMORIES ARE STORED IN LIGHT.
MY MIND, A NONLINEAR, PHOTONIC ARRAY WITH VIRTUALLY INSTANTANEOUS RECALL, MEANING THERE IS LITTLE DIFFERENCE BETWEEN NOW, AND THEN.
MY MEMORIES, ALWAYS DOMINATED BY MY LIFE'S MOST SIGNIFICANT EVENT.
YESTERDAY, I SAW MY EARTH COLLIDE WITH ANOTHER EARTH AND DIE. I SEE IT NOW, AND I WILL SEE IT TOMORROW.
SO I WORK TO CREATE BETTER MEMORIES, I WORK TO MAKE THIS WORLD BETTER.
I WORK TO SAVE IT.
WE'VE BROKEN THE CHILDREN INTO SMALL GROUPS FOR AN INFORMAL, HANDS-ON LEARNING EXPERIENCE WITH THEIR DESIGNATED INSTRUCTOR.
THE HOPE IS IF WE CAN MAKE THE PROCESS OF DISCOVERY SOMETHING INTIMATE, AND INDIVIDUALIZED, THEY'LL IN TURN WANT TO SHARE THAT NEW KNOWLEDGE WITH THEIR PEERS OUTSIDE THE GROUP--
TEACHING THEM THE INHERENT MEANING OF VALUE ITSELF. THAT'S GOOD, HYPERION. I LIKE THAT.
HMM. I'VE TRIED TO TAILOR THESE LESSONS TO SUIT OUR PEOPLE THE BEST I CAN, BUT MY EXPERIENCE IS LIMITED...
SO I WOULD BE GRATEFUL FOR ANY INPUT YOU MIGHT HAVE REGARDING MY CHOICES.
GOOD IDEA. SO, SPIDER-MAN...
WHAT'S HE SUPPOSED TO BE TEACHING THEM?
--WITH HIM DISTRACTED BY YOUR SUDDEN GENEROSITY, YOU TAKE THE OPPORTUNITY TO STRIKE--
TRUST.
AND THEN YOU CAN DO WITH YOUR ENEMY AS YOU WILL!

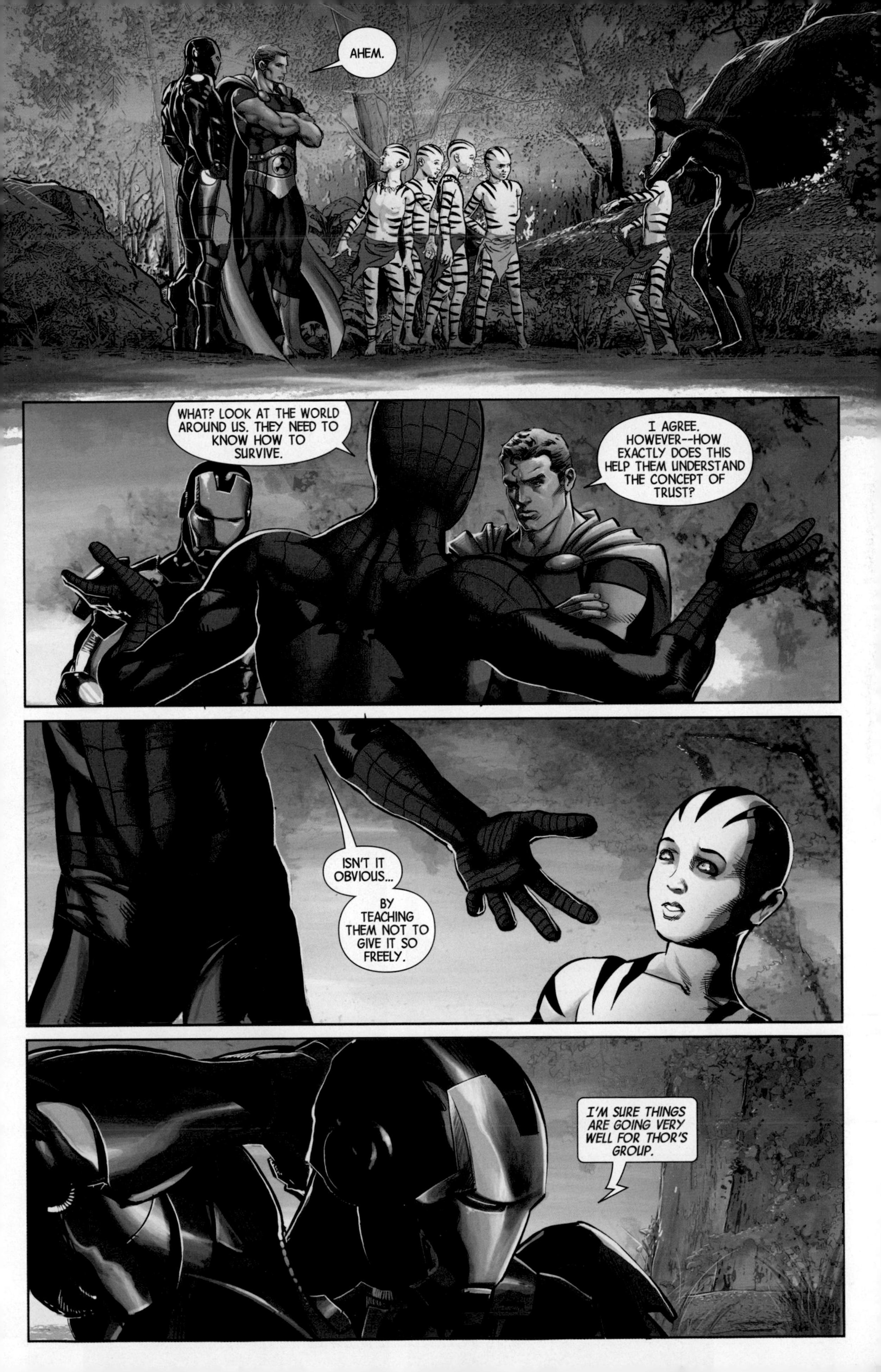
AHEM.
WHAT? LOOK AT THE WORLD AROUND US. THEY NEED TO KNOW HOW TO SURVIVE.
I AGREE. HOWEVER--HOW EXACTLY DOES THIS HELP THEM UNDERSTAND THE CONCEPT OF TRUST?
ISN'T IT OBVIOUS...
BY TEACHING THEM NOT TO GIVE IT SO FREELY.
I'M SURE THINGS ARE GOING VERY WELL FOR THOR'S GROUP.

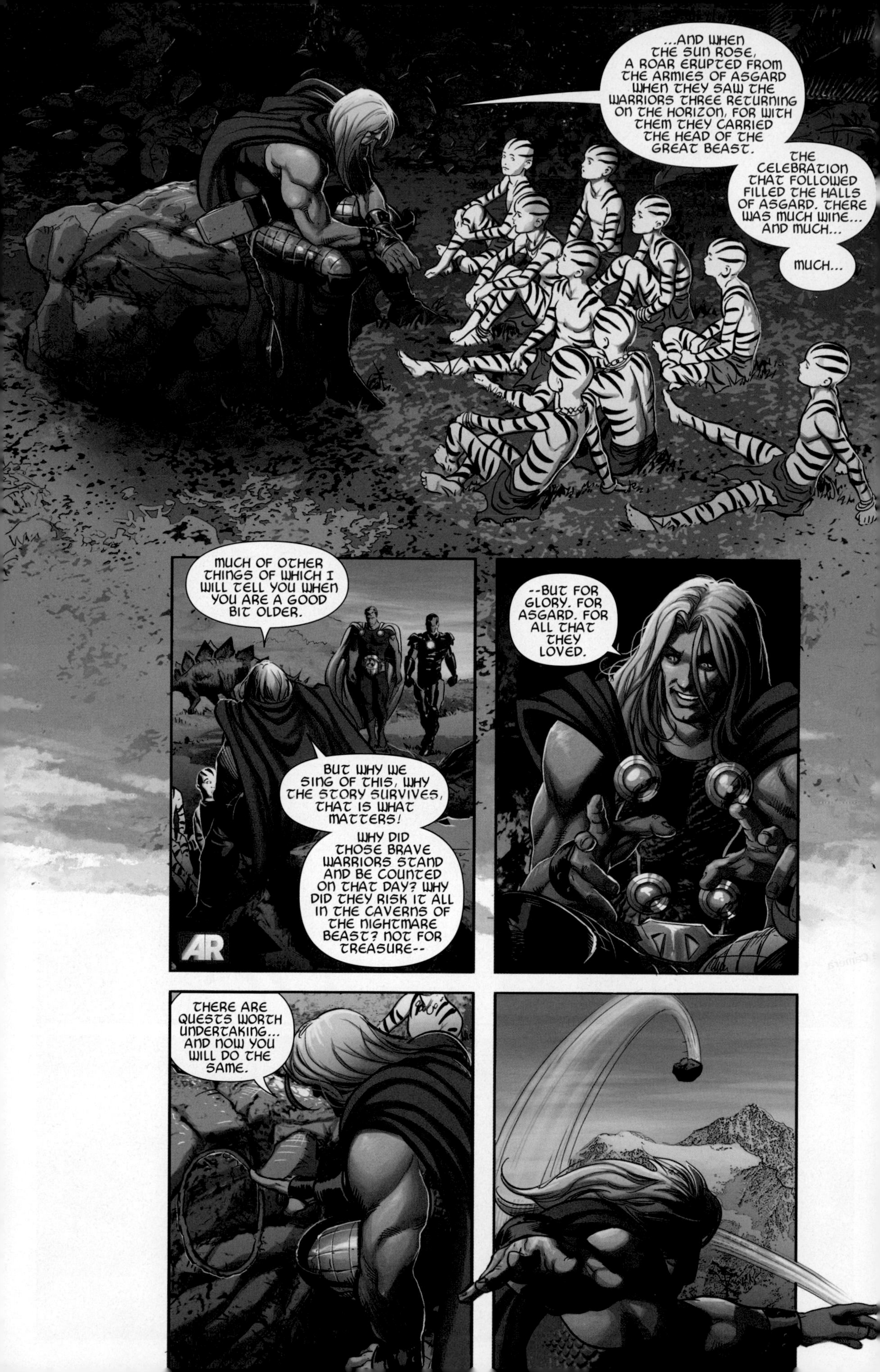
...AND WHEN THE SUN ROSE, A ROAR ERUPTED FROM THE ARMIES OF ASGARD WHEN THEY SAW THE WARRIORS THREE RETURNING ON THE HORIZON, FOR WITH THEM THEY CARRIED THE HEAD OF THE GREAT BEAST.
THE CELEBRATION THAT FOLLOWED FILLED THE HALLS OF ASGARD. THERE WAS MUCH WINE... AND MUCH...
MUCH...
MUCH OF OTHER THINGS OF WHICH I WILL TELL YOU WHEN YOU ARE A GOOD BIT OLDER.
BUT WHY WE SING OF THIS, WHY THE STORY SURVIVES, THAT IS WHAT MATTERS!
WHY DID THOSE BRAVE WARRIORS STAND AND BE COUNTED ON THAT DAY? WHY DID THEY RISK IT ALL IN THE CAVERNS OF THE NIGHTMARE BEAST? NOT FOR TREASURE--
AR
--BUT FOR GLORY. FOR ASGARD. FOR ALL THAT THEY LOVED.
THERE ARE QUESTS WORTH UNDERTAKING... AND NOW YOU WILL DO THE SAME.

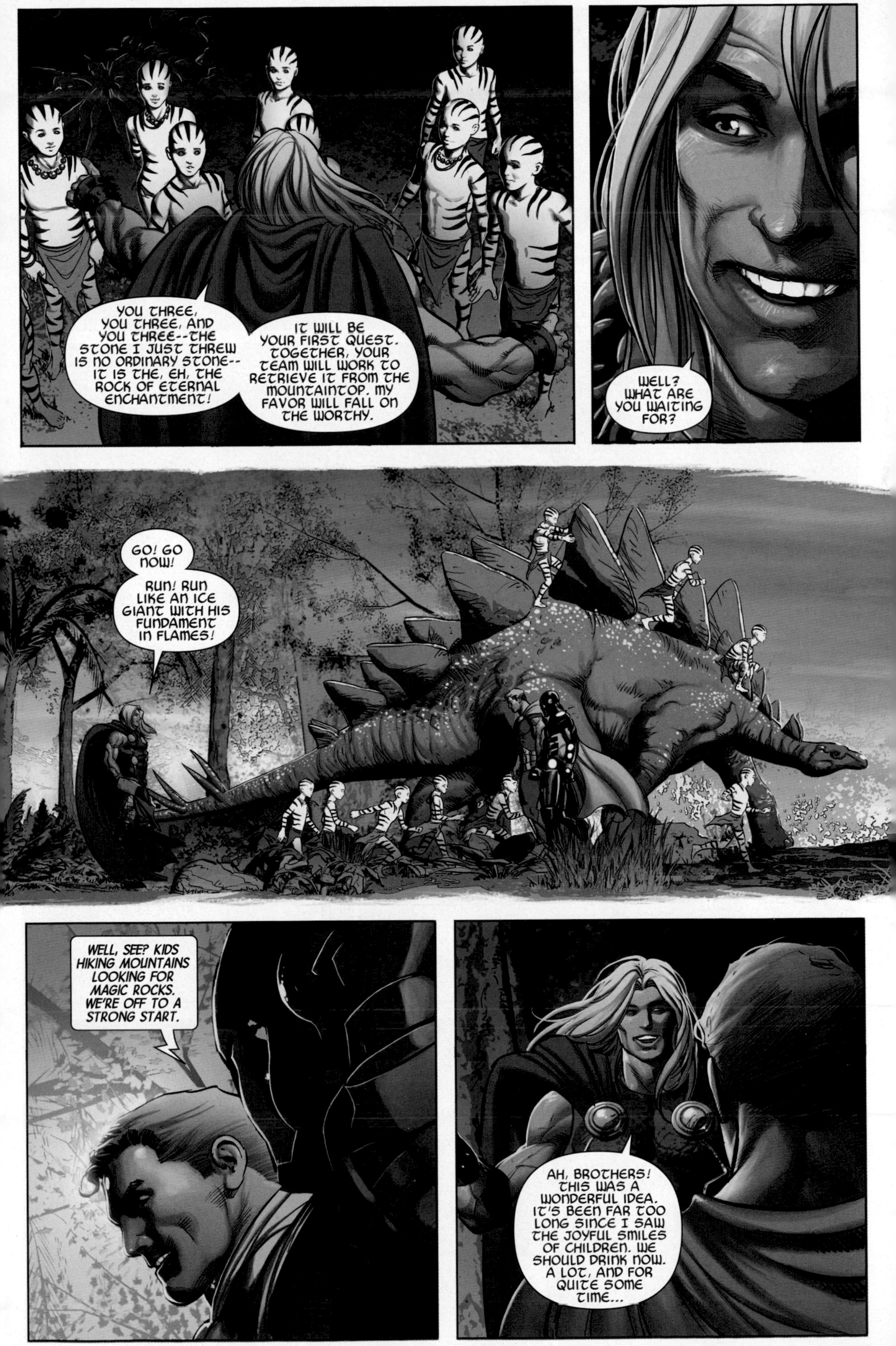

YOU THREE, YOU THREE, AND YOU THREE--THE STONE I JUST THREW IS NO ORDINARY STONE-- IT IS THE, EH, THE ROCK OF ETERNAL ENCHANTMENT!
IT WILL BE YOUR FIRST QUEST. TOGETHER, YOUR TEAM WILL WORK TO RETRIEVE IT FROM THE MOUNTAINTOP. MY FAVOR WILL FALL ON THE WORTHY.
WELL? WHAT ARE YOU WAITING FOR?
GO! GO NOW!
RUN! RUN LIKE AN ICE GIANT WITH HIS FUNDAMENT IN FLAMES!
WELL, SEE? KIDS HIKING MOUNTAINS LOOKING FOR MAGIC ROCKS. WE'RE OFF TO A STRONG START.
AH, BROTHERS! THIS WAS A WONDERFUL IDEA. IT'S BEEN FAR TOO LONG SINCE I SAW THE JOYFUL SMILES OF CHILDREN. WE SHOULD DRINK NOW. A LOT, AND FOR QUITE SOME TIME...

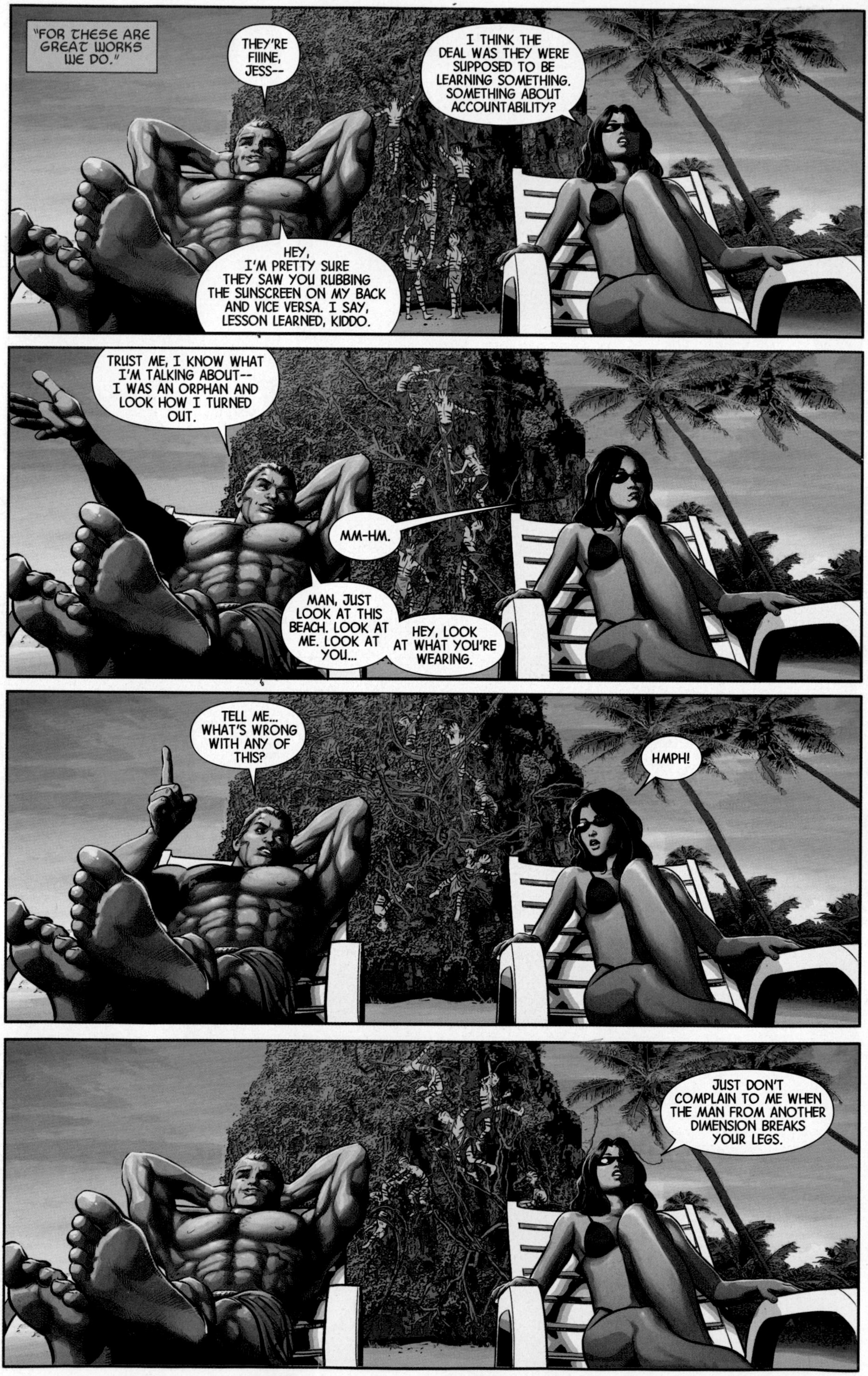
"FOR THESE ARE GREAT WORKS WE DO."
THEY'RE FIIINE, JESS--
I THINK THE DEAL WAS THEY WERE SUPPOSED TO BE LEARNING SOMETHING. SOMETHING ABOUT ACCOUNTABILITY?
HEY, I'M PRETTY SURE THEY SAW YOU RUBBING THE SUNSCREEN ON MY BACK AND VICE VERSA. I SAY, LESSON LEARNED, KIDDO.
TRUST ME, I KNOW WHAT I'M TALKING ABOUT-- I WAS AN ORPHAN AND LOOK HOW I TURNED OUT.
MM-HM.
MAN, JUST LOOK AT THIS BEACH. LOOK AT ME. LOOK AT YOU...
HEY, LOOK AT WHAT YOU'RE WEARING.
TELL ME... WHAT'S WRONG WITH ANY OF THIS?
HMPH!
JUST DON'T COMPLAIN TO ME WHEN THE MAN FROM ANOTHER DIMENSION BREAKS YOUR LEGS.

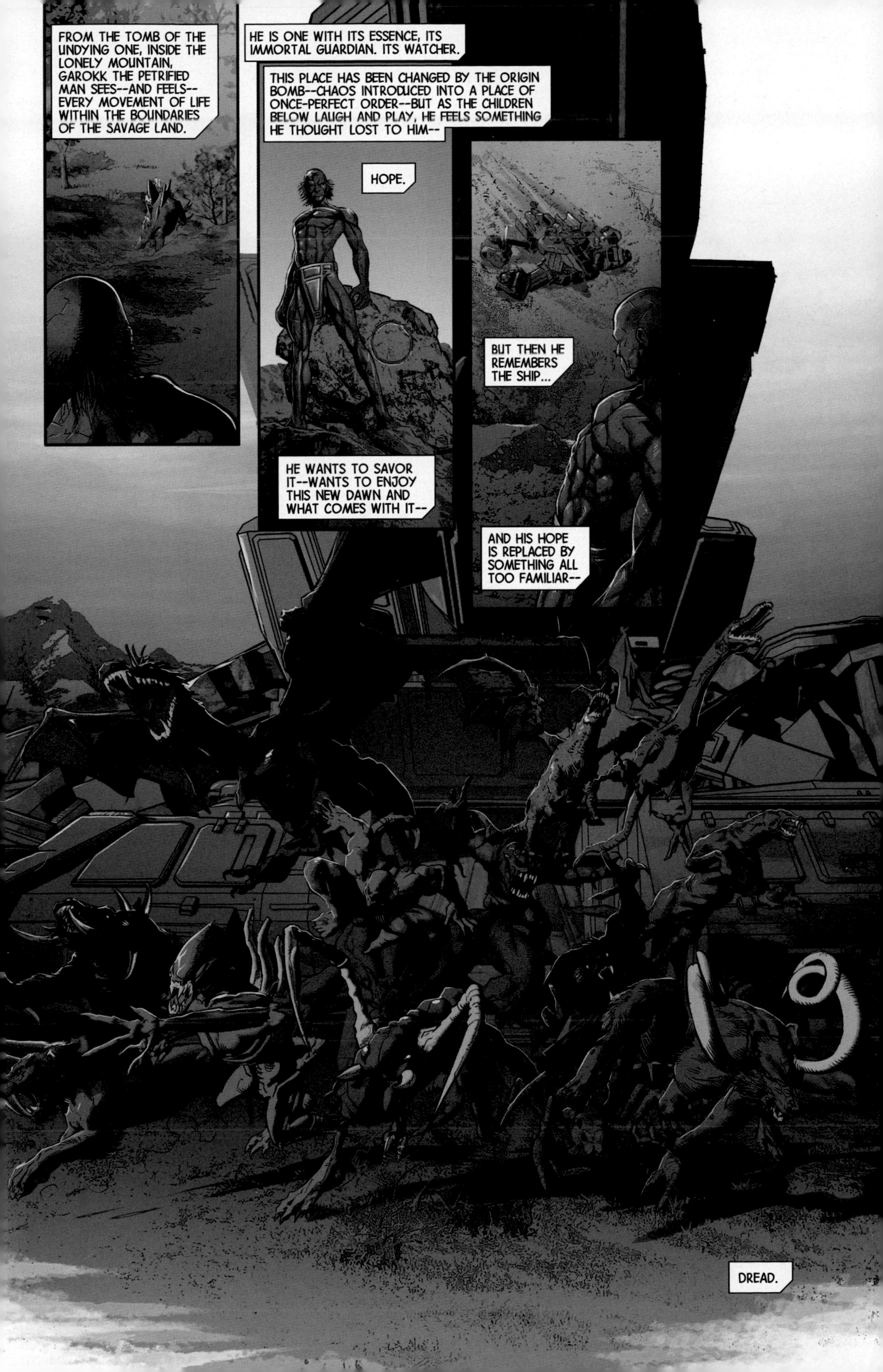
FROM THE TOMB OF THE UNDYING ONE, INSIDE THE LONELY MOUNTAIN, GAROKK THE PETRIFIED MAN SEES--AND FEELS--EVERY MOVEMENT OF LIFE WITHIN THE BOUNDARIES OF THE SAVAGE LAND.
HE IS ONE WITH ITS ESSENCE, ITS IMMORTAL GUARDIAN. ITS WATCHER.
THIS PLACE HAS BEEN CHANGED BY THE ORIGIN BOMB--CHAOS INTRODUCED INTO A PLACE OF ONCE-PERFECT ORDER--BUT AS THE CHILDREN BELOW LAUGH AND PLAY, HE FEELS SOMETHING HE THOUGHT LOST TO HIM--
HOPE.
HE WANTS TO SAVOR IT--WANTS TO ENJOY THIS NEW DAWN AND WHAT COMES WITH IT--
BUT THEN HE REMEMBERS THE SHIP...
AND HIS HOPE IS REPLACED BY SOMETHING ALL TOO FAMILIAR--
DREAD.

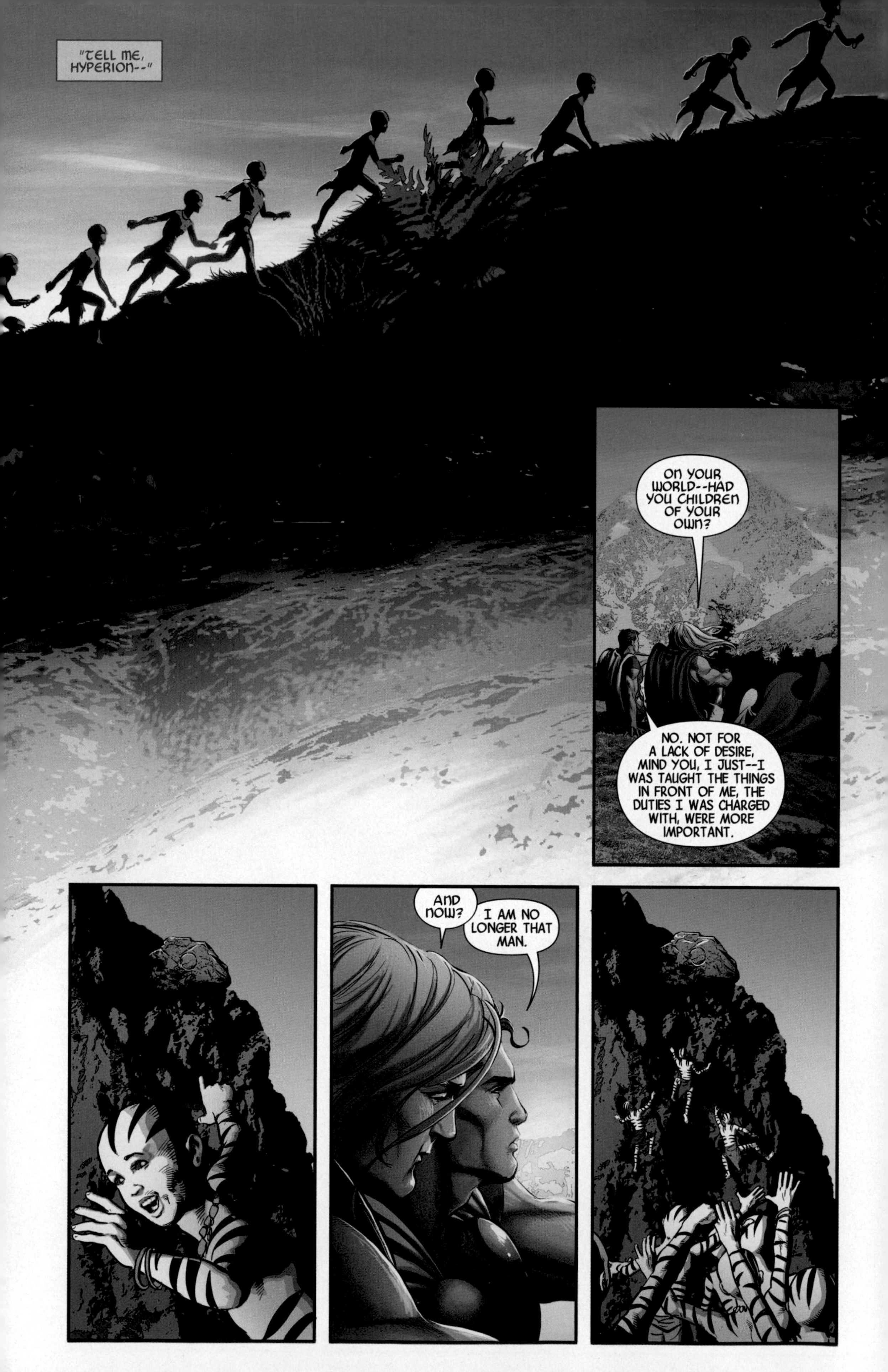
"TELL ME, HYPERION--"
ON YOUR WORLD--HAD YOU CHILDREN OF YOUR OWN?
NO. NOT FOR A LACK OF DESIRE, MIND YOU, I JUST--I WAS TAUGHT THE THINGS IN FRONT OF ME, THE DUTIES I WAS CHARGED WITH, WERE MORE IMPORTANT.
AND NOW?
I AM NO LONGER THAT MAN.

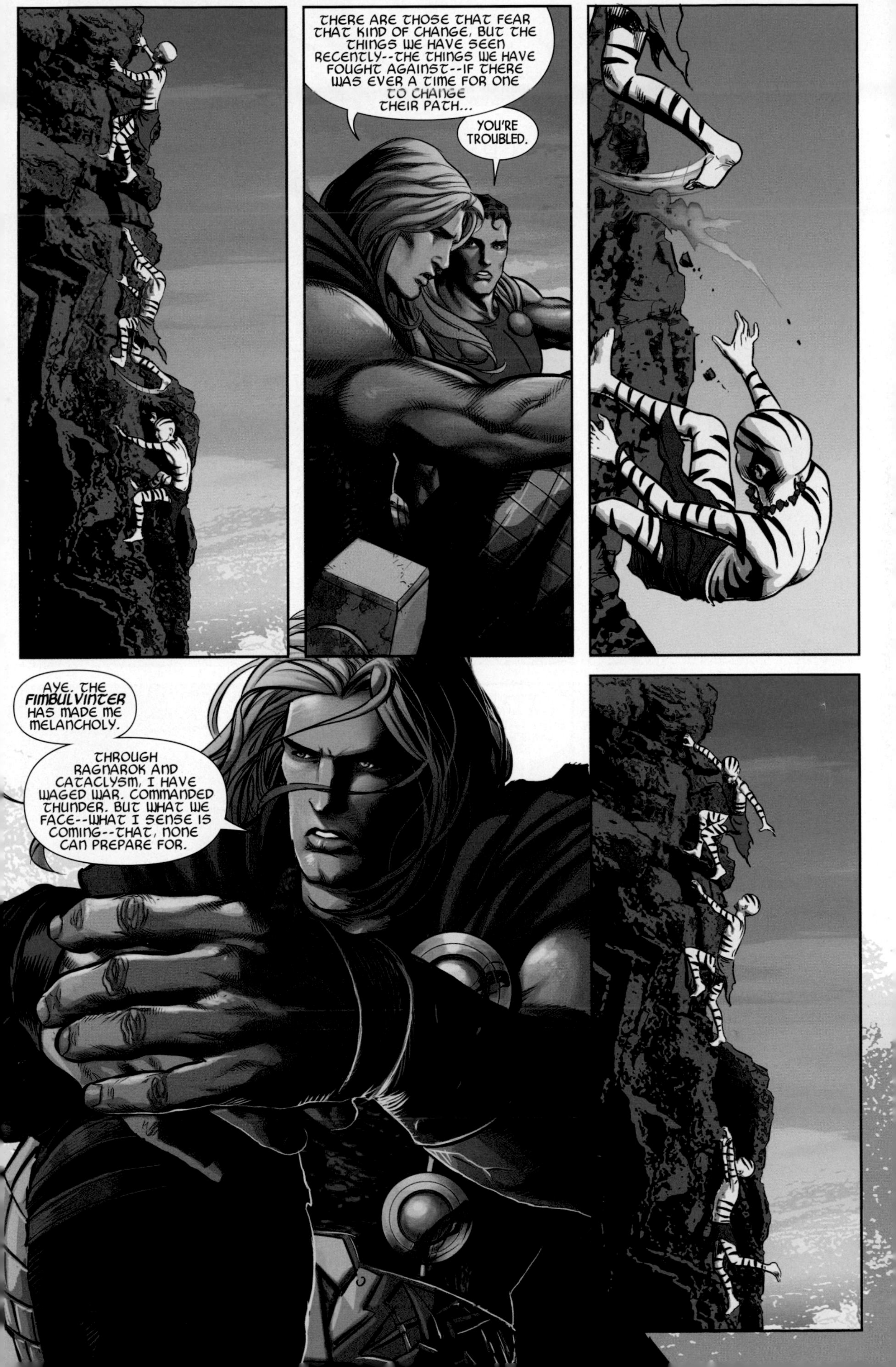

THERE ARE THOSE THAT FEAR THAT KIND OF CHANGE, BUT THE THINGS WE HAVE SEEN RECENTLY--THE THINGS WE HAVE FOUGHT AGAINST--IF THERE WAS EVER A TIME FOR ONE TO CHANGE THEIR PATH...
YOU'RE TROUBLED.
AYE. THE FIMBULVINTER HAS MADE ME MELANCHOLY.
THROUGH RAGNAROK AND CATACLYSM, I HAVE WAGED WAR. COMMANDED THUNDER. BUT WHAT WE FACE--WHAT I SENSE IS COMING--THAT, NONE CAN PREPARE FOR.

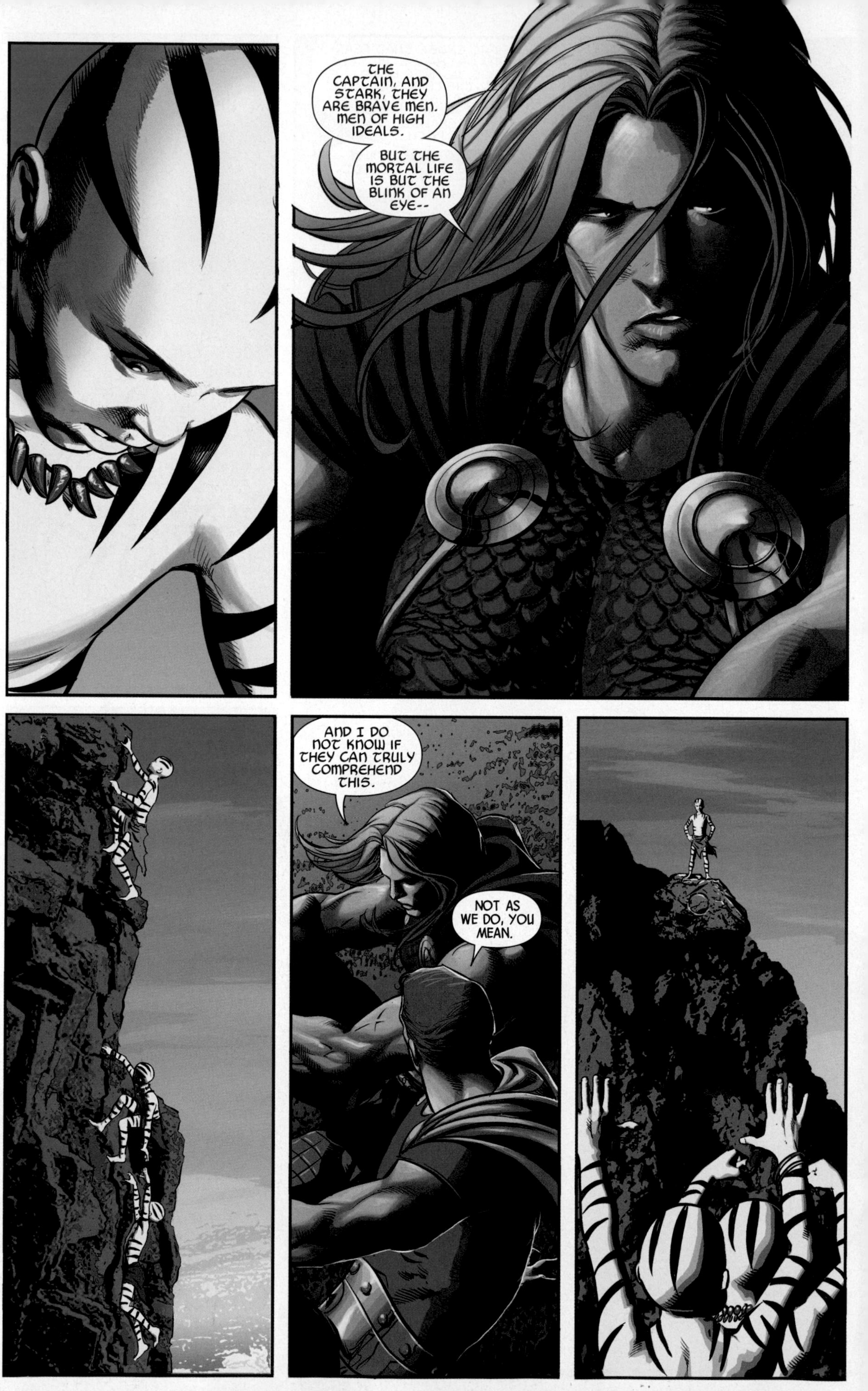
THE CAPTAIN, AND STARK, THEY ARE BRAVE MEN. MEN OF HIGH IDEALS.
BUT THE MORTAL LIFE IS BUT THE BLINK OF AN EYE--
AND I DO NOT KNOW IF THEY CAN TRULY COMPREHEND THIS.
NOT AS WE DO, YOU MEAN.

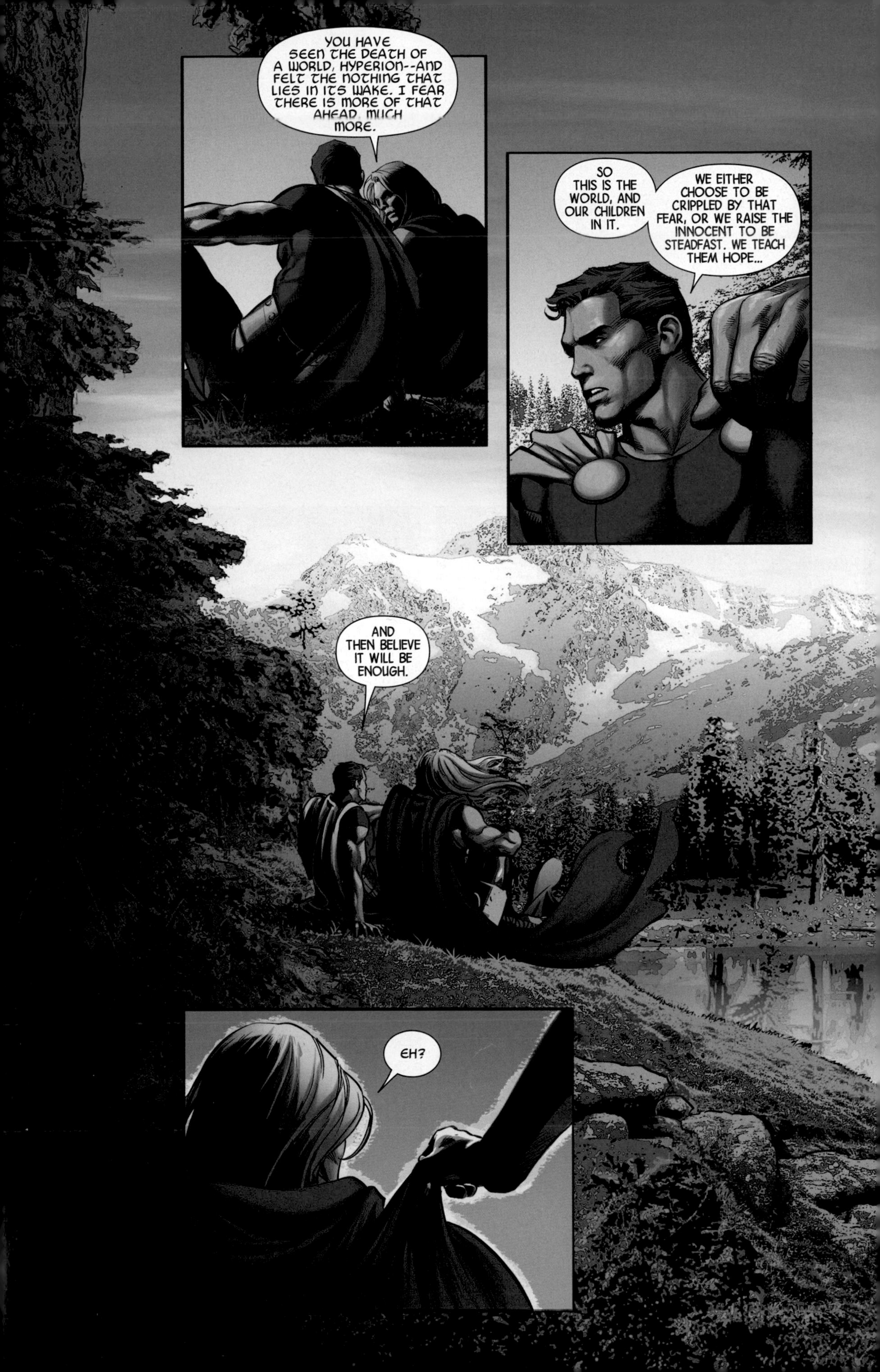
YOU HAVE SEEN THE DEATH OF A WORLD, HYPERION--AND FELT THE NOTHING THAT LIES IN ITS WAKE. I FEAR THERE IS MORE OF THAT AHEAD. MUCH MORE.
SO THIS IS THE WORLD, AND OUR CHILDREN IN IT.
WE EITHER CHOOSE TO BE CRIPPLED BY THAT FEAR, OR WE RAISE THE INNOCENT TO BE STEADFAST. WE TEACH THEM HOPE...
AND THEN BELIEVE IT WILL BE ENOUGH.
EH?

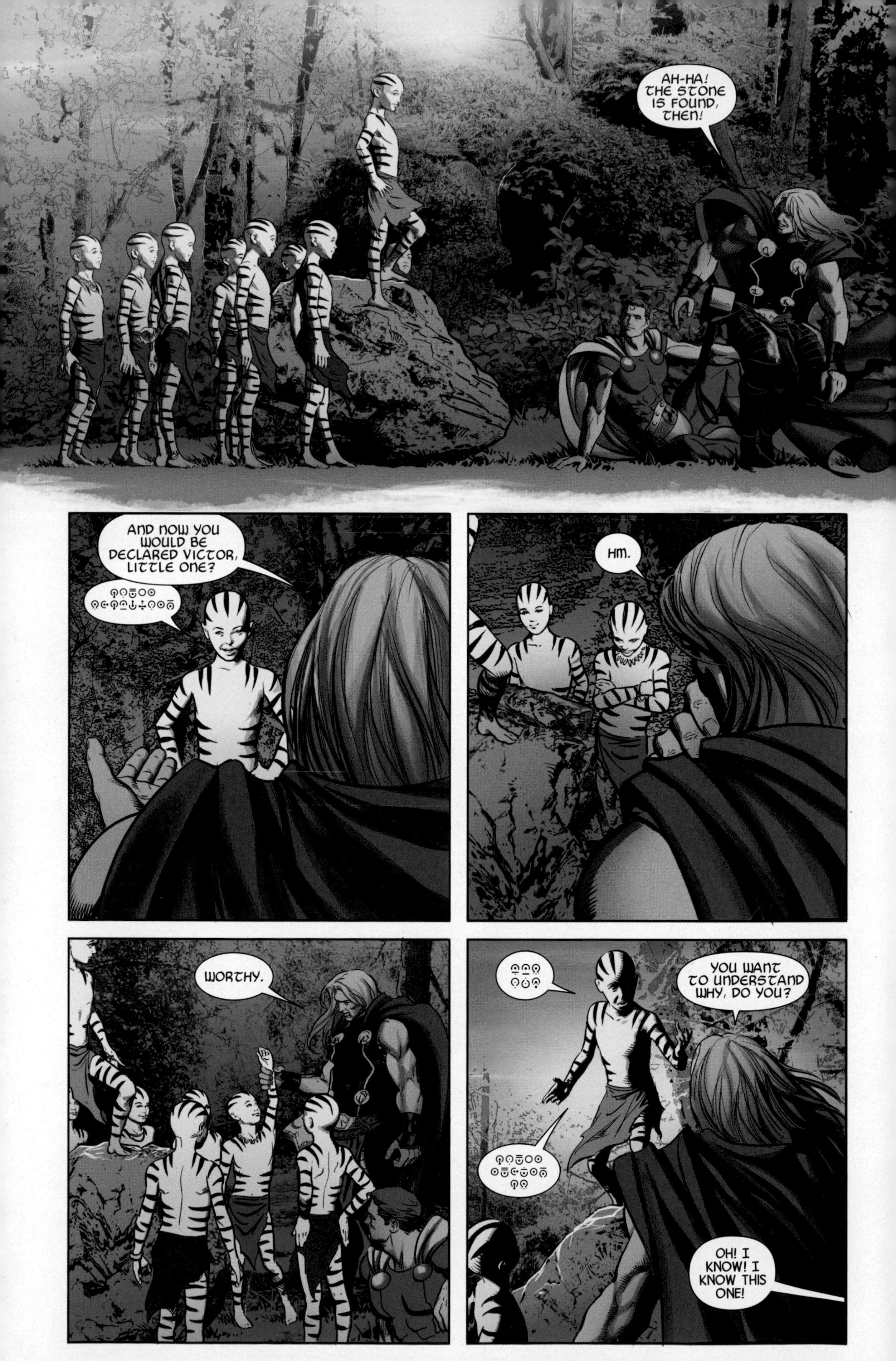
AH-HA! THE STONE IS FOUND, THEN!
AND NOW YOU WOULD BE DECLARED VICTOR, LITTLE ONE?
HM.
WORTHY.
YOU WANT TO UNDERSTAND WHY, DO YOU?
OH! I KNOW! I KNOW THIS ONE!

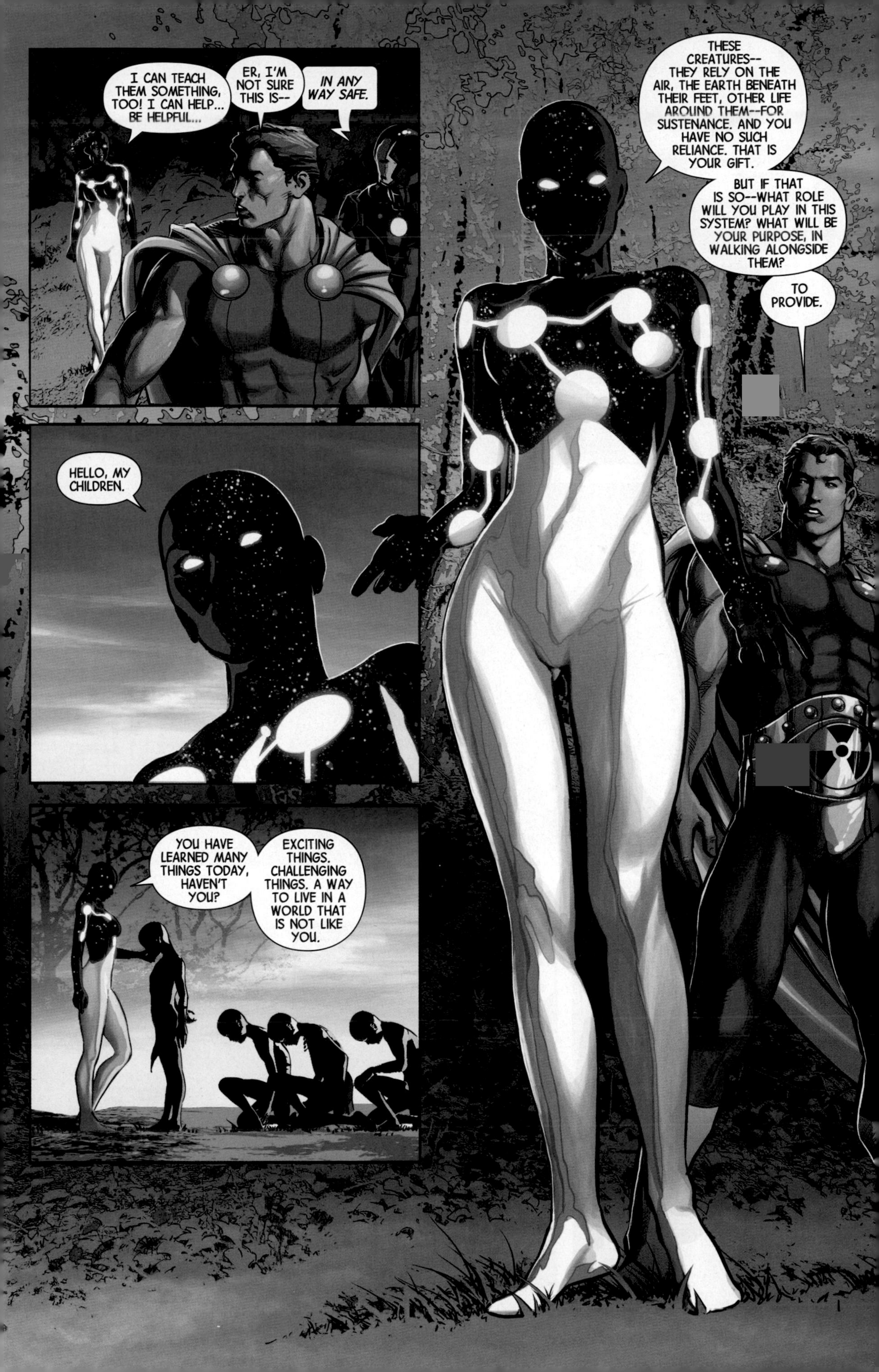

I CAN TEACH THEM SOMETHING, TOO! I CAN HELP... BE HELPFUL...
ER, I'M NOT SURE THIS IS--
IN ANY WAY SAFE.
HELLO, MY CHILDREN.
YOU HAVE LEARNED MANY THINGS TODAY, HAVEN'T YOU?
EXCITING THINGS. CHALLENGING THINGS. A WAY TO LIVE IN A WORLD THAT IS NOT LIKE YOU.
THESE CREATURES-- THEY RELY ON THE AIR, THE EARTH BENEATH THEIR FEET, OTHER LIFE AROUND THEM--FOR SUSTENANCE. AND YOU HAVE NO SUCH RELIANCE. THAT IS YOUR GIFT.
BUT IF THAT IS SO--WHAT ROLE WILL YOU PLAY IN THIS SYSTEM? WHAT WILL BE YOUR PURPOSE, IN WALKING ALONGSIDE THEM?
TO PROVIDE.

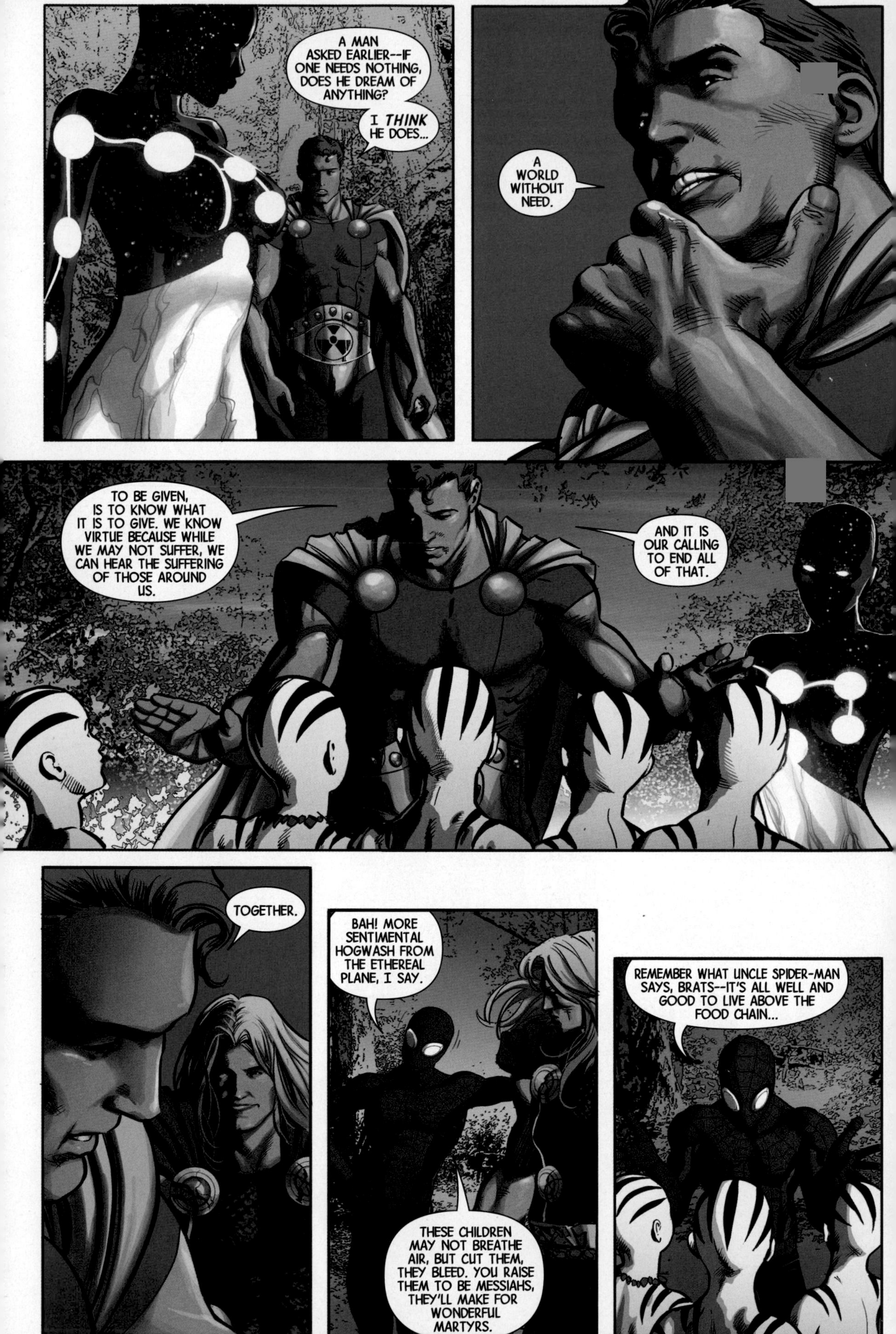
A MAN ASKED EARLIER--IF ONE NEEDS NOTHING, DOES HE DREAM OF ANYTHING?
I *THINK* HE DOES...
A WORLD WITHOUT NEED.
TO BE GIVEN, IS TO KNOW WHAT IT IS TO GIVE. WE KNOW VIRTUE BECAUSE WHILE WE MAY NOT SUFFER, WE CAN HEAR THE SUFFERING OF THOSE AROUND US.
AND IT IS OUR CALLING TO END ALL OF THAT.
TOGETHER.
BAH! MORE SENTIMENTAL HOGWASH FROM THE ETHEREAL PLANE, I SAY.
THESE CHILDREN MAY NOT BREATHE AIR, BUT CUT THEM, THEY BLEED. YOU RAISE THEM TO BE MESSIAHS, THEY'LL MAKE FOR WONDERFUL MARTYRS.
REMEMBER WHAT UNCLE SPIDER-MAN SAYS, BRATS--IT'S ALL WELL AND GOOD TO LIVE ABOVE THE FOOD CHAIN...

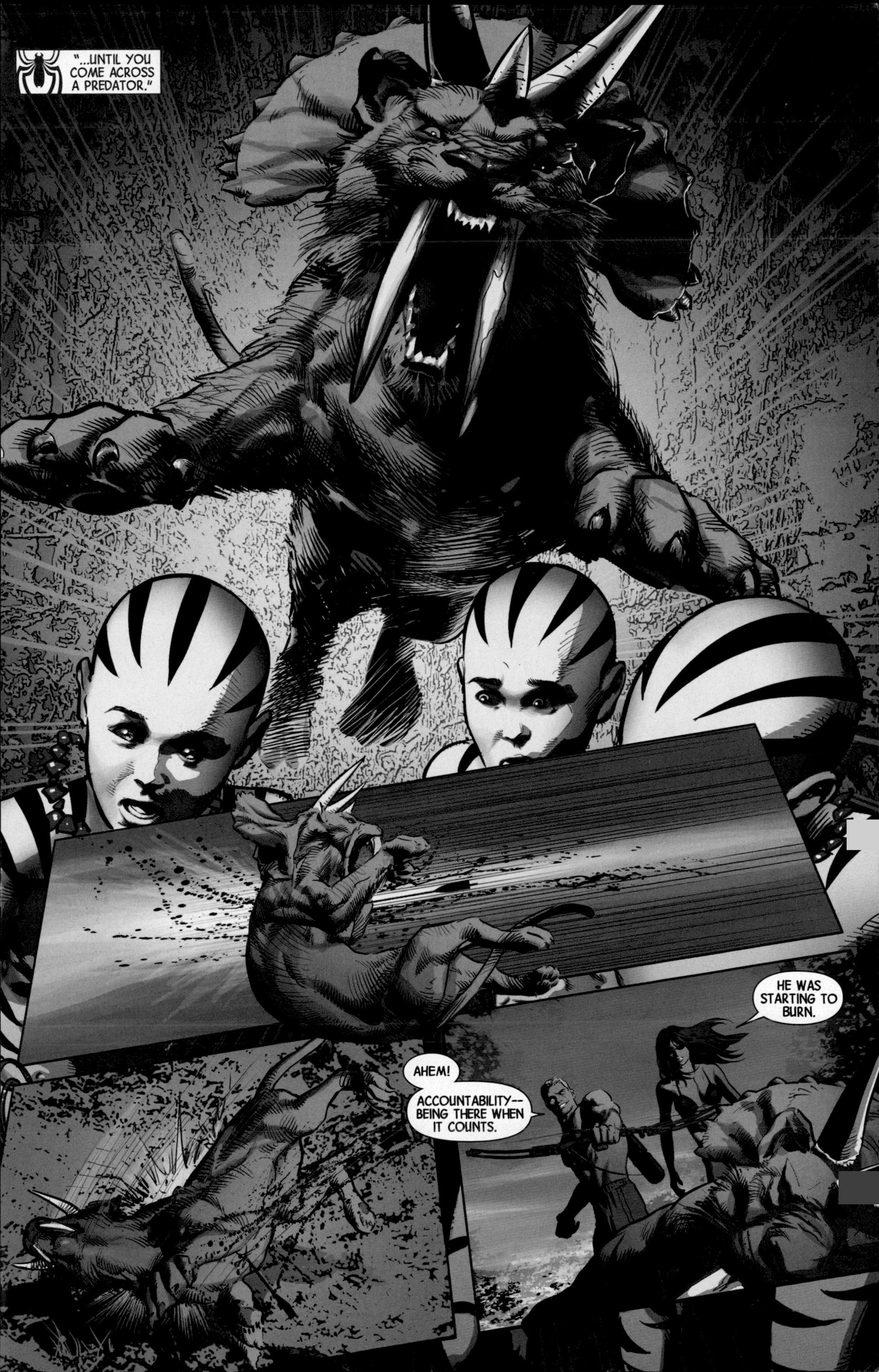
"...UNTIL YOU COME ACROSS A PREDATOR."
HE WAS STARTING TO BURN.
AHEM!
ACCOUNTABILITY-- BEING THERE WHEN IT COUNTS.

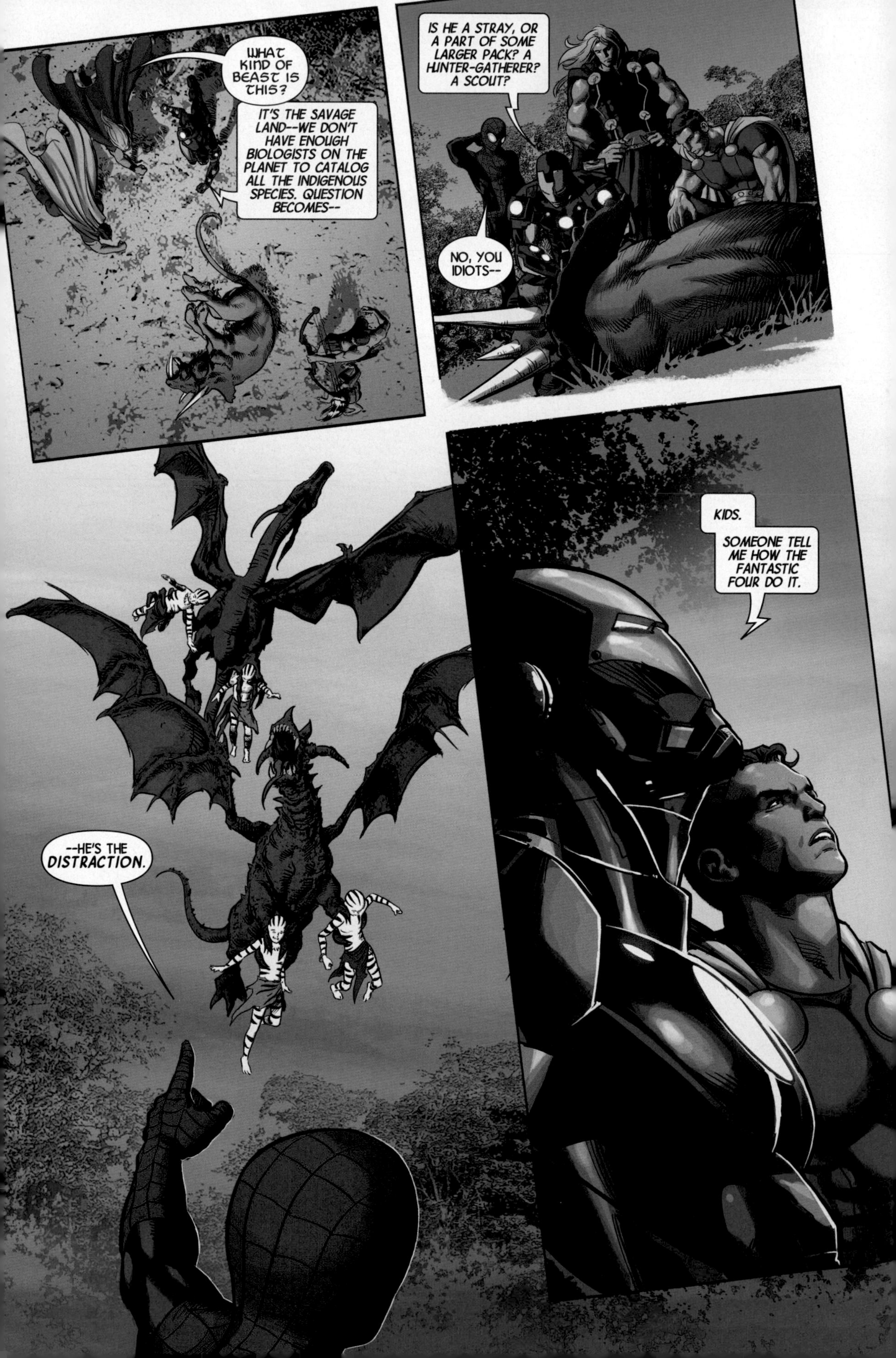
WHAT KIND OF BEAST IS THIS?
IT'S THE SAVAGE LAND--WE DON'T HAVE ENOUGH BIOLOGISTS ON THE PLANET TO CATALOG ALL THE INDIGENOUS SPECIES. QUESTION BECOMES--
IS HE A STRAY, OR A PART OF SOME LARGER PACK? A HUNTER-GATHERER? A SCOUT?
NO, YOU IDIOTS--
--HE'S THE DISTRACTION.
KIDS.
SOMEONE TELL ME HOW THE FANTASTIC FOUR DO IT.

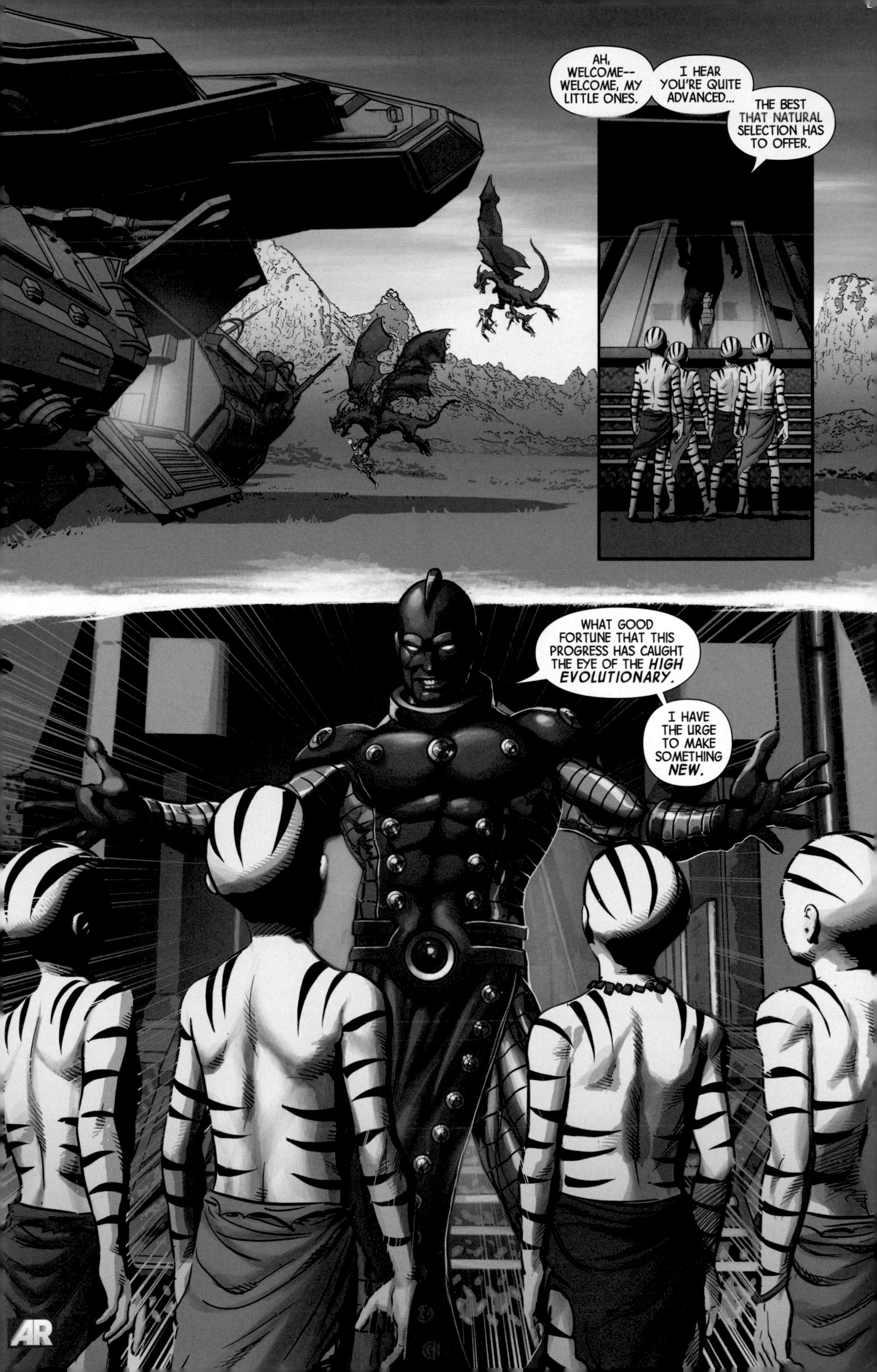
AH, WELCOME-- WELCOME, MY LITTLE ONES.
I HEAR YOU'RE QUITE ADVANCED...
THE BEST THAT NATURAL SELECTION HAS TO OFFER.
WHAT GOOD FORTUNE THAT THIS PROGRESS HAS CAUGHT THE EYE OF THE HIGH EVOLUTIONARY.
I HAVE THE URGE TO MAKE SOMETHING NEW.
AR

"STRONG"

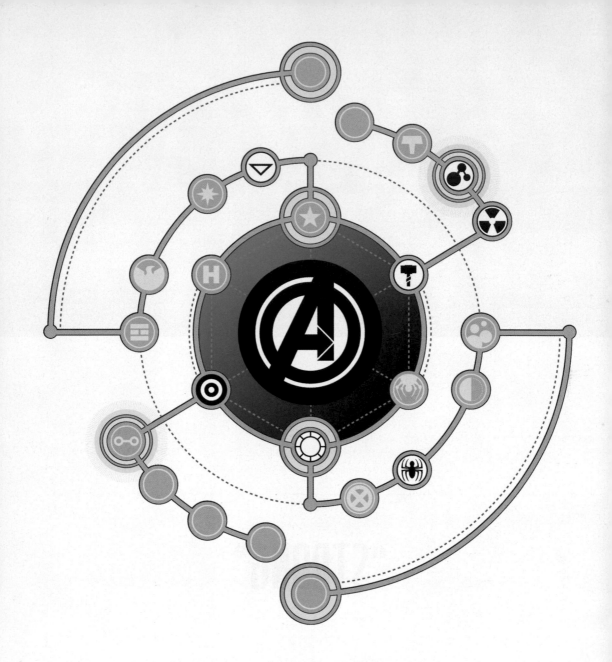

EARTH'S MIGHTIEST HEROES

CAPTAIN AMERICA · IRON MAN · THOR · HAWKEYE · BLACK WIDOW · HULK
WOLVERINE · SPIDER-MAN · CAPTAIN MARVEL · SPIDER-WOMAN
FALCON · SHANG-CHI · SUNSPOT · CANNONBALL · MANIFOLD
SMASHER · CAPTAIN UNIVERSE · HYPERION

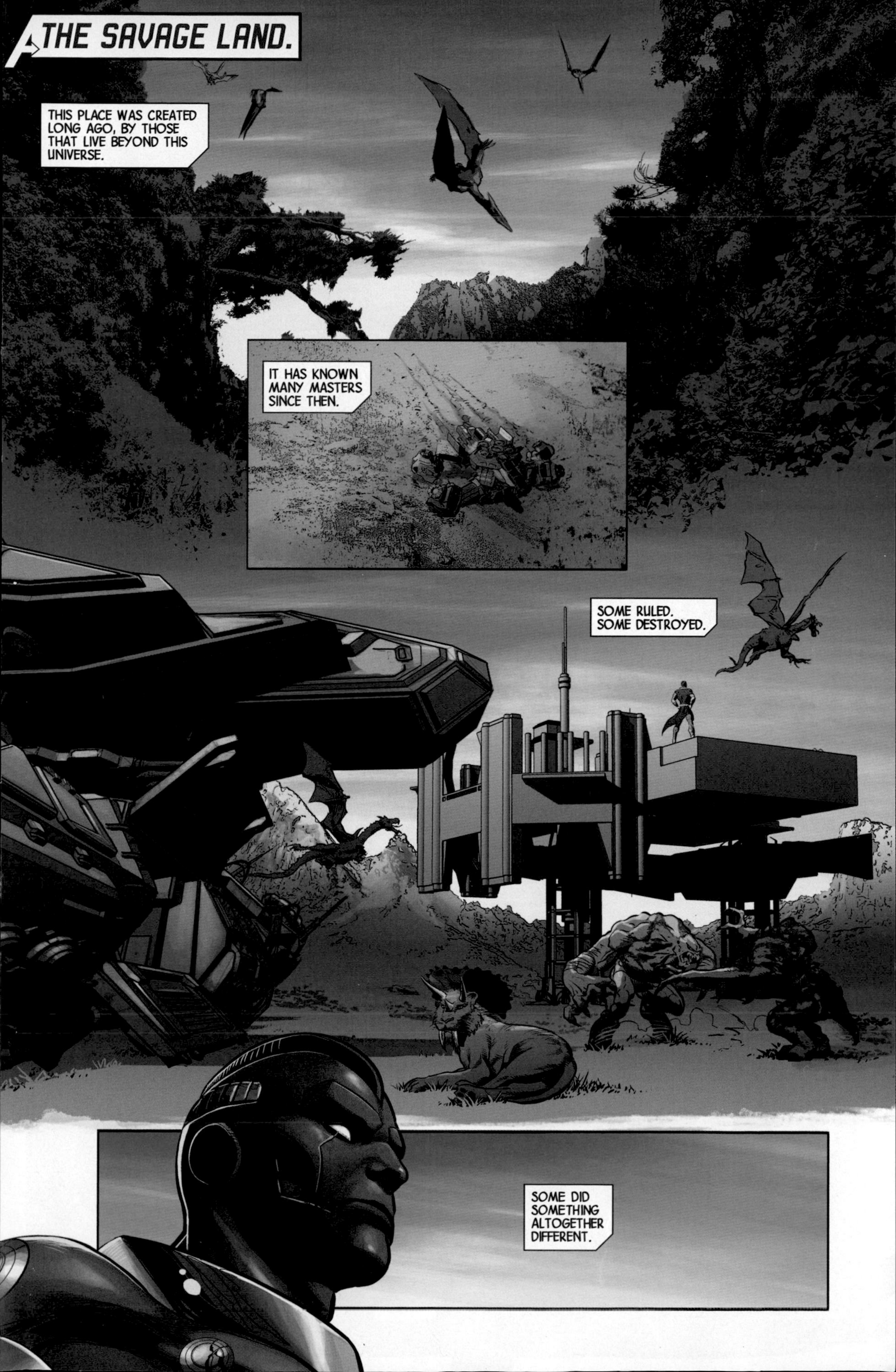
THE SAVAGE LAND.
THIS PLACE WAS CREATED LONG AGO, BY THOSE THAT LIVE BEYOND THIS UNIVERSE.
IT HAS KNOWN MANY MASTERS SINCE THEN.
SOME RULED. SOME DESTROYED.
SOME DID SOMETHING ALTOGETHER DIFFERENT.

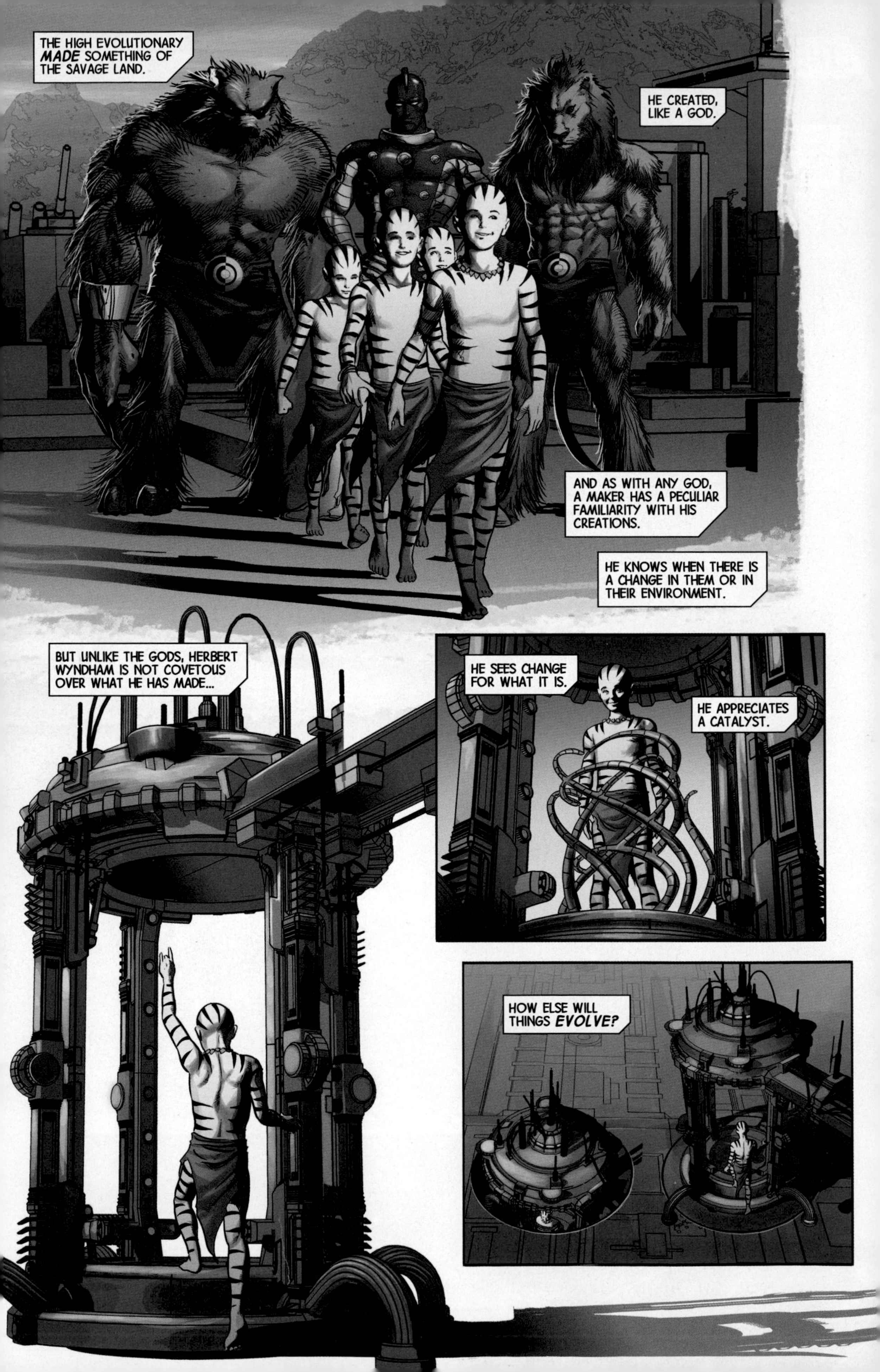
THE HIGH EVOLUTIONARY MADE SOMETHING OF THE SAVAGE LAND.
HE CREATED, LIKE A GOD.
AND AS WITH ANY GOD, A MAKER HAS A PECULIAR FAMILIARITY WITH HIS CREATIONS.
HE KNOWS WHEN THERE IS A CHANGE IN THEM OR IN THEIR ENVIRONMENT.
BUT UNLIKE THE GODS, HERBERT WYNDHAM IS NOT COVETOUS OVER WHAT HE HAS MADE...
HE SEES CHANGE FOR WHAT IT IS.
HE APPRECIATES A CATALYST.
HOW ELSE WILL THINGS EVOLVE?

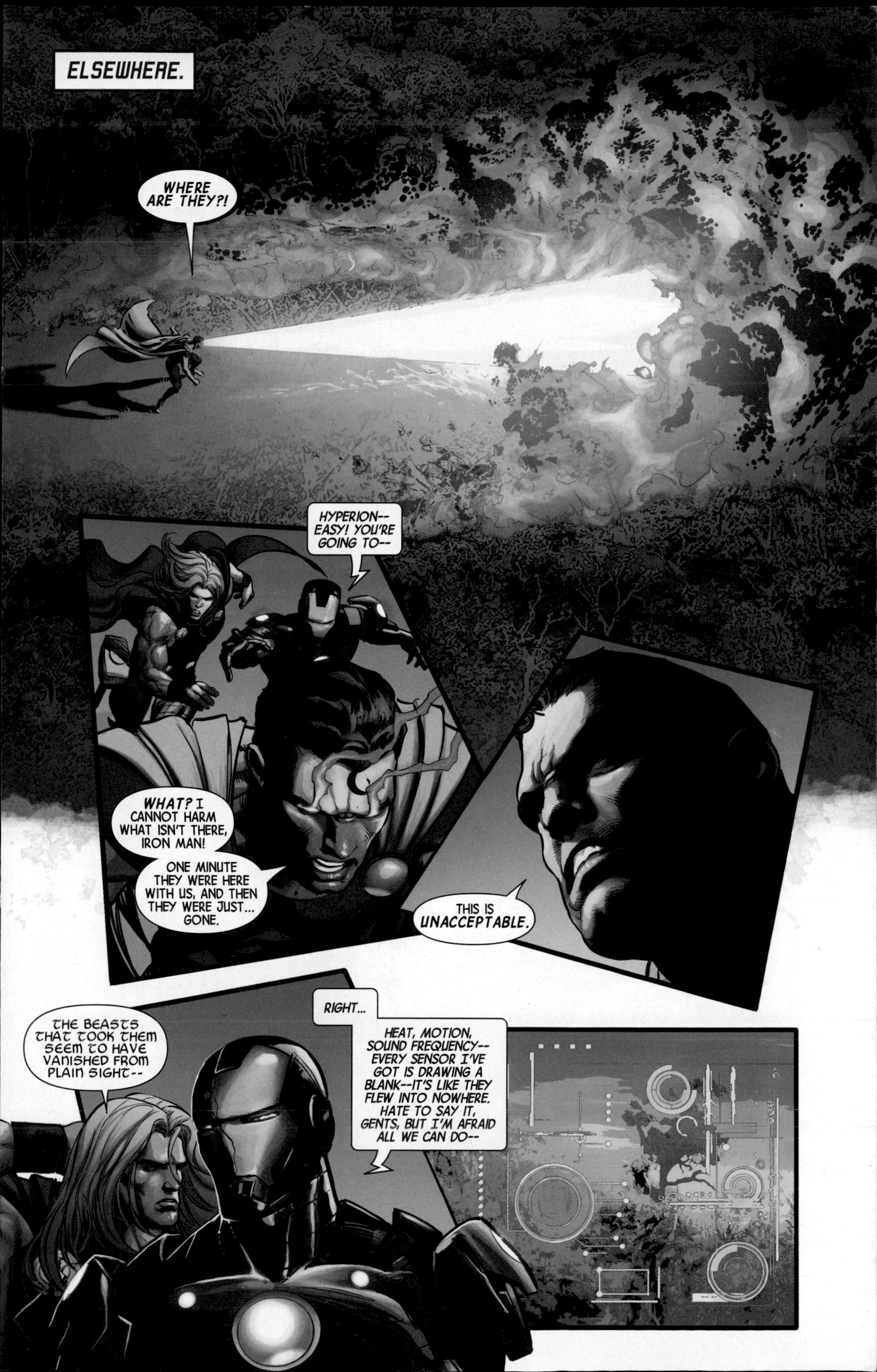
ELSEWHERE.
WHERE ARE THEY?!
HYPERION-- EASY! YOU'RE GOING TO--
WHAT? I CANNOT HARM WHAT ISN'T THERE, IRON MAN!
ONE MINUTE THEY WERE HERE WITH US, AND THEN THEY WERE JUST... GONE.
THIS IS UNACCEPTABLE.
THE BEASTS THAT TOOK THEM SEEM TO HAVE VANISHED FROM PLAIN SIGHT--
RIGHT...
HEAT, MOTION, SOUND FREQUENCY-- EVERY SENSOR I'VE GOT IS DRAWING A BLANK--IT'S LIKE THEY FLEW INTO NOWHERE. HATE TO SAY IT, GENTS, BUT I'M AFRAID ALL WE CAN DO--

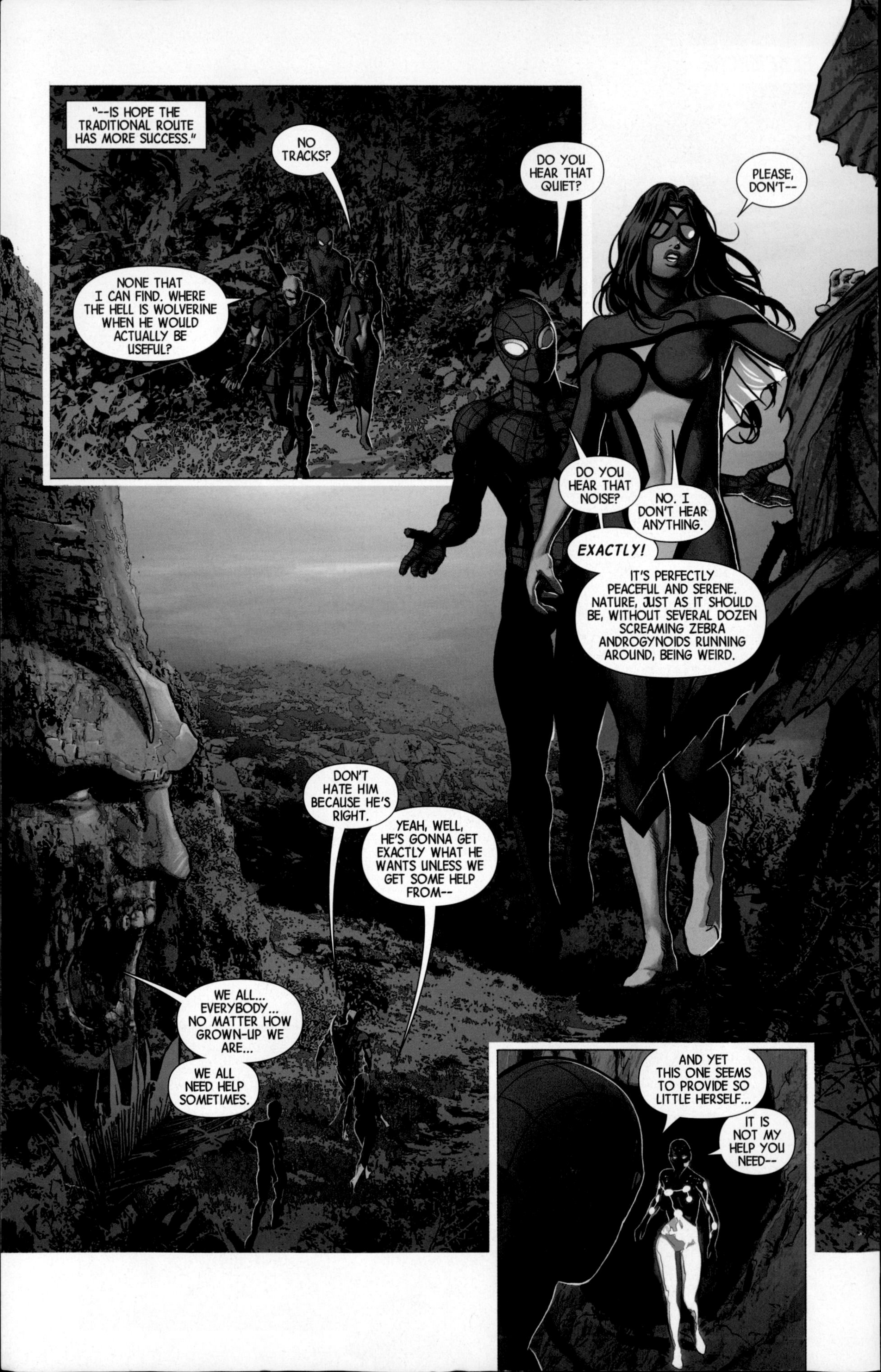
"--IS HOPE THE TRADITIONAL ROUTE HAS MORE SUCCESS."
NO TRACKS?
NONE THAT I CAN FIND. WHERE THE HELL IS WOLVERINE WHEN HE WOULD ACTUALLY BE USEFUL?
DO YOU HEAR THAT QUIET?
PLEASE, DON'T--
DO YOU HEAR THAT NOISE?
NO. I DON'T HEAR ANYTHING.
EXACTLY!
IT'S PERFECTLY PEACEFUL AND SERENE. NATURE, JUST AS IT SHOULD BE, WITHOUT SEVERAL DOZEN SCREAMING ZEBRA ANDROGYNOIDS RUNNING AROUND, BEING WEIRD.
DON'T HATE HIM BECAUSE HE'S RIGHT.
YEAH, WELL, HE'S GONNA GET EXACTLY WHAT HE WANTS UNLESS WE GET SOME HELP FROM--
WE ALL... EVERYBODY... NO MATTER HOW GROWN-UP WE ARE...
WE ALL NEED HELP SOMETIMES.
AND YET THIS ONE SEEMS TO PROVIDE SO LITTLE HERSELF...
IT IS NOT MY HELP YOU NEED--

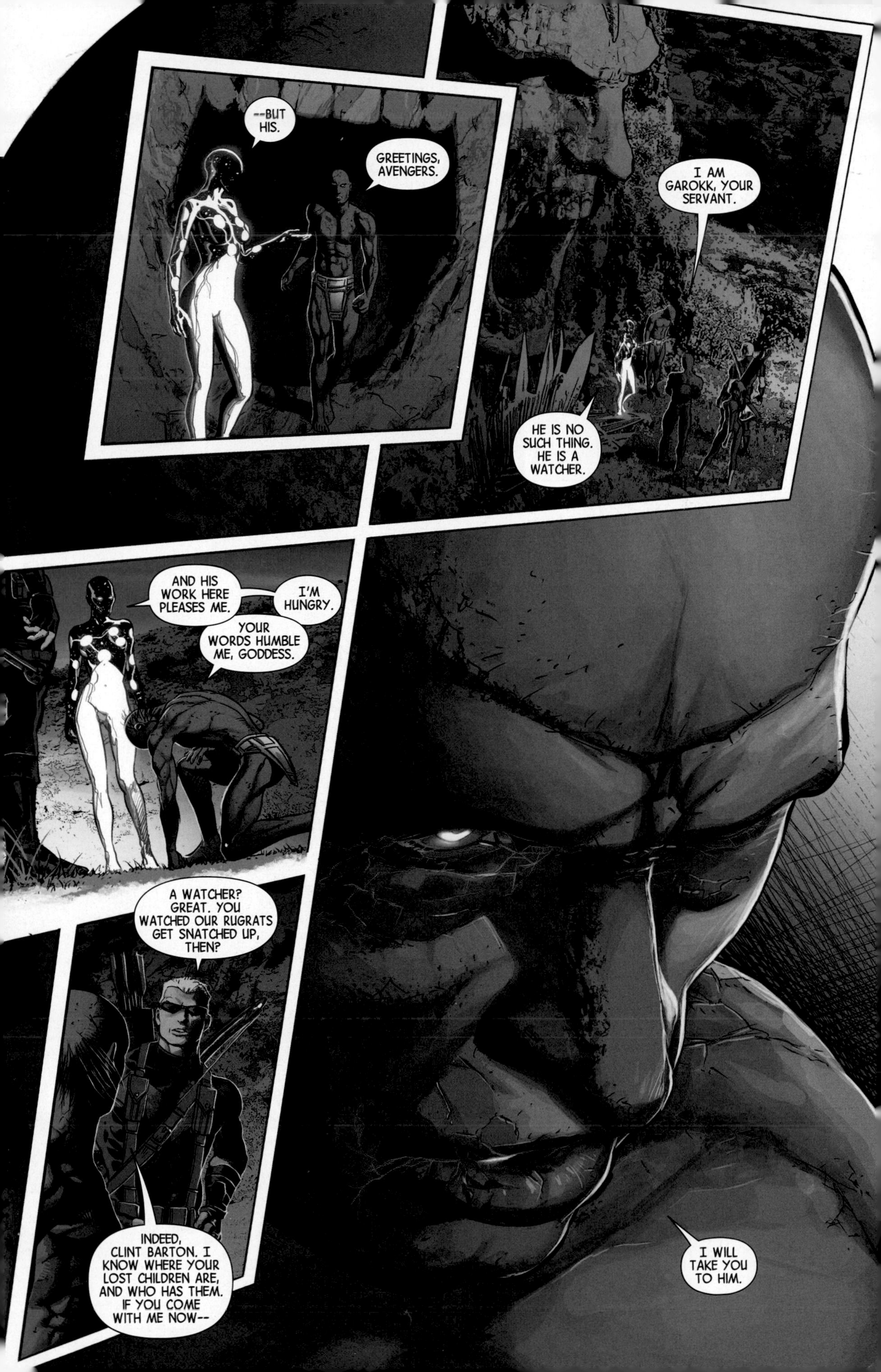
--BUT HIS.
GREETINGS, AVENGERS.
I AM GAROKK, YOUR SERVANT.
HE IS NO SUCH THING. HE IS A WATCHER.
AND HIS WORK HERE PLEASES ME.
I'M HUNGRY.
YOUR WORDS HUMBLE ME, GODDESS.
A WATCHER? GREAT. YOU WATCHED OUR RUGRATS GET SNATCHED UP, THEN?
INDEED, CLINT BARTON. I KNOW WHERE YOUR LOST CHILDREN ARE, AND WHO HAS THEM. IF YOU COME WITH ME NOW--
I WILL TAKE YOU TO HIM.

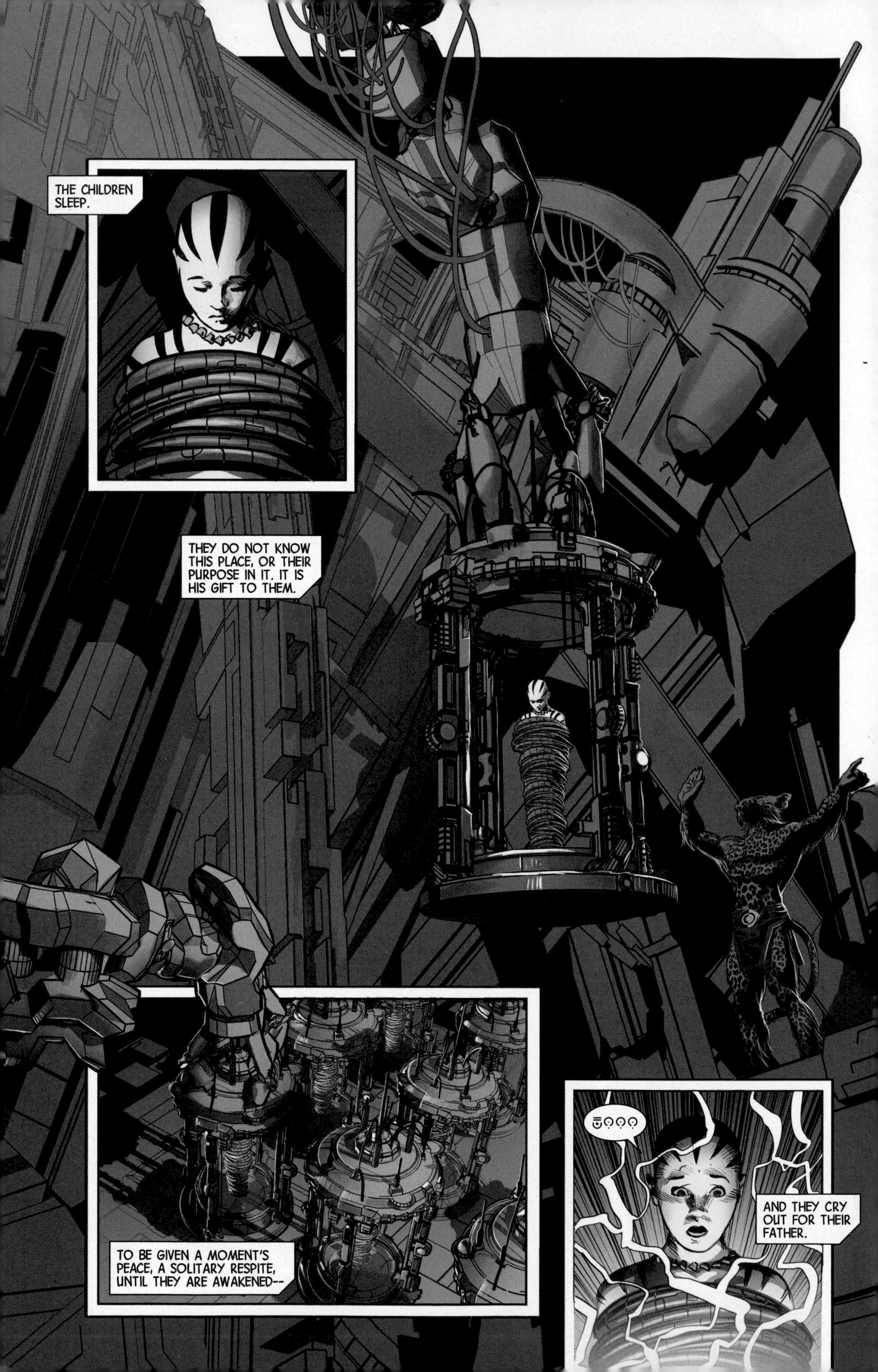
THE CHILDREN SLEEP.
THEY DO NOT KNOW THIS PLACE, OR THEIR PURPOSE IN IT. IT IS HIS GIFT TO THEM.
TO BE GIVEN A MOMENT'S PEACE, A SOLITARY RESPITE, UNTIL THEY ARE AWAKENED--
AND THEY CRY OUT FOR THEIR FATHER.

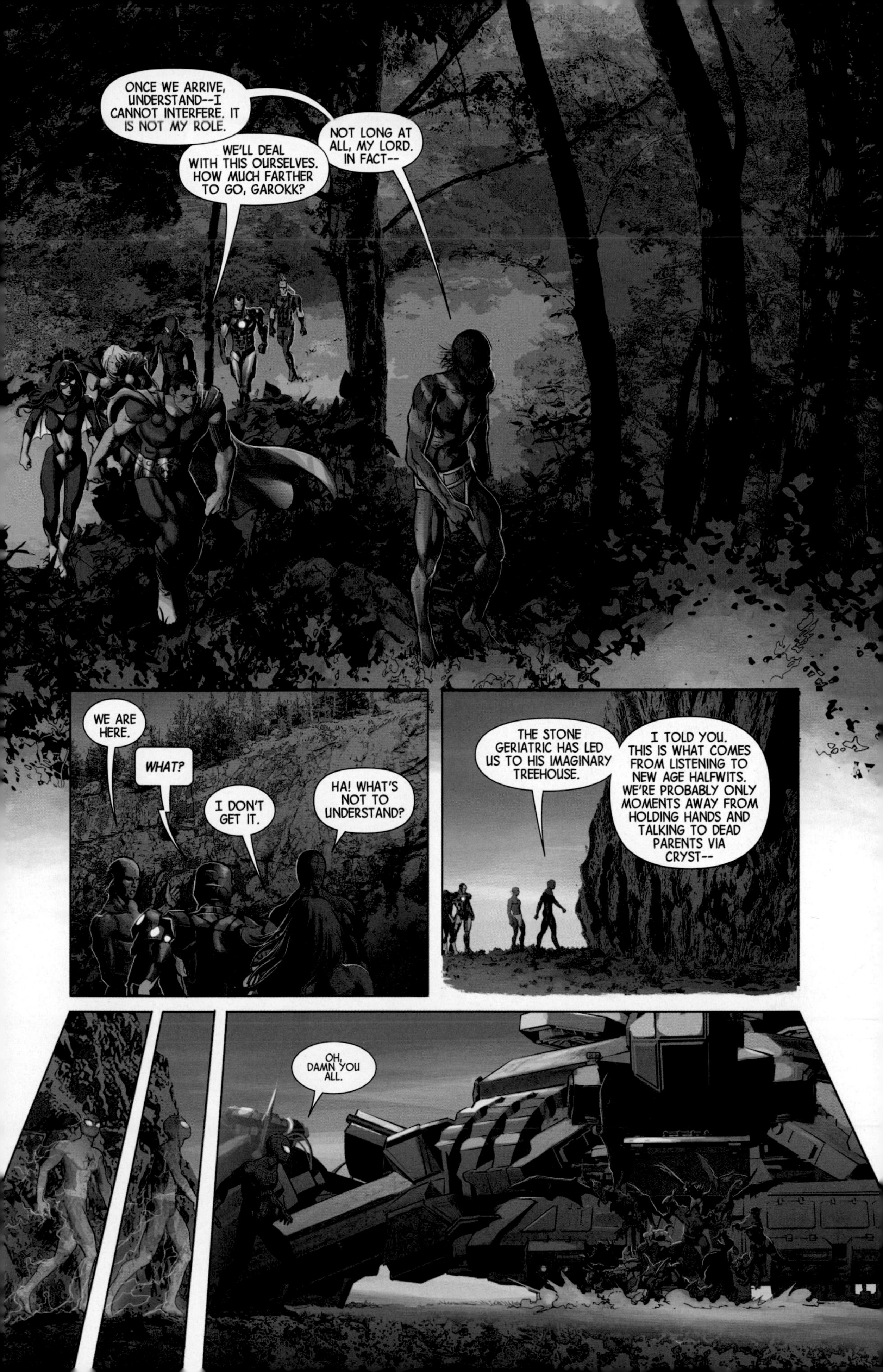
ONCE WE ARRIVE, UNDERSTAND--I CANNOT INTERFERE. IT IS NOT MY ROLE.
WE'LL DEAL WITH THIS OURSELVES. HOW MUCH FARTHER TO GO, GAROKK?
NOT LONG AT ALL, MY LORD. IN FACT--
WE ARE HERE.
WHAT?
I DON'T GET IT.
HA! WHAT'S NOT TO UNDERSTAND?
THE STONE GERIATRIC HAS LED US TO HIS IMAGINARY TREEHOUSE.
I TOLD YOU. THIS IS WHAT COMES FROM LISTENING TO NEW AGE HALFWITS. WE'RE PROBABLY ONLY MOMENTS AWAY FROM HOLDING HANDS AND TALKING TO DEAD PARENTS VIA CRYST--
OH, DAMN YOU ALL.

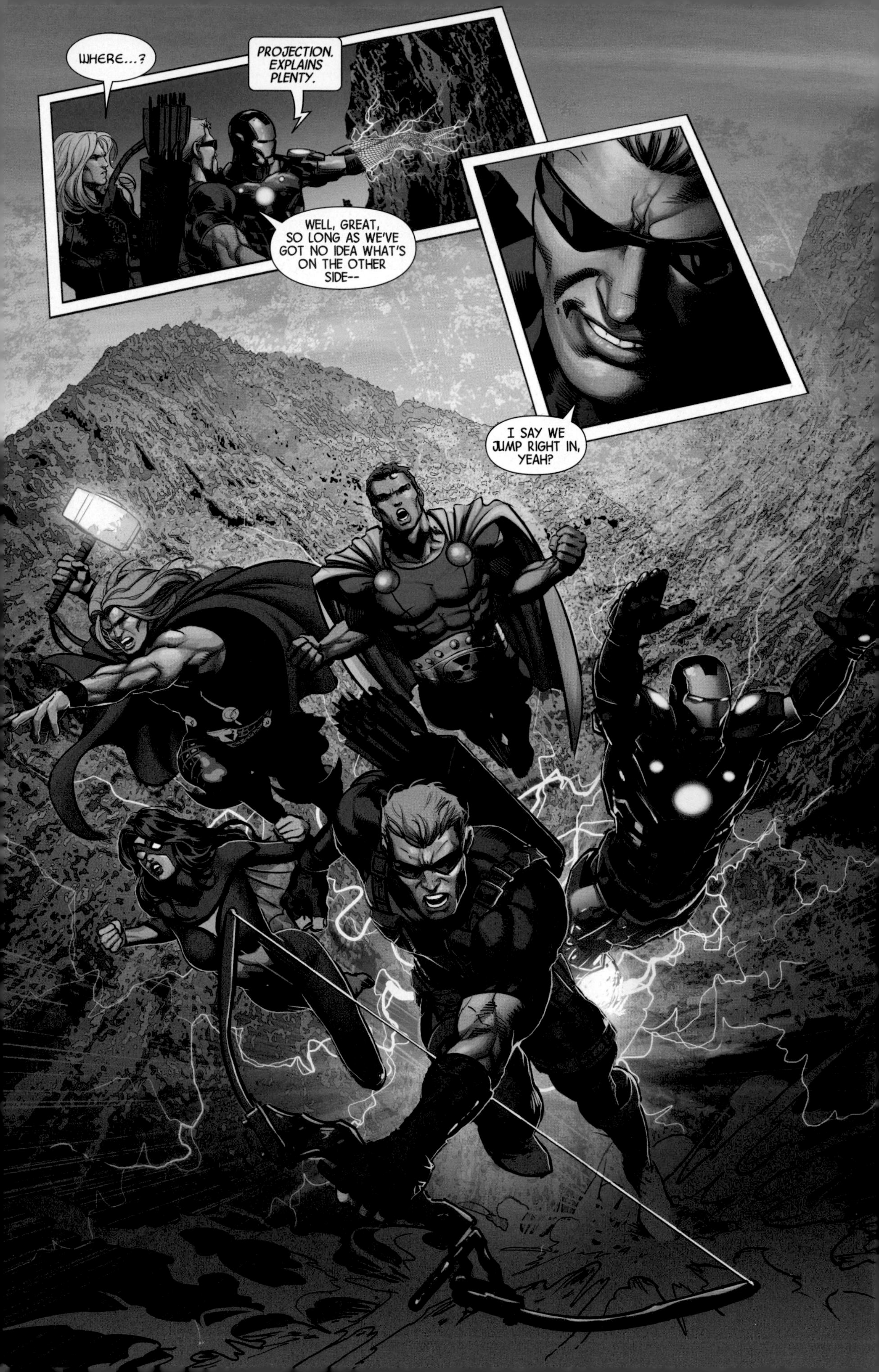
WHERE...?
PROJECTION. EXPLAINS PLENTY.
WELL, GREAT, SO LONG AS WE'VE GOT NO IDEA WHAT'S ON THE OTHER SIDE--
I SAY WE JUMP RIGHT IN, YEAH?

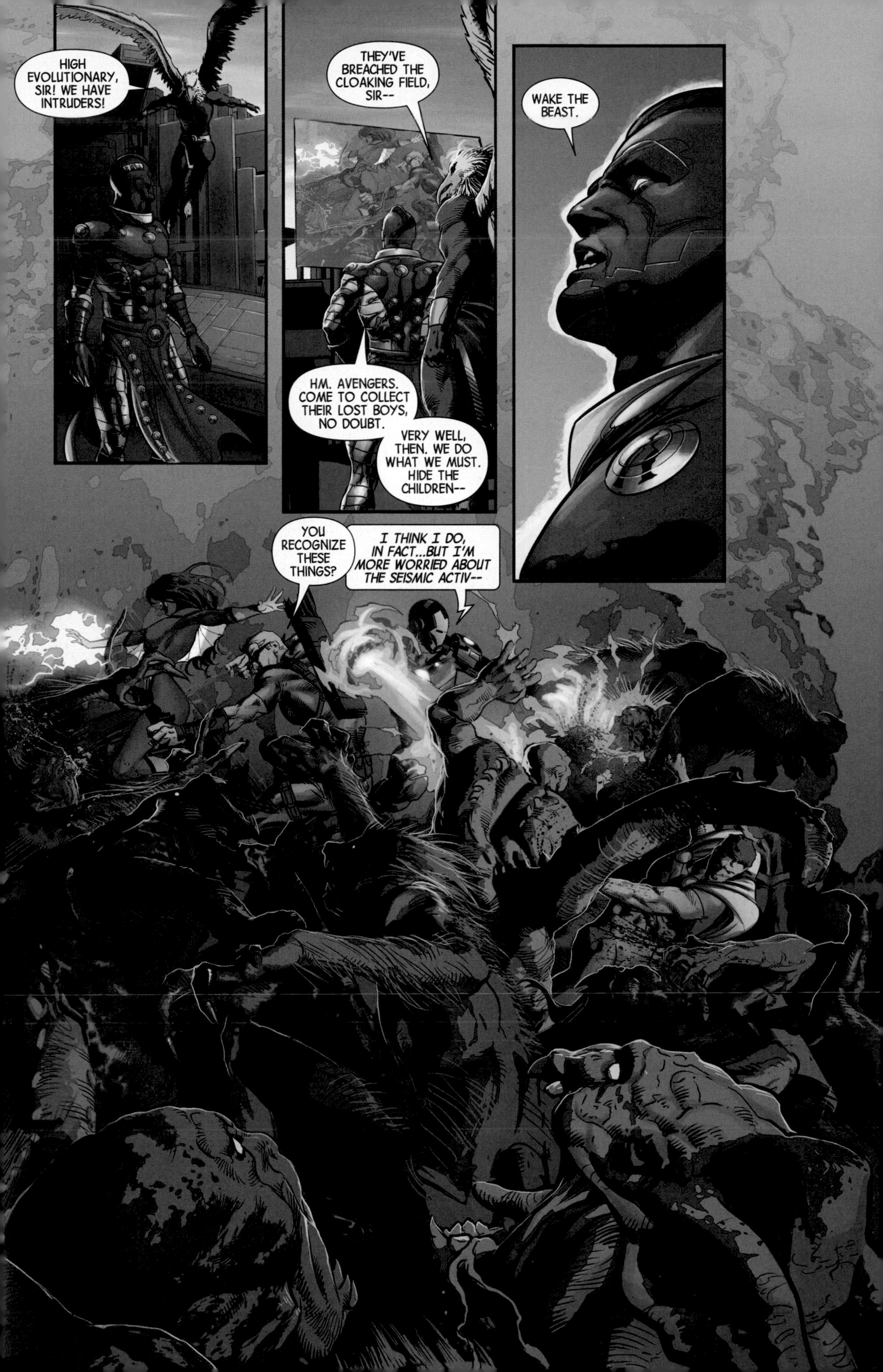
HIGH EVOLUTIONARY, SIR! WE HAVE INTRUDERS!
THEY'VE BREACHED THE CLOAKING FIELD, SIR--
HM. AVENGERS. COME TO COLLECT THEIR LOST BOYS, NO DOUBT.
VERY WELL, THEN. WE DO WHAT WE MUST. HIDE THE CHILDREN--
WAKE THE BEAST.
YOU RECOGNIZE THESE THINGS?
I THINK I DO, IN FACT...BUT I'M MORE WORRIED ABOUT THE SEISMIC ACTIV--

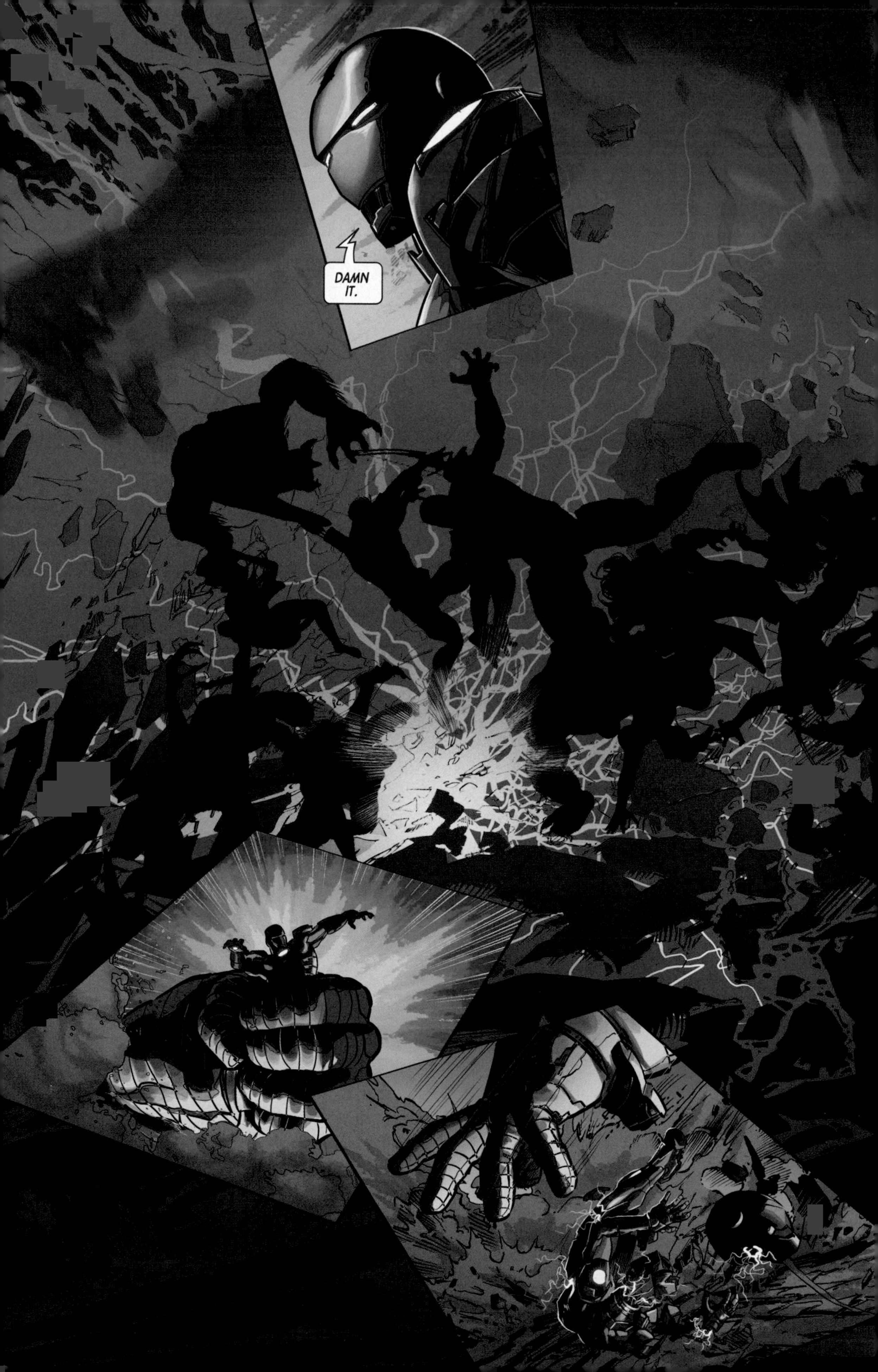
DAMN IT.

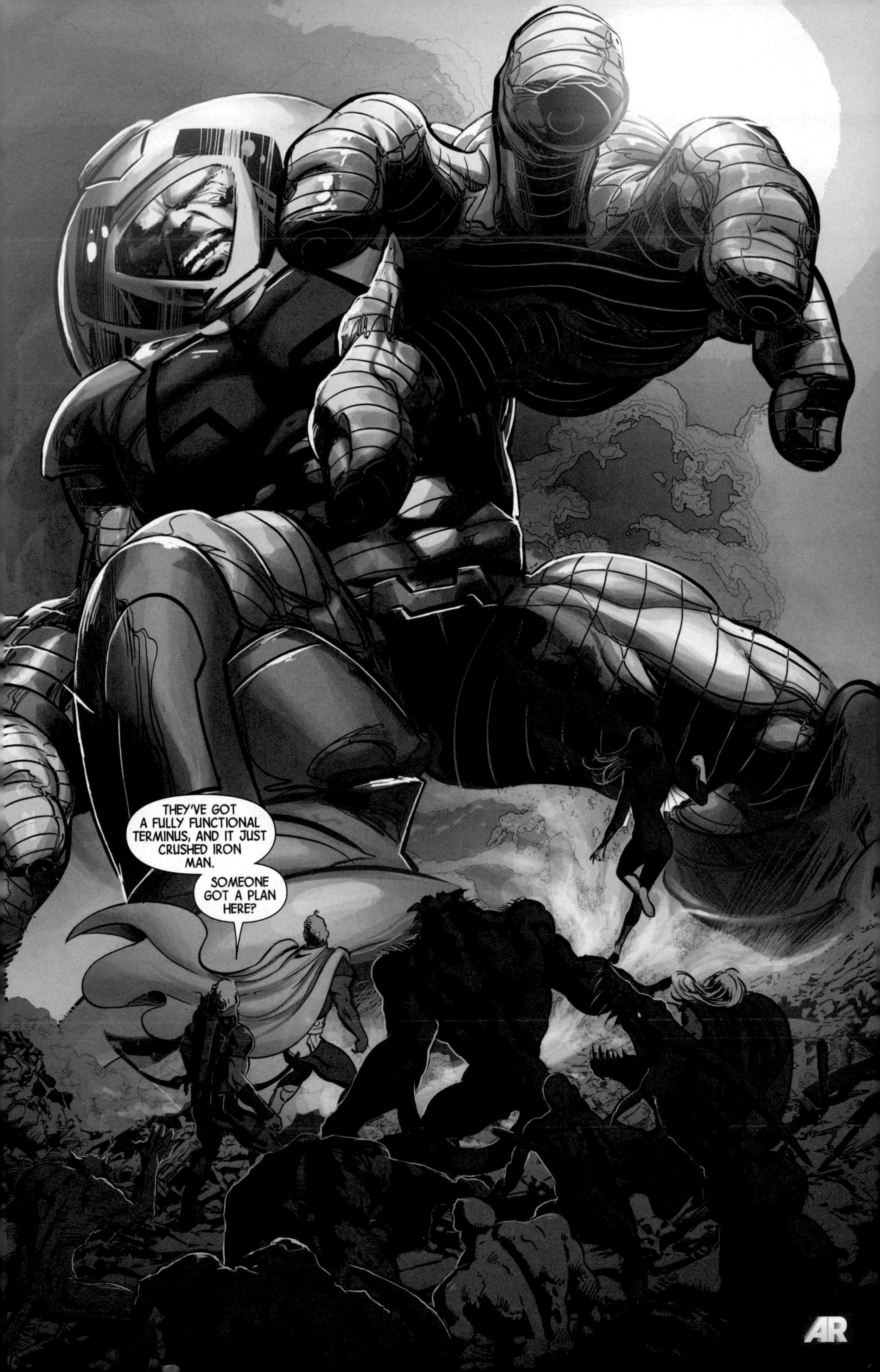
THEY'VE GOT A FULLY FUNCTIONAL TERMINUS, AND IT JUST CRUSHED IRON MAN.
SOMEONE GOT A PLAN HERE?

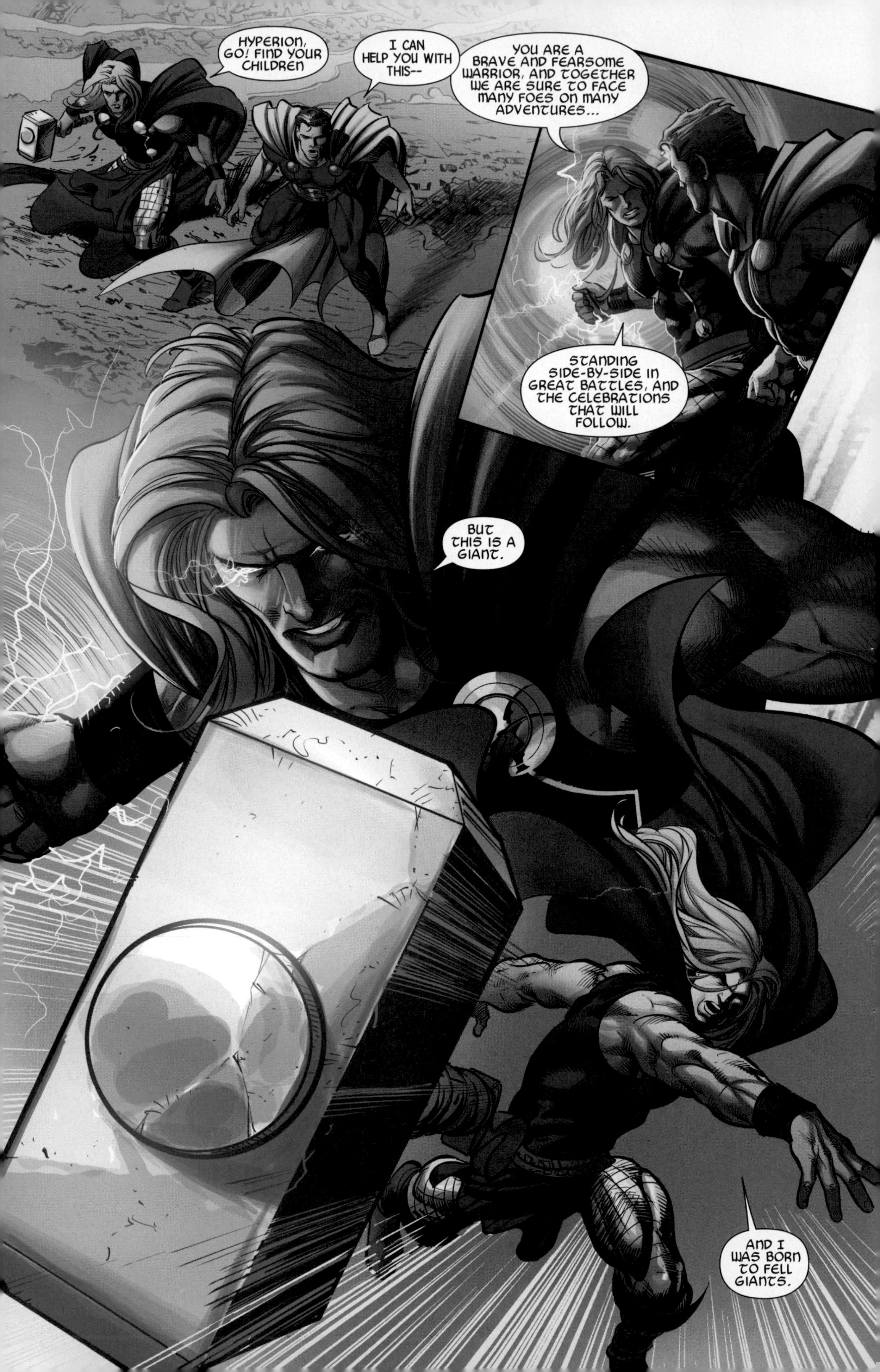
HYPERION, GO! FIND YOUR CHILDREN
I CAN HELP YOU WITH THIS--
YOU ARE A BRAVE AND FEARSOME WARRIOR, AND TOGETHER WE ARE SURE TO FACE MANY FOES ON MANY ADVENTURES...
STANDING SIDE-BY-SIDE IN GREAT BATTLES, AND THE CELEBRATIONS THAT WILL FOLLOW.
BUT THIS IS A GIANT.
AND I WAS BORN TO FELL GIANTS.

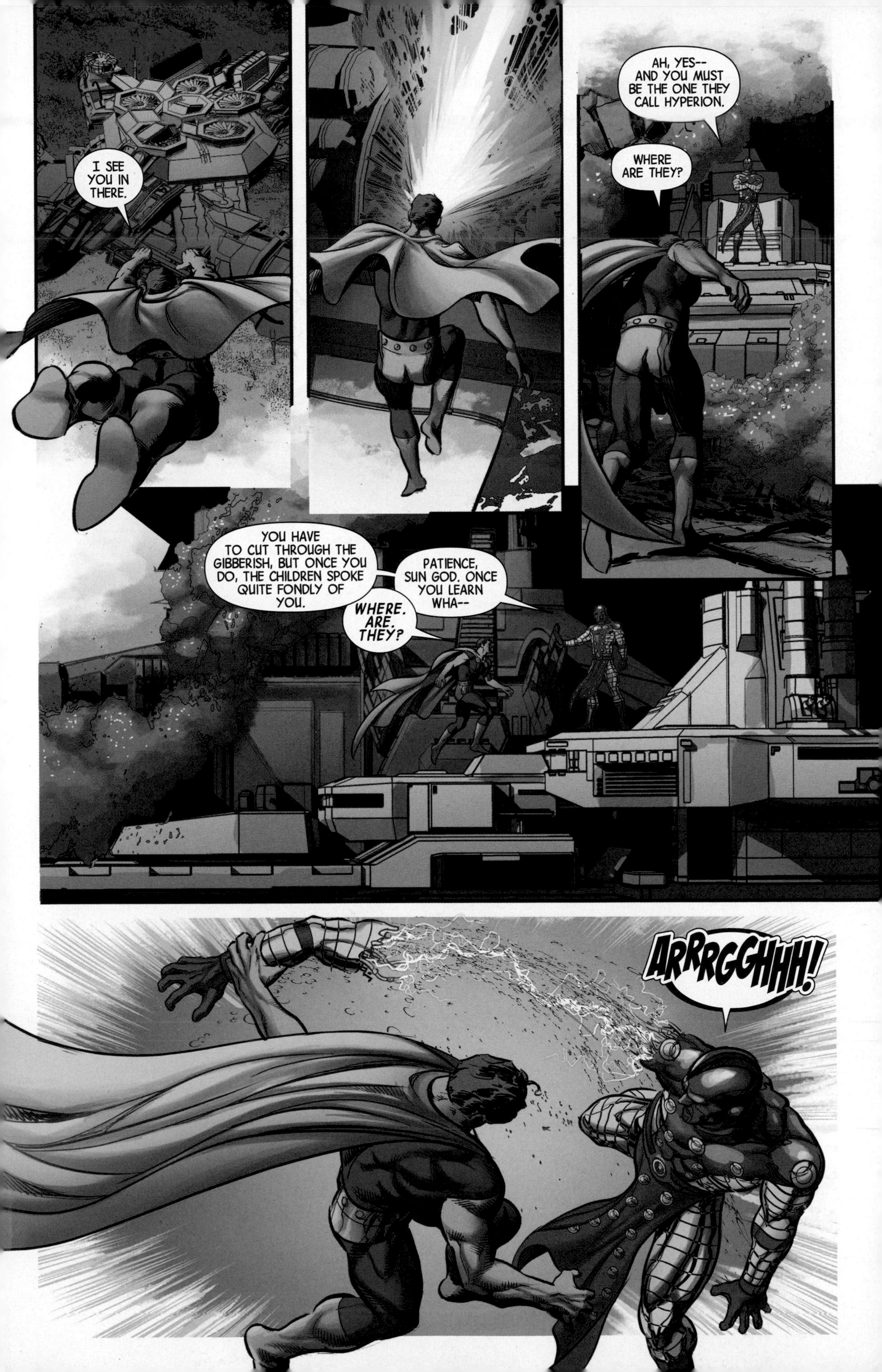
I SEE YOU IN THERE.
AH, YES-- AND YOU MUST BE THE ONE THEY CALL HYPERION.
WHERE ARE THEY?
YOU HAVE TO CUT THROUGH THE GIBBERISH, BUT ONCE YOU DO, THE CHILDREN SPOKE QUITE FONDLY OF YOU.
PATIENCE, SUN GOD. ONCE YOU LEARN WHA--
WHERE. ARE. THEY?
ARRRGGHHH!

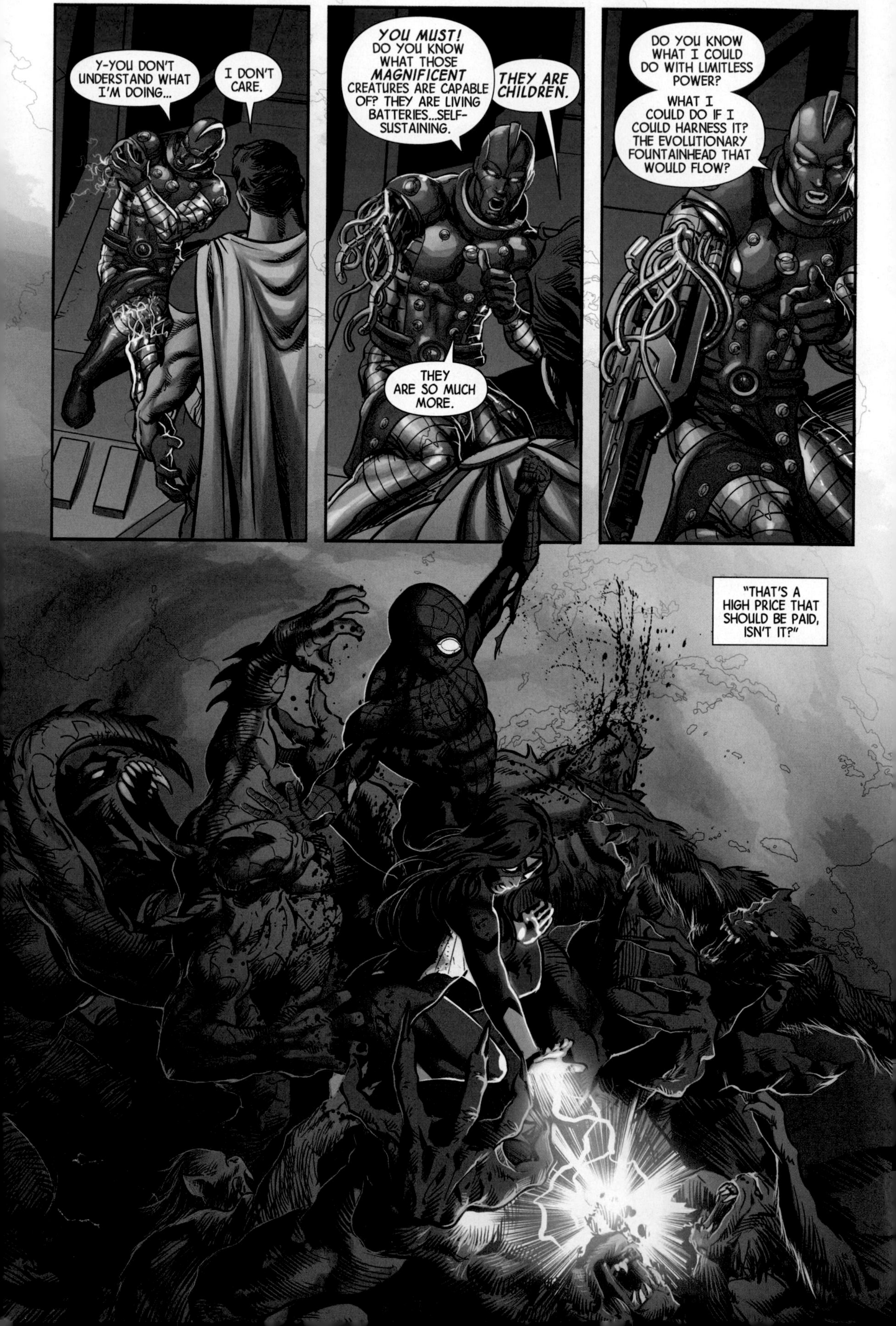
Y-YOU DON'T UNDERSTAND WHAT I'M DOING...
I DON'T CARE.
YOU MUST! DO YOU KNOW WHAT THOSE MAGNIFICENT CREATURES ARE CAPABLE OF? THEY ARE LIVING BATTERIES...SELF-SUSTAINING.
THEY ARE CHILDREN.
THEY ARE SO MUCH MORE.
DO YOU KNOW WHAT I COULD DO WITH LIMITLESS POWER?
WHAT I COULD DO IF I COULD HARNESS IT? THE EVOLUTIONARY FOUNTAINHEAD THAT WOULD FLOW?
"THAT'S A HIGH PRICE THAT SHOULD BE PAID, ISN'T IT?"

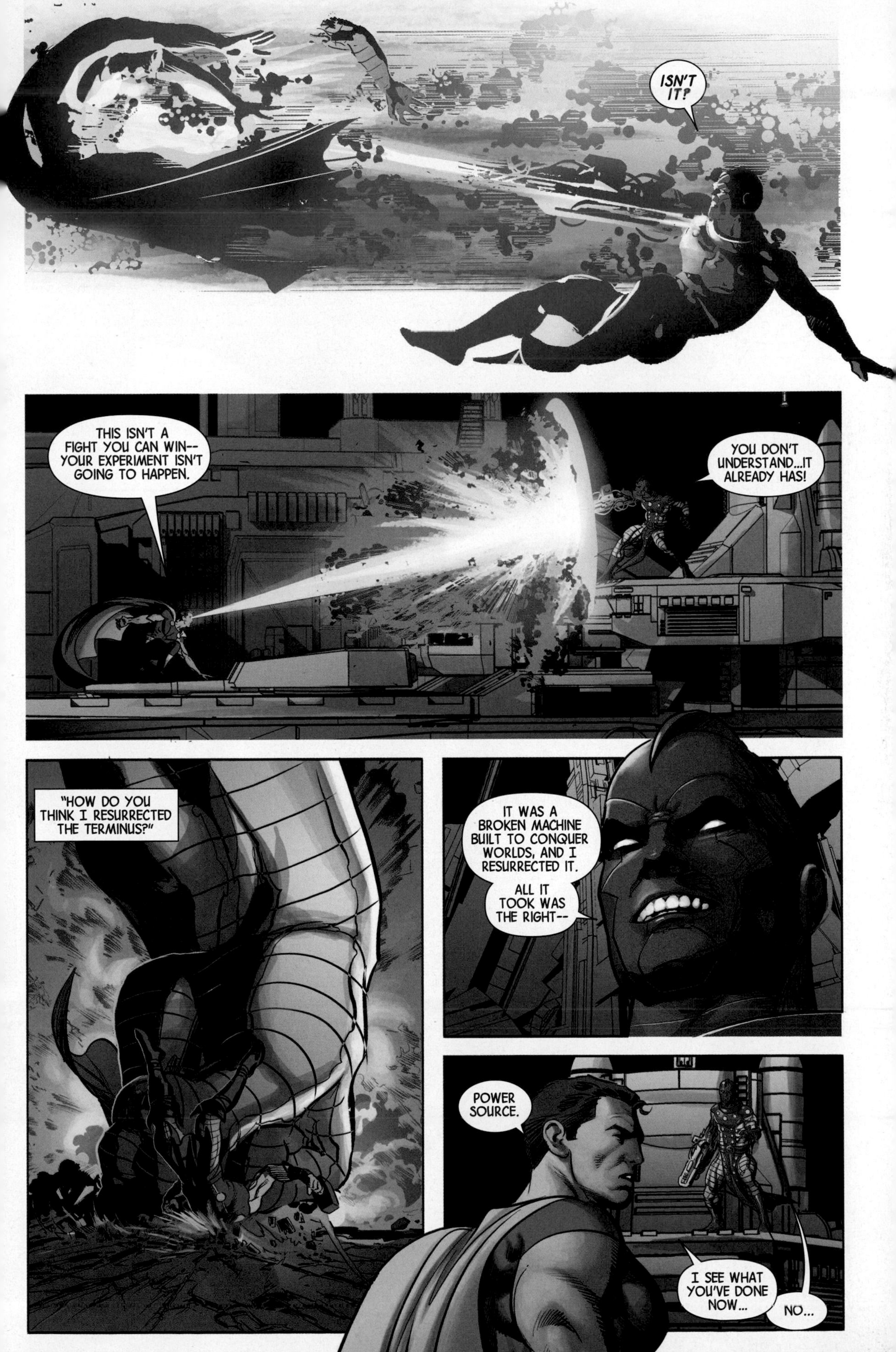
ISN'T IT?
THIS ISN'T A FIGHT YOU CAN WIN-- YOUR EXPERIMENT ISN'T GOING TO HAPPEN.
YOU DON'T UNDERSTAND...IT ALREADY HAS!
"HOW DO YOU THINK I RESURRECTED THE TERMINUS?"
IT WAS A BROKEN MACHINE BUILT TO CONQUER WORLDS, AND I RESURRECTED IT.
ALL IT TOOK WAS THE RIGHT--
POWER SOURCE.
I SEE WHAT YOU'VE DONE NOW...
NO...

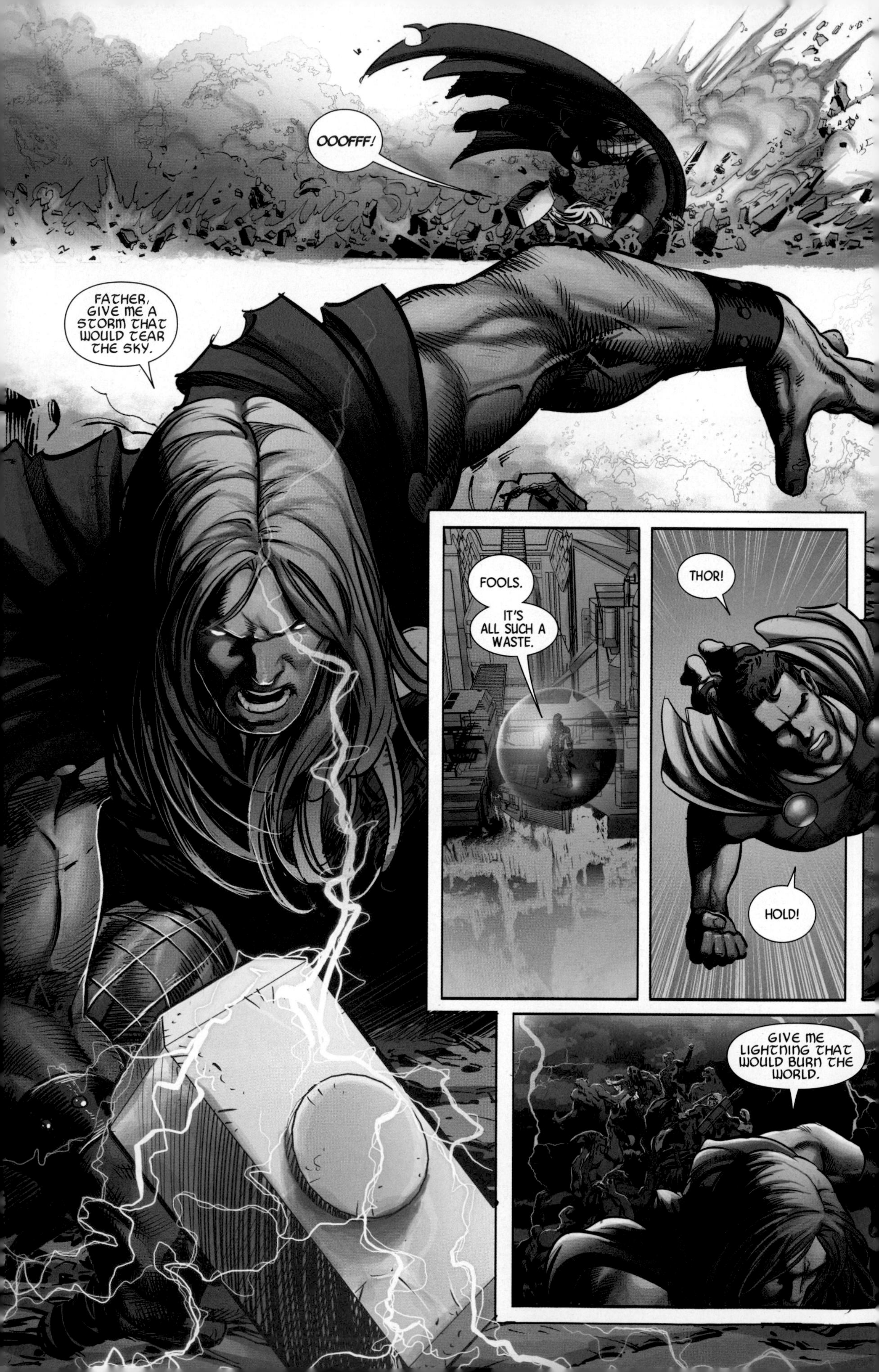
OOOFFF!
FATHER, GIVE ME A STORM THAT WOULD TEAR THE SKY.
FOOLS.
IT'S ALL SUCH A WASTE.
THOR!
HOLD!
GIVE ME LIGHTNING THAT WOULD BURN THE WORLD.

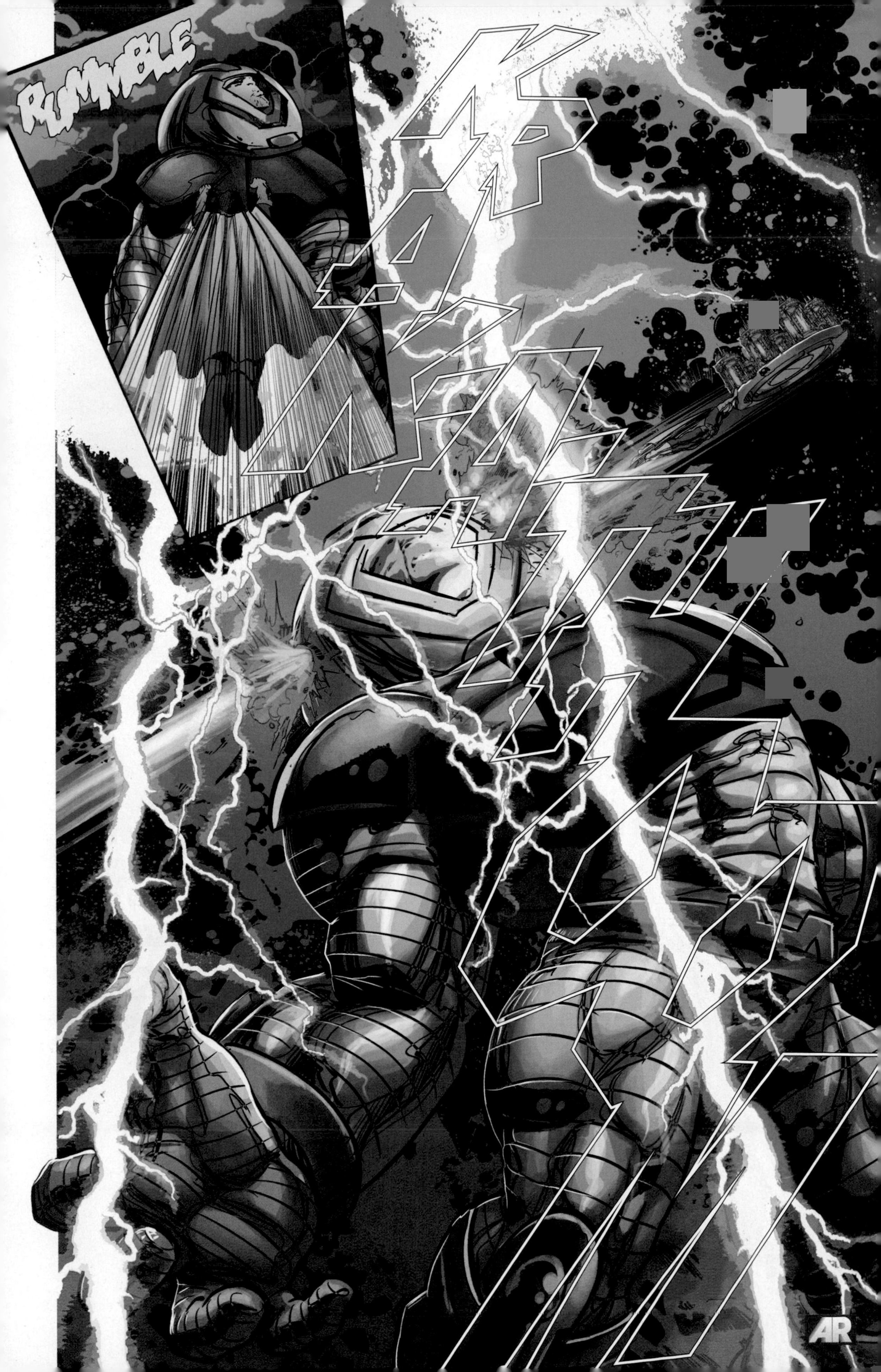
RUMMBLE

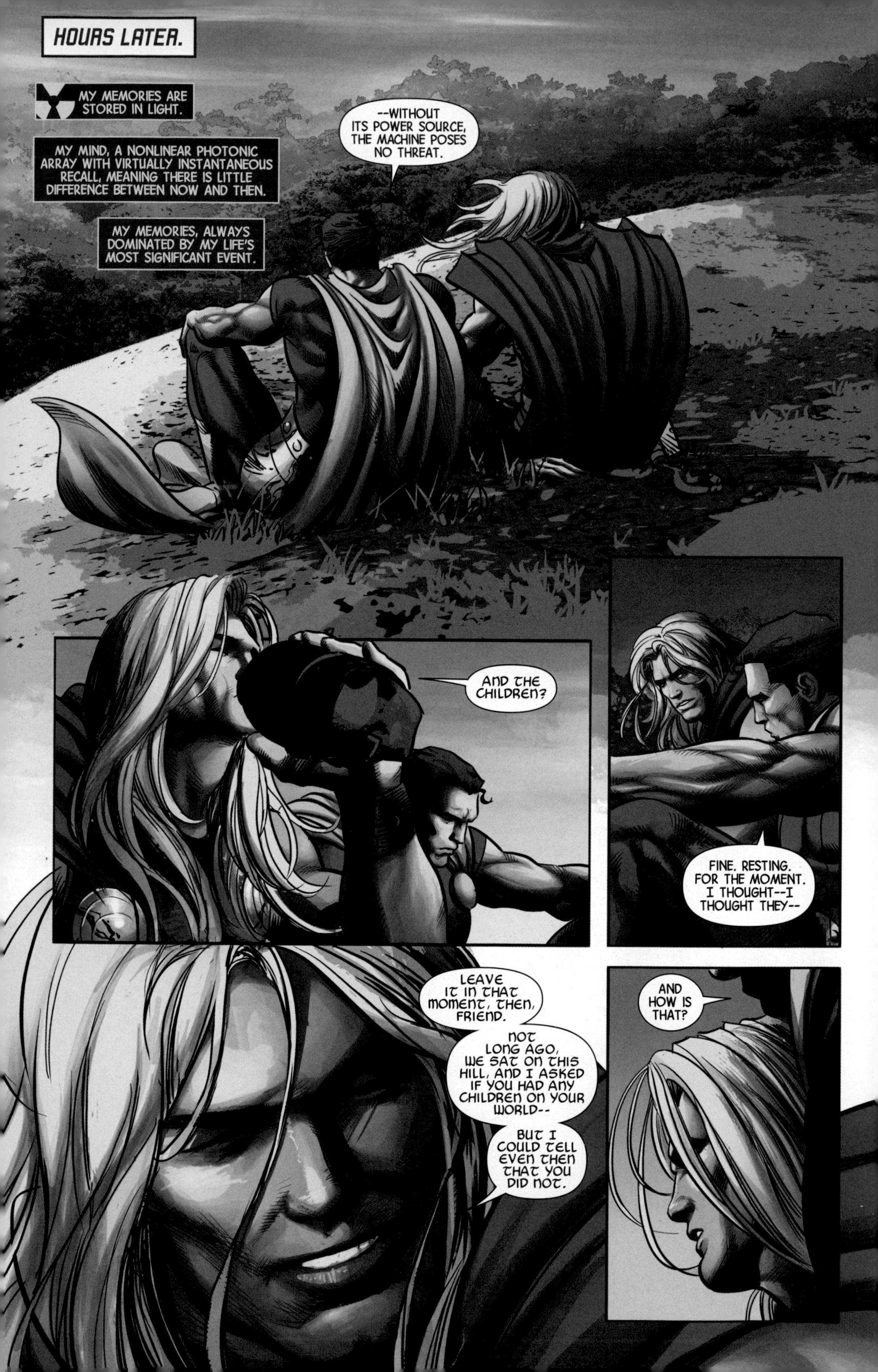
HOURS LATER.
MY MEMORIES ARE STORED IN LIGHT.
MY MIND, A NONLINEAR PHOTONIC ARRAY WITH VIRTUALLY INSTANTANEOUS RECALL, MEANING THERE IS LITTLE DIFFERENCE BETWEEN NOW AND THEN.
MY MEMORIES, ALWAYS DOMINATED BY MY LIFE'S MOST SIGNIFICANT EVENT.
--WITHOUT ITS POWER SOURCE, THE MACHINE POSES NO THREAT.
AND THE CHILDREN?
FINE. RESTING. FOR THE MOMENT. I THOUGHT--I THOUGHT THEY--
LEAVE IT IN THAT MOMENT, THEN, FRIEND.
NOT LONG AGO, WE SAT ON THIS HILL, AND I ASKED IF YOU HAD ANY CHILDREN ON YOUR WORLD--
BUT I COULD TELL EVEN THEN THAT YOU DID NOT.
AND HOW IS THAT?

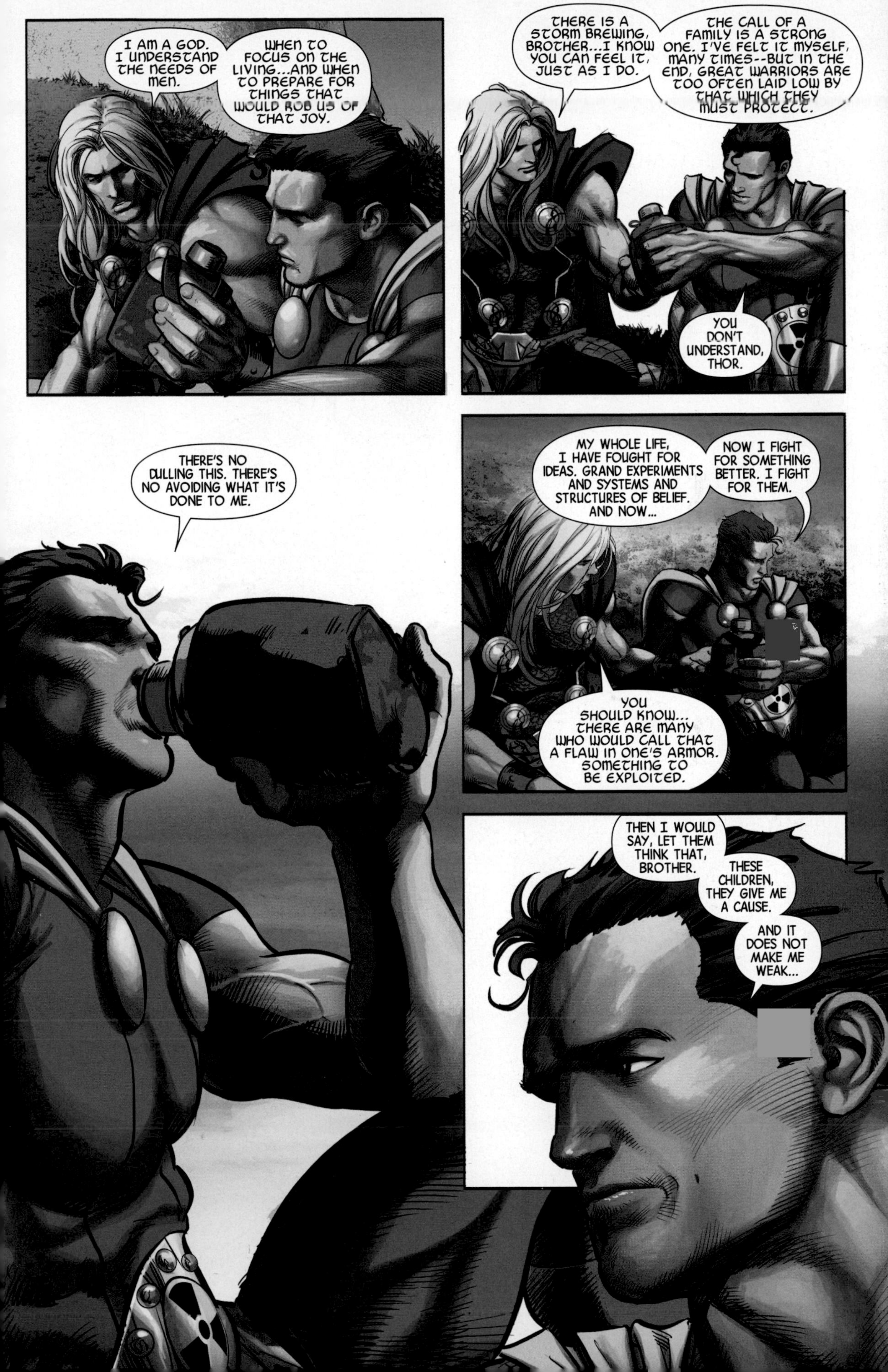
I AM A GOD. I UNDERSTAND THE NEEDS OF MEN.
WHEN TO FOCUS ON THE LIVING...AND WHEN TO PREPARE FOR THINGS THAT WOULD ROB US OF THAT JOY.
THERE IS A STORM BREWING, BROTHER...I KNOW YOU CAN FEEL IT, JUST AS I DO.
THE CALL OF A FAMILY IS A STRONG ONE. I'VE FELT IT MYSELF, MANY TIMES--BUT IN THE END, GREAT WARRIORS ARE TOO OFTEN LAID LOW BY THAT WHICH THEY MUST PROTECT.
YOU DON'T UNDERSTAND, THOR.
THERE'S NO DULLING THIS. THERE'S NO AVOIDING WHAT IT'S DONE TO ME.
MY WHOLE LIFE, I HAVE FOUGHT FOR IDEAS. GRAND EXPERIMENTS AND SYSTEMS AND STRUCTURES OF BELIEF. AND NOW...
NOW I FIGHT FOR SOMETHING BETTER. I FIGHT FOR THEM.
YOU SHOULD KNOW... THERE ARE MANY WHO WOULD CALL THAT A FLAW IN ONE'S ARMOR. SOMETHING TO BE EXPLOITED.
THEN I WOULD SAY, LET THEM THINK THAT, BROTHER.
THESE CHILDREN, THEY GIVE ME A CAUSE.
AND IT DOES NOT MAKE ME WEAK...

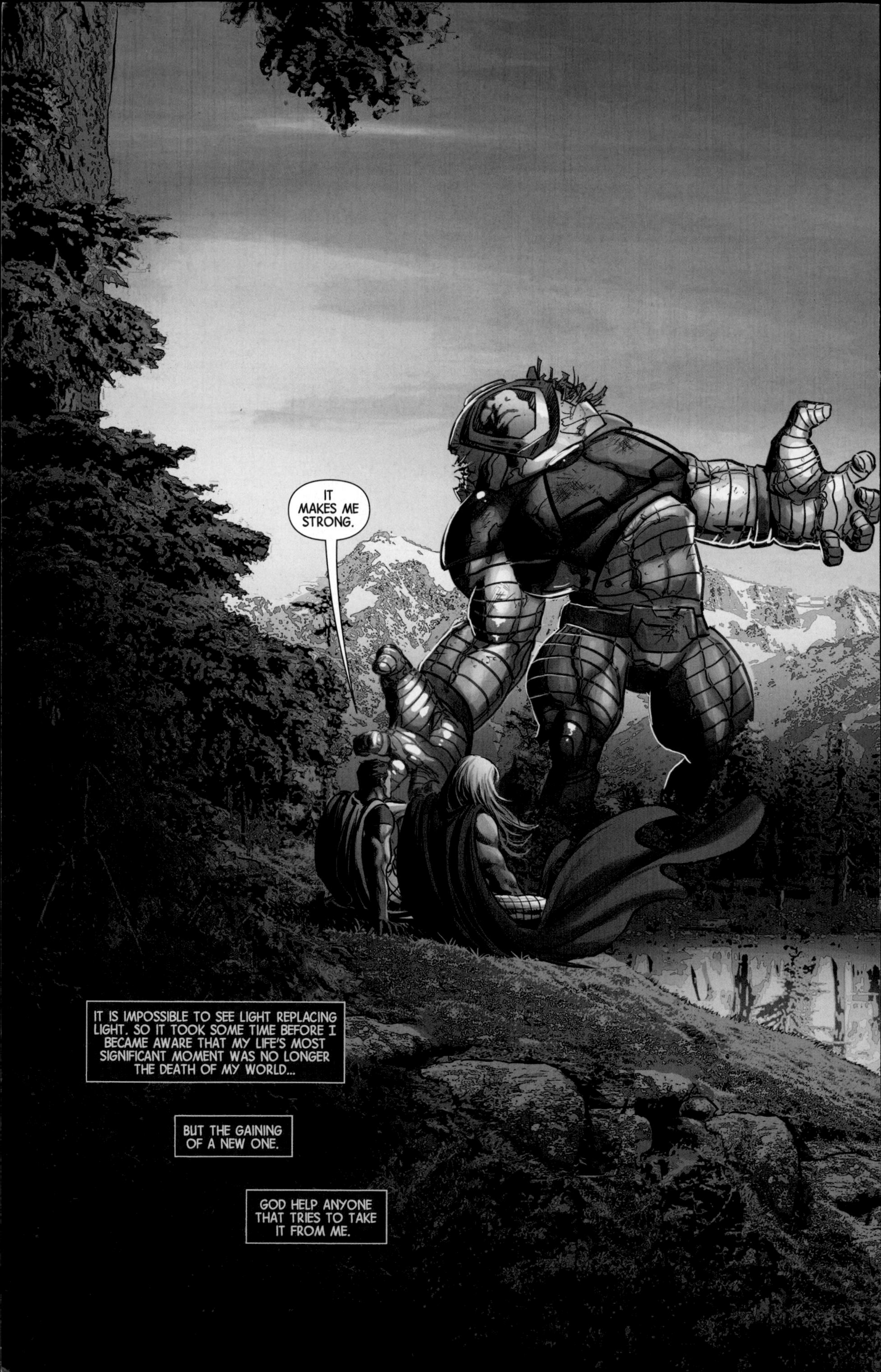
IT MAKES ME STRONG.
IT IS IMPOSSIBLE TO SEE LIGHT REPLACING LIGHT. SO IT TOOK SOME TIME BEFORE I BECAME AWARE THAT MY LIFE'S MOST SIGNIFICANT MOMENT WAS NO LONGER THE DEATH OF MY WORLD...
BUT THE GAINING OF A NEW ONE.
GOD HELP ANYONE THAT TRIES TO TAKE IT FROM ME.

"THE SIGNAL"

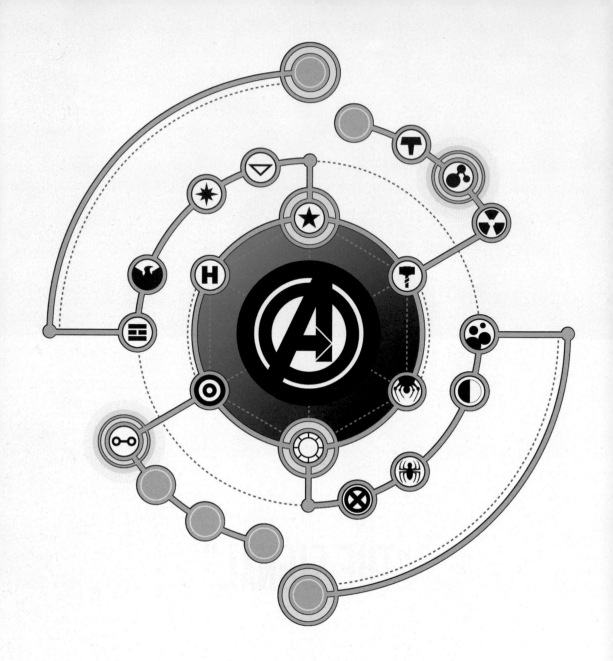

EARTH'S MIGHTIEST HEROES

CAPTAIN AMERICA · IRON MAN · THOR · HAWKEYE · BLACK WIDOW · HULK
WOLVERINE · SPIDER-MAN · CAPTAIN MARVEL · SPIDER-WOMAN
FALCON · SHANG-CHI · SUNSPOT · CANNONBALL · MANIFOLD
SMASHER · CAPTAIN UNIVERSE · HYPERION

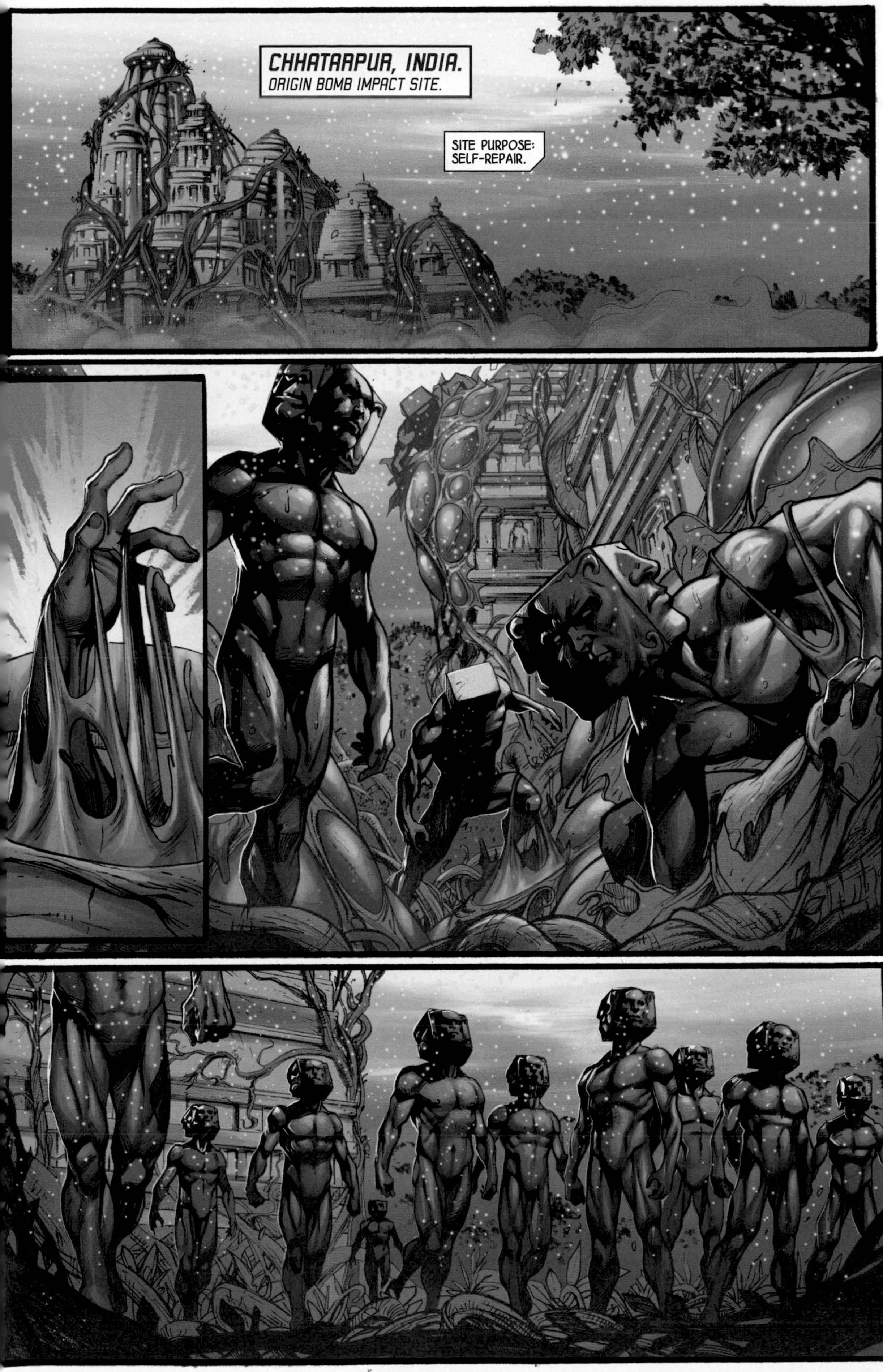
CHHATARPUR, INDIA.
ORIGIN BOMB IMPACT SITE.
SITE PURPOSE: SELF-REPAIR.

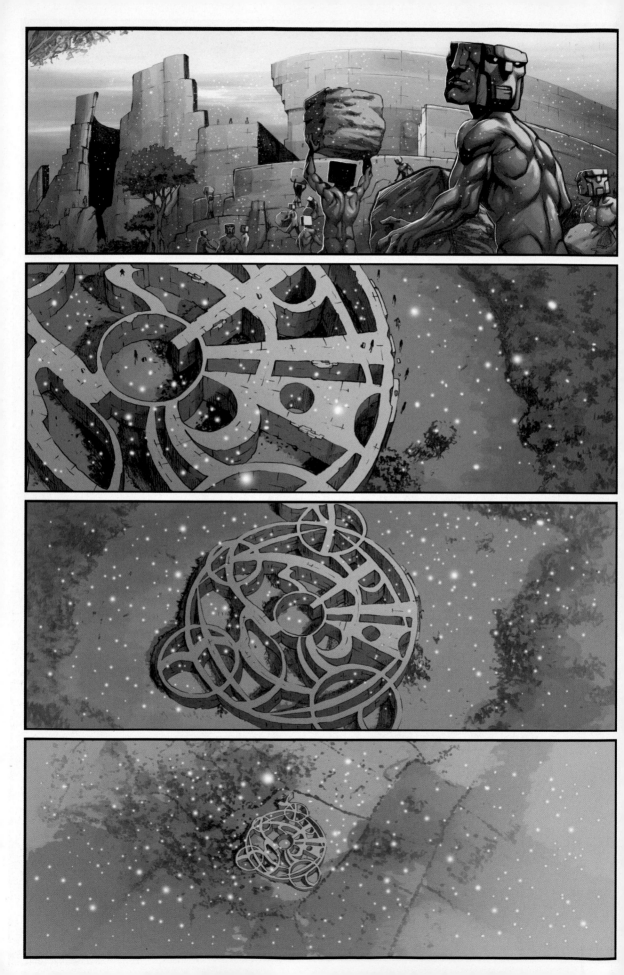

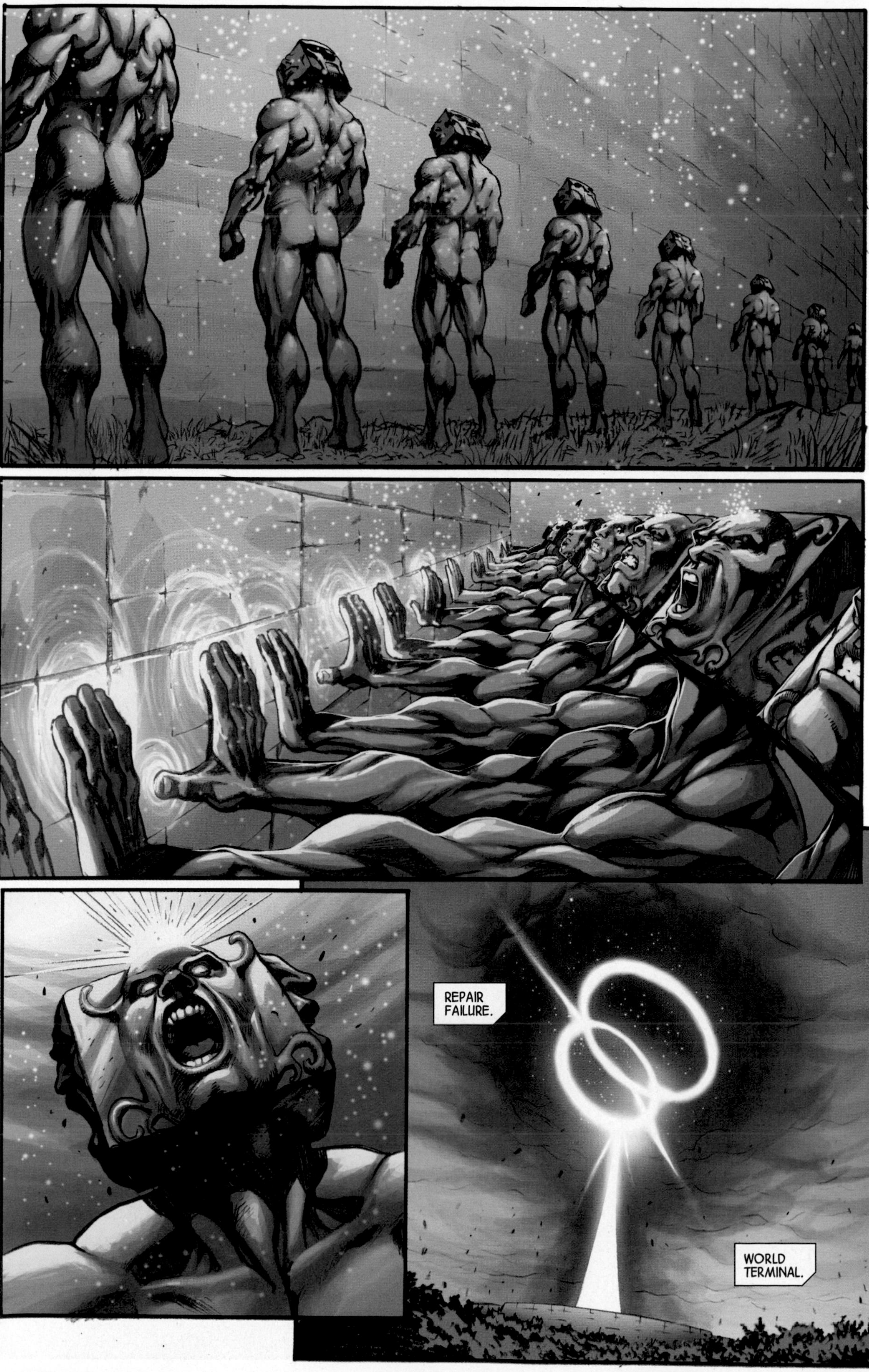
REPAIR FAILURE.
WORLD TERMINAL.

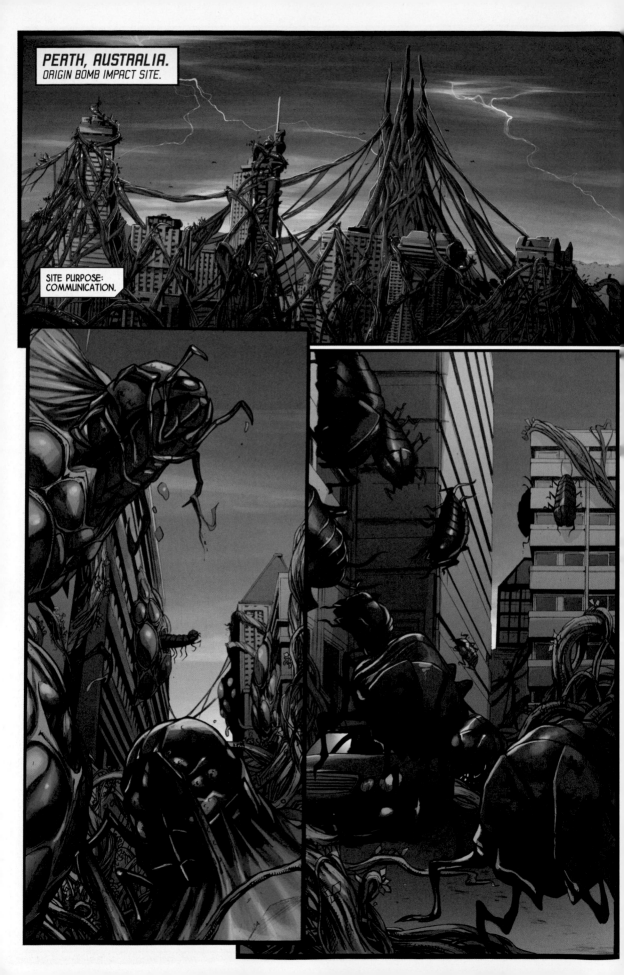

PERTH, AUSTRALIA.
ORIGIN BOMB IMPACT SITE.

SITE PURPOSE:
COMMUNICATION.

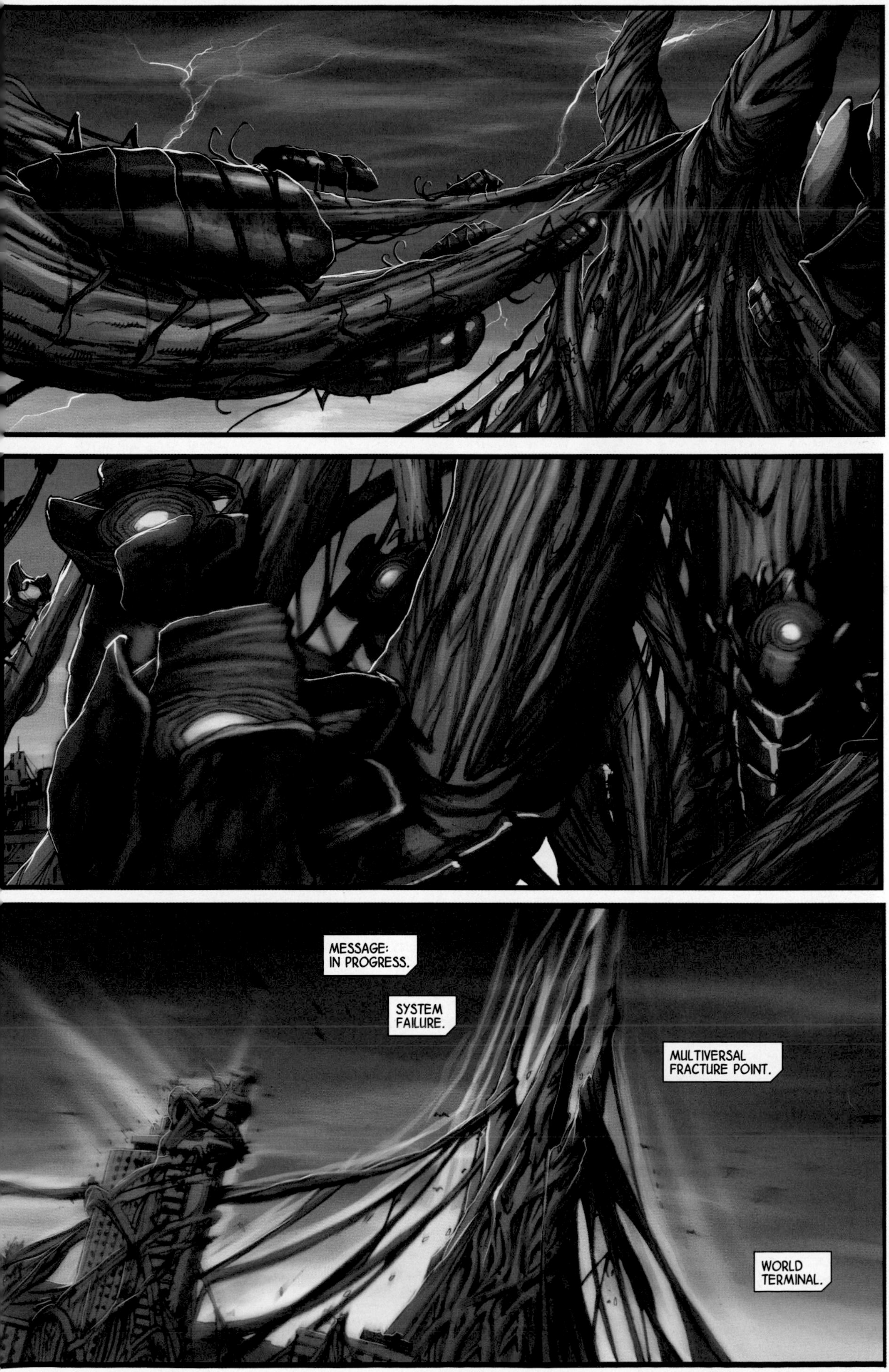
MESSAGE:
IN PROGRESS.
SYSTEM
FAILURE.
MULTIVERSAL
FRACTURE POINT.
WORLD
TERMINAL.

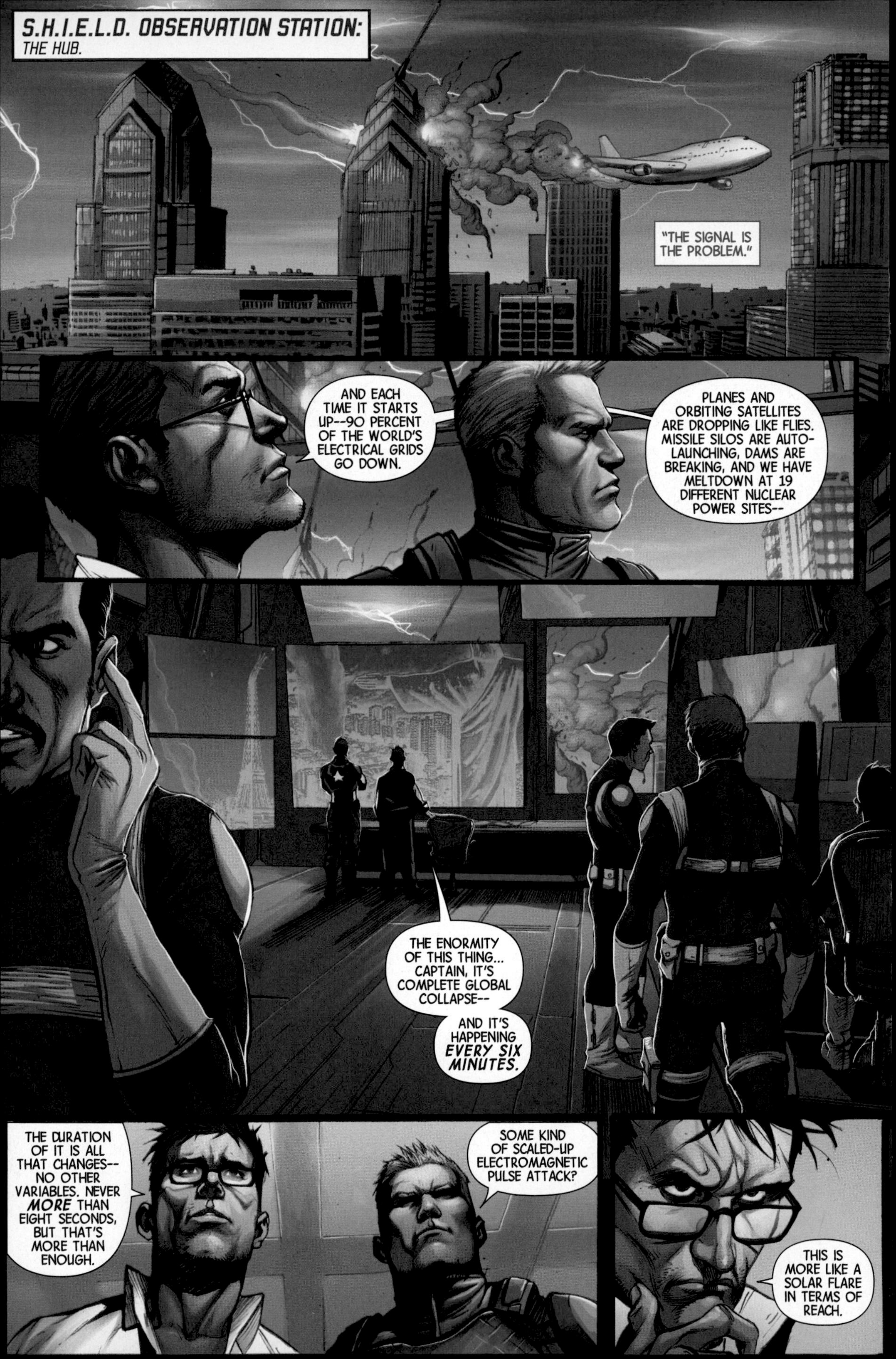
S.H.I.E.L.D. OBSERVATION STATION: THE HUB.
"THE SIGNAL IS THE PROBLEM."
AND EACH TIME IT STARTS UP--90 PERCENT OF THE WORLD'S ELECTRICAL GRIDS GO DOWN.
PLANES AND ORBITING SATELLITES ARE DROPPING LIKE FLIES. MISSILE SILOS ARE AUTO-LAUNCHING, DAMS ARE BREAKING, AND WE HAVE MELTDOWN AT 19 DIFFERENT NUCLEAR POWER SITES--
THE ENORMITY OF THIS THING... CAPTAIN, IT'S COMPLETE GLOBAL COLLAPSE--
AND IT'S HAPPENING EVERY SIX MINUTES.
THE DURATION OF IT IS ALL THAT CHANGES-- NO OTHER VARIABLES. NEVER MORE THAN EIGHT SECONDS, BUT THAT'S MORE THAN ENOUGH.
SOME KIND OF SCALED-UP ELECTROMAGNETIC PULSE ATTACK?
THIS IS MORE LIKE A SOLAR FLARE IN TERMS OF REACH.

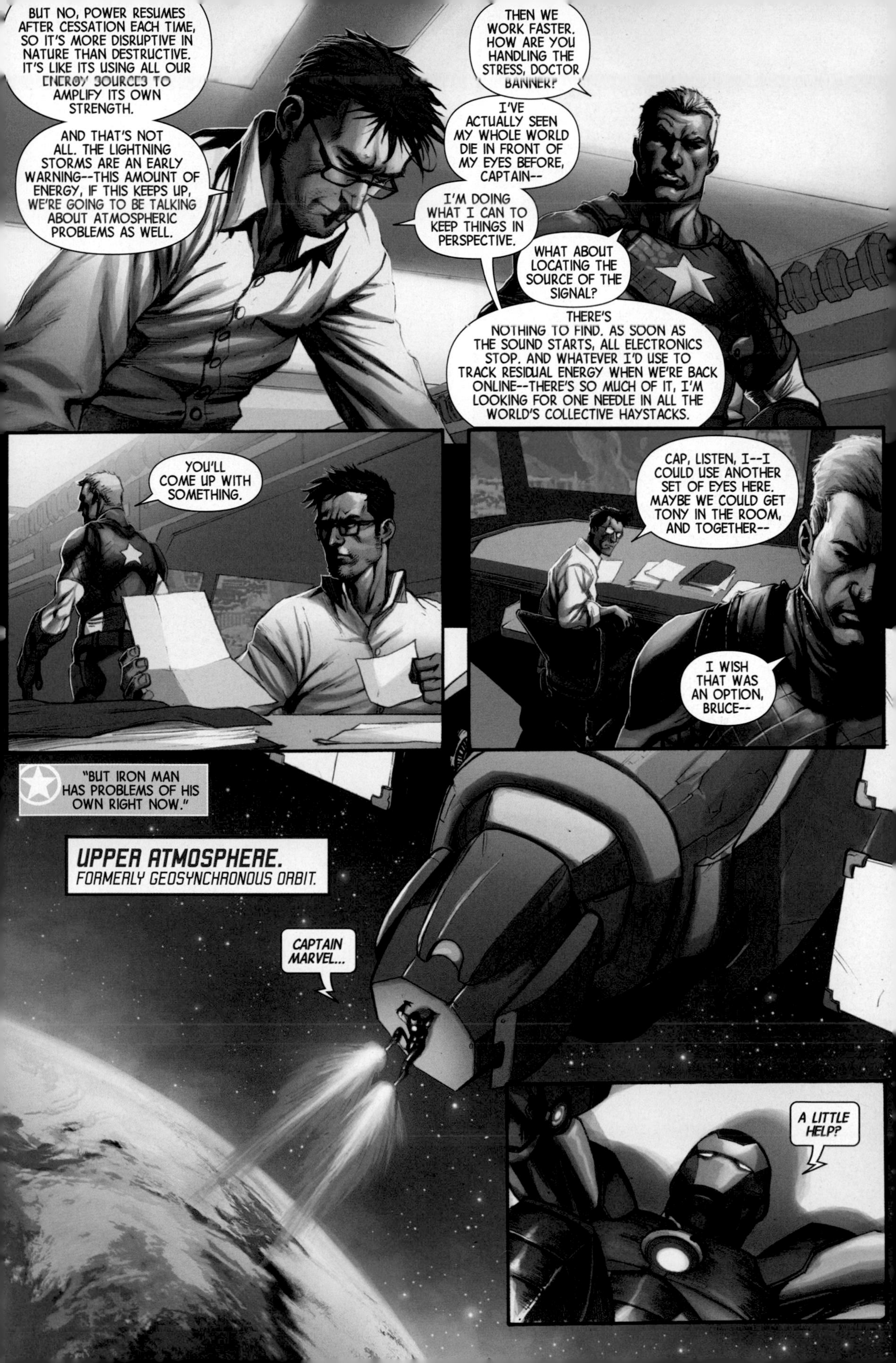
BUT NO, POWER RESUMES AFTER CESSATION EACH TIME, SO IT'S MORE DISRUPTIVE IN NATURE THAN DESTRUCTIVE. IT'S LIKE ITS USING ALL OUR ENERGY SOURCES TO AMPLIFY ITS OWN STRENGTH.
AND THAT'S NOT ALL. THE LIGHTNING STORMS ARE AN EARLY WARNING--THIS AMOUNT OF ENERGY, IF THIS KEEPS UP, WE'RE GOING TO BE TALKING ABOUT ATMOSPHERIC PROBLEMS AS WELL.
THEN WE WORK FASTER. HOW ARE YOU HANDLING THE STRESS, DOCTOR BANNER?
I'VE ACTUALLY SEEN MY WHOLE WORLD DIE IN FRONT OF MY EYES BEFORE, CAPTAIN--
I'M DOING WHAT I CAN TO KEEP THINGS IN PERSPECTIVE.
WHAT ABOUT LOCATING THE SOURCE OF THE SIGNAL?
THERE'S NOTHING TO FIND. AS SOON AS THE SOUND STARTS, ALL ELECTRONICS STOP. AND WHATEVER I'D USE TO TRACK RESIDUAL ENERGY WHEN WE'RE BACK ONLINE--THERE'S SO MUCH OF IT, I'M LOOKING FOR ONE NEEDLE IN ALL THE WORLD'S COLLECTIVE HAYSTACKS.
YOU'LL COME UP WITH SOMETHING.
CAP, LISTEN, I--I COULD USE ANOTHER SET OF EYES HERE. MAYBE WE COULD GET TONY IN THE ROOM, AND TOGETHER--
I WISH THAT WAS AN OPTION, BRUCE--
"BUT IRON MAN HAS PROBLEMS OF HIS OWN RIGHT NOW."
UPPER ATMOSPHERE.
FORMERLY GEOSYNCHRONOUS ORBIT.
CAPTAIN MARVEL...
A LITTLE HELP?

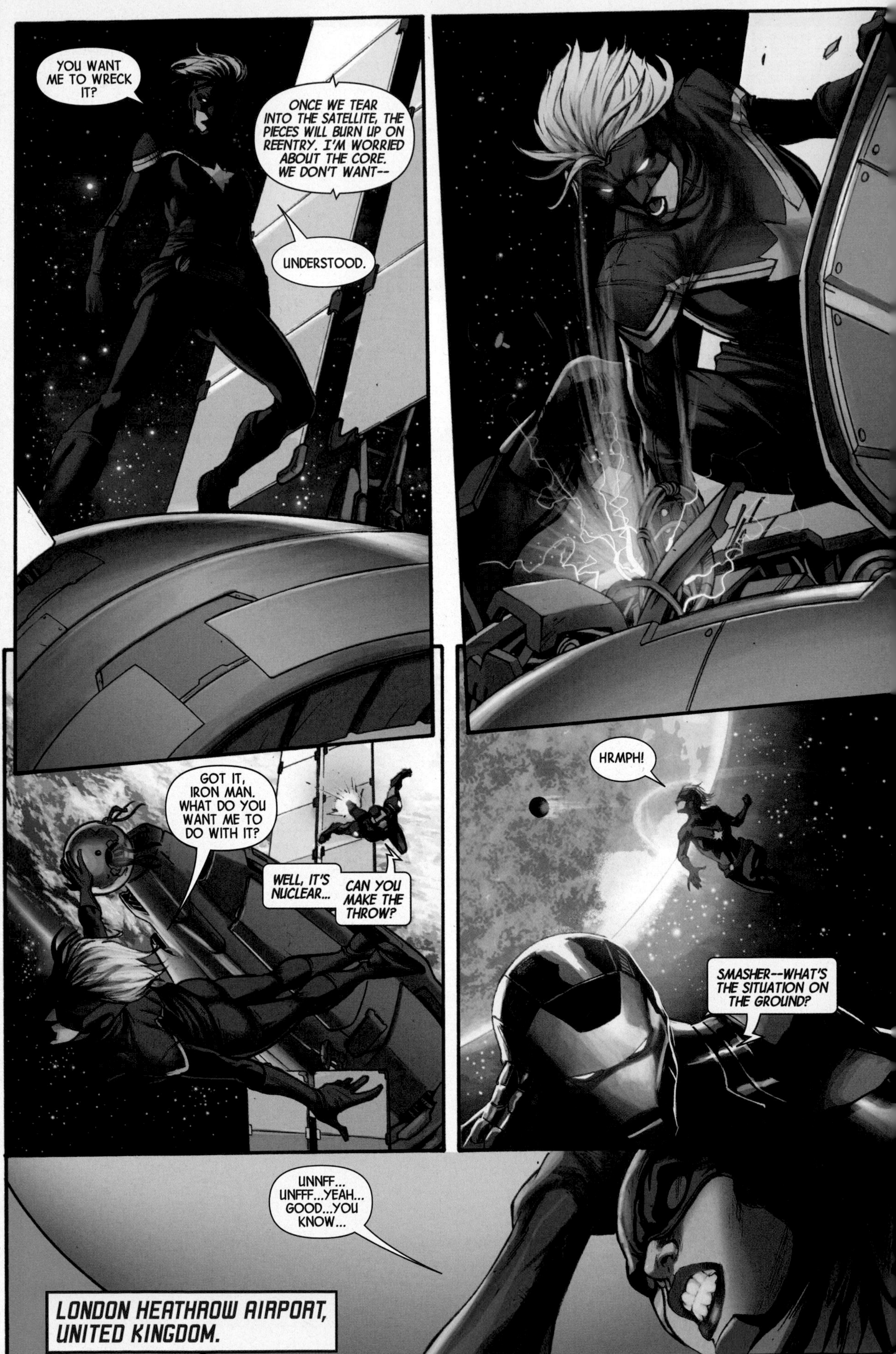
YOU WANT ME TO WRECK IT?
ONCE WE TEAR INTO THE SATELLITE, THE PIECES WILL BURN UP ON REENTRY. I'M WORRIED ABOUT THE CORE. WE DON'T WANT--
UNDERSTOOD.
GOT IT, IRON MAN. WHAT DO YOU WANT ME TO DO WITH IT?
WELL, IT'S NUCLEAR...
CAN YOU MAKE THE THROW?
HRMPH!
SMASHER--WHAT'S THE SITUATION ON THE GROUND?
UNNFF... UNFFF...YEAH... GOOD...YOU KNOW...
LONDON HEATHROW AIRPORT, UNITED KINGDOM.

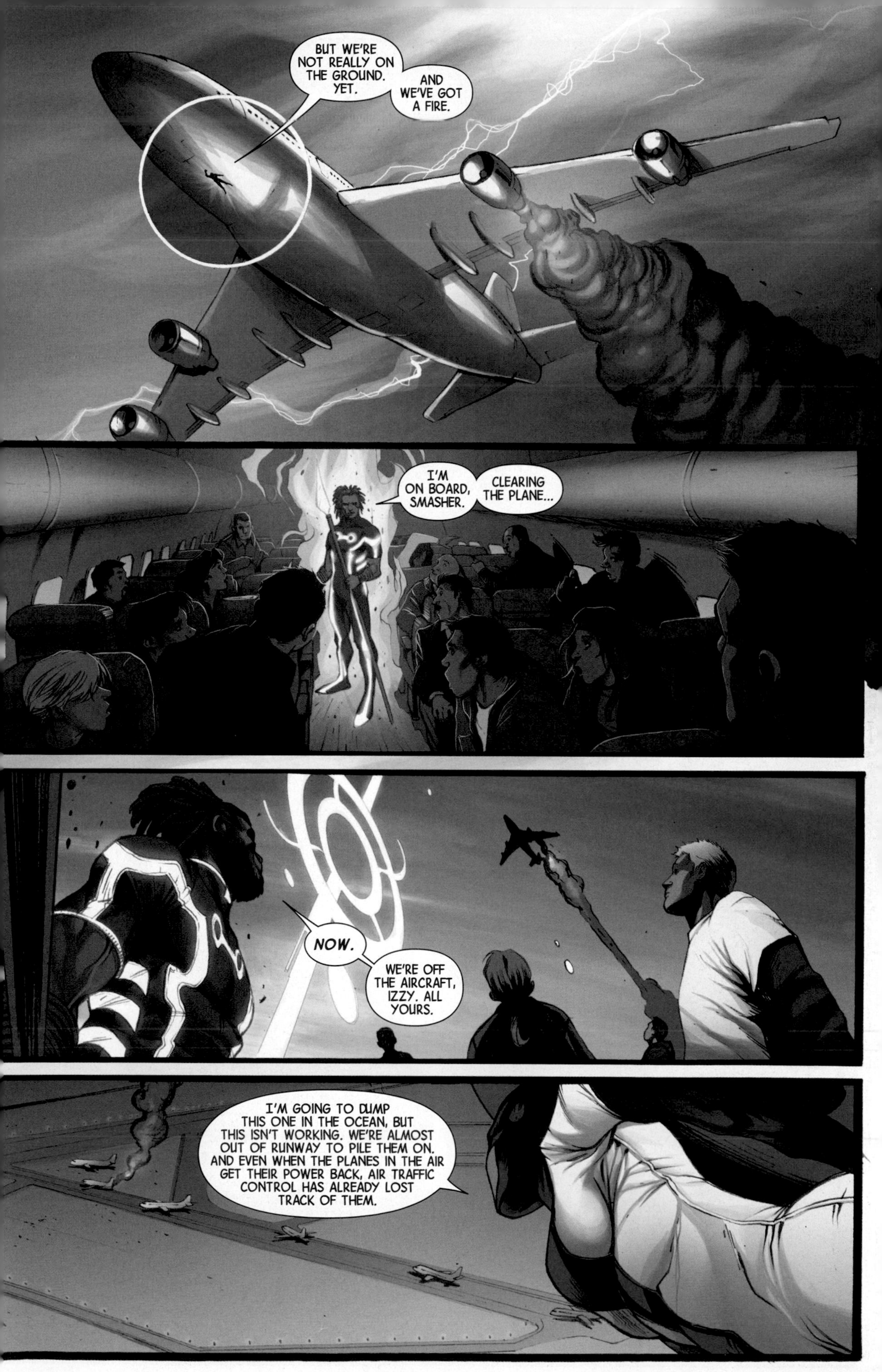
BUT WE'RE NOT REALLY ON THE GROUND. YET.
AND WE'VE GOT A FIRE.
I'M ON BOARD, SMASHER.
CLEARING THE PLANE...
NOW.
WE'RE OFF THE AIRCRAFT, IZZY. ALL YOURS.
I'M GOING TO DUMP THIS ONE IN THE OCEAN, BUT THIS ISN'T WORKING. WE'RE ALMOST OUT OF RUNWAY TO PILE THEM ON. AND EVEN WHEN THE PLANES IN THE AIR GET THEIR POWER BACK, AIR TRAFFIC CONTROL HAS ALREADY LOST TRACK OF THEM.

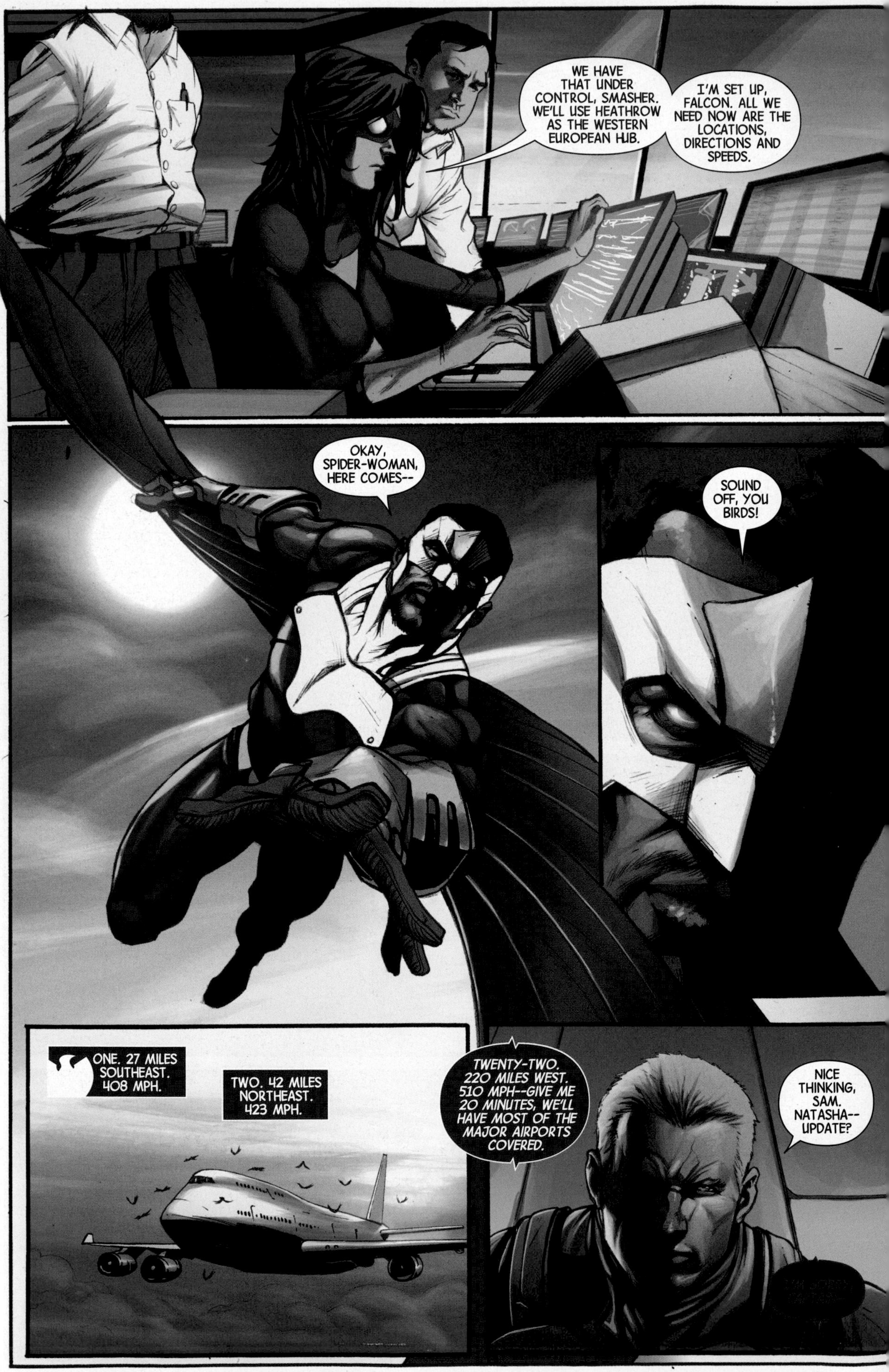
WE HAVE THAT UNDER CONTROL, SMASHER. WE'LL USE HEATHROW AS THE WESTERN EUROPEAN HUB.
I'M SET UP, FALCON. ALL WE NEED NOW ARE THE LOCATIONS, DIRECTIONS AND SPEEDS.
OKAY, SPIDER-WOMAN, HERE COMES--
SOUND OFF, YOU BIRDS!
ONE. 27 MILES SOUTHEAST. 408 MPH.
TWO. 42 MILES NORTHEAST. 423 MPH.
TWENTY-TWO. 220 MILES WEST. 510 MPH--GIVE ME 20 MINUTES, WE'LL HAVE MOST OF THE MAJOR AIRPORTS COVERED.
NICE THINKING, SAM. NATASHA-- UPDATE?

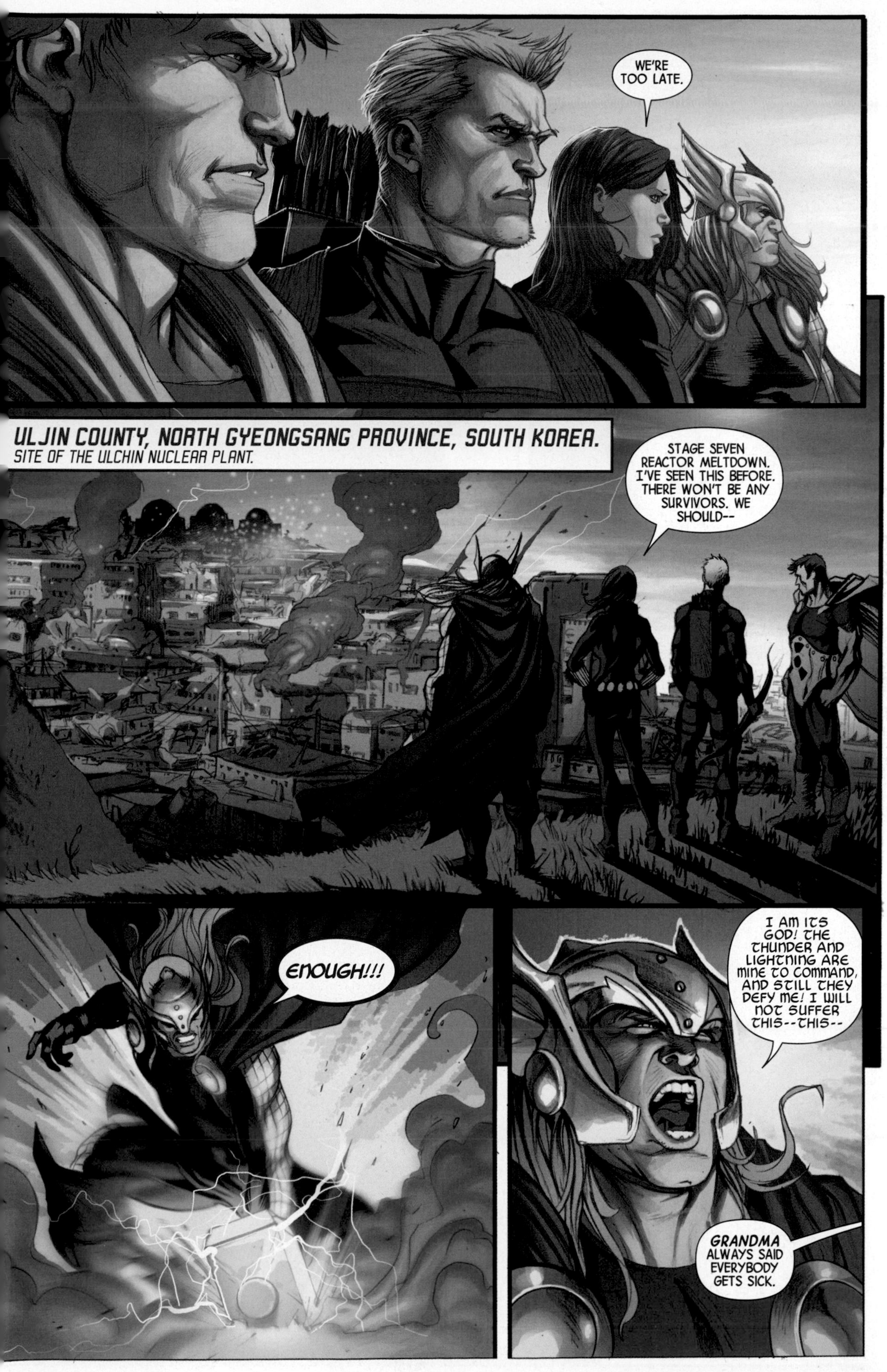
WE'RE TOO LATE.
ULJIN COUNTY, NORTH GYEONGSANG PROVINCE, SOUTH KOREA.
SITE OF THE ULCHIN NUCLEAR PLANT.
STAGE SEVEN REACTOR MELTDOWN. I'VE SEEN THIS BEFORE. THERE WON'T BE ANY SURVIVORS. WE SHOULD--
ENOUGH!!!
I AM ITS GOD! THE THUNDER AND LIGHTNING ARE MINE TO COMMAND, AND STILL THEY DEFY ME! I WILL NOT SUFFER THIS--THIS--
GRANDMA ALWAYS SAID EVERYBODY GETS SICK.

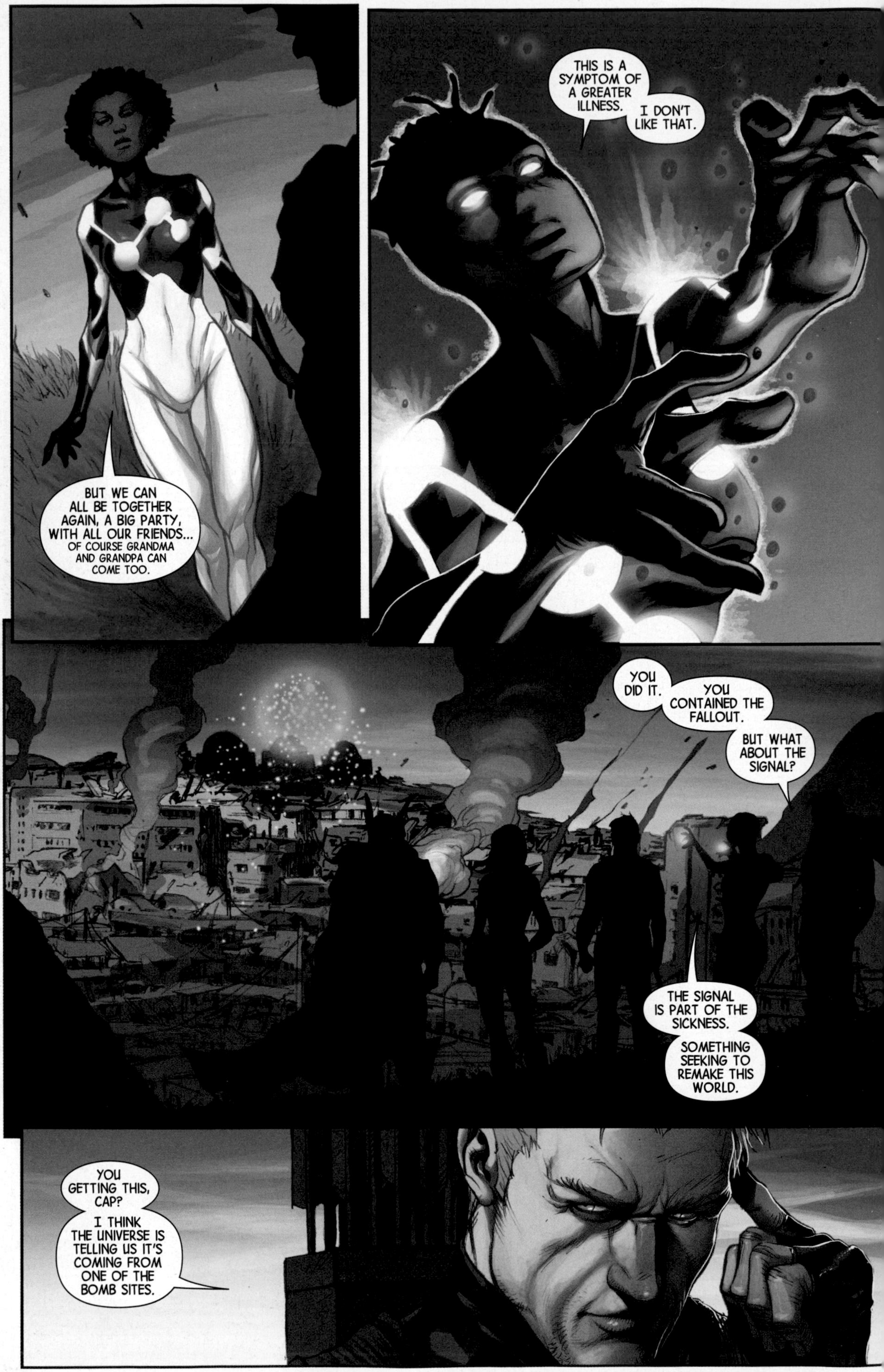
BUT WE CAN ALL BE TOGETHER AGAIN, A BIG PARTY, WITH ALL OUR FRIENDS... OF COURSE GRANDMA AND GRANDPA CAN COME TOO.
THIS IS A SYMPTOM OF A GREATER ILLNESS.
I DON'T LIKE THAT.
YOU DID IT.
YOU CONTAINED THE FALLOUT.
BUT WHAT ABOUT THE SIGNAL?
THE SIGNAL IS PART OF THE SICKNESS.
SOMETHING SEEKING TO REMAKE THIS WORLD.
YOU GETTING THIS, CAP?
I THINK THE UNIVERSE IS TELLING US IT'S COMING FROM ONE OF THE BOMB SITES.

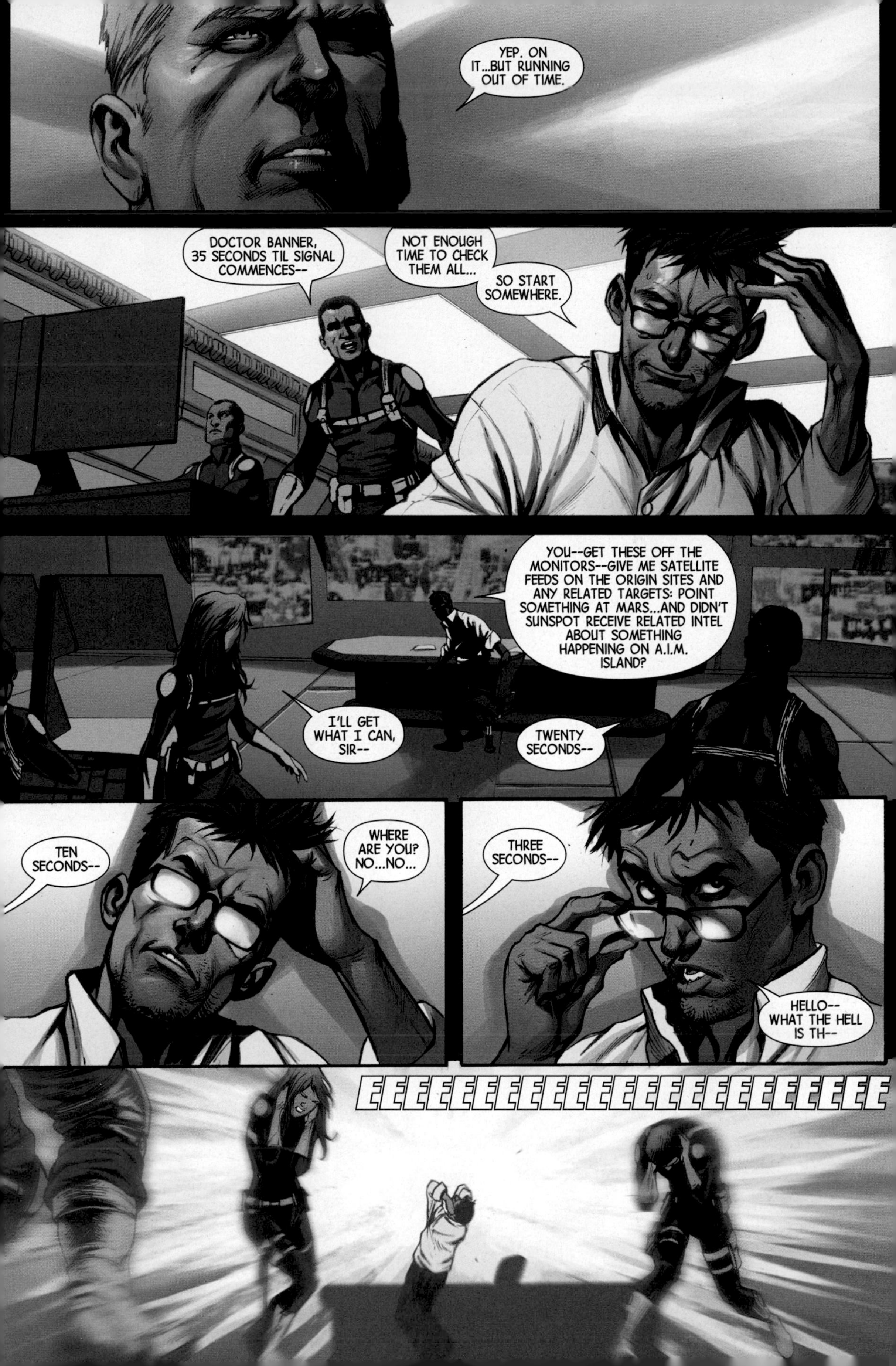
YEP. ON IT...BUT RUNNING OUT OF TIME.
DOCTOR BANNER, 35 SECONDS TIL SIGNAL COMMENCES--
NOT ENOUGH TIME TO CHECK THEM ALL...
SO START SOMEWHERE.
YOU--GET THESE OFF THE MONITORS--GIVE ME SATELLITE FEEDS ON THE ORIGIN SITES AND ANY RELATED TARGETS: POINT SOMETHING AT MARS...AND DIDN'T SUNSPOT RECEIVE RELATED INTEL ABOUT SOMETHING HAPPENING ON A.I.M. ISLAND?
I'LL GET WHAT I CAN, SIR--
TWENTY SECONDS--
TEN SECONDS--
WHERE ARE YOU? NO...NO...
THREE SECONDS--
HELLO-- WHAT THE HELL IS TH--
EEEEEEEEEEEEEEEEEEEEEEEEE

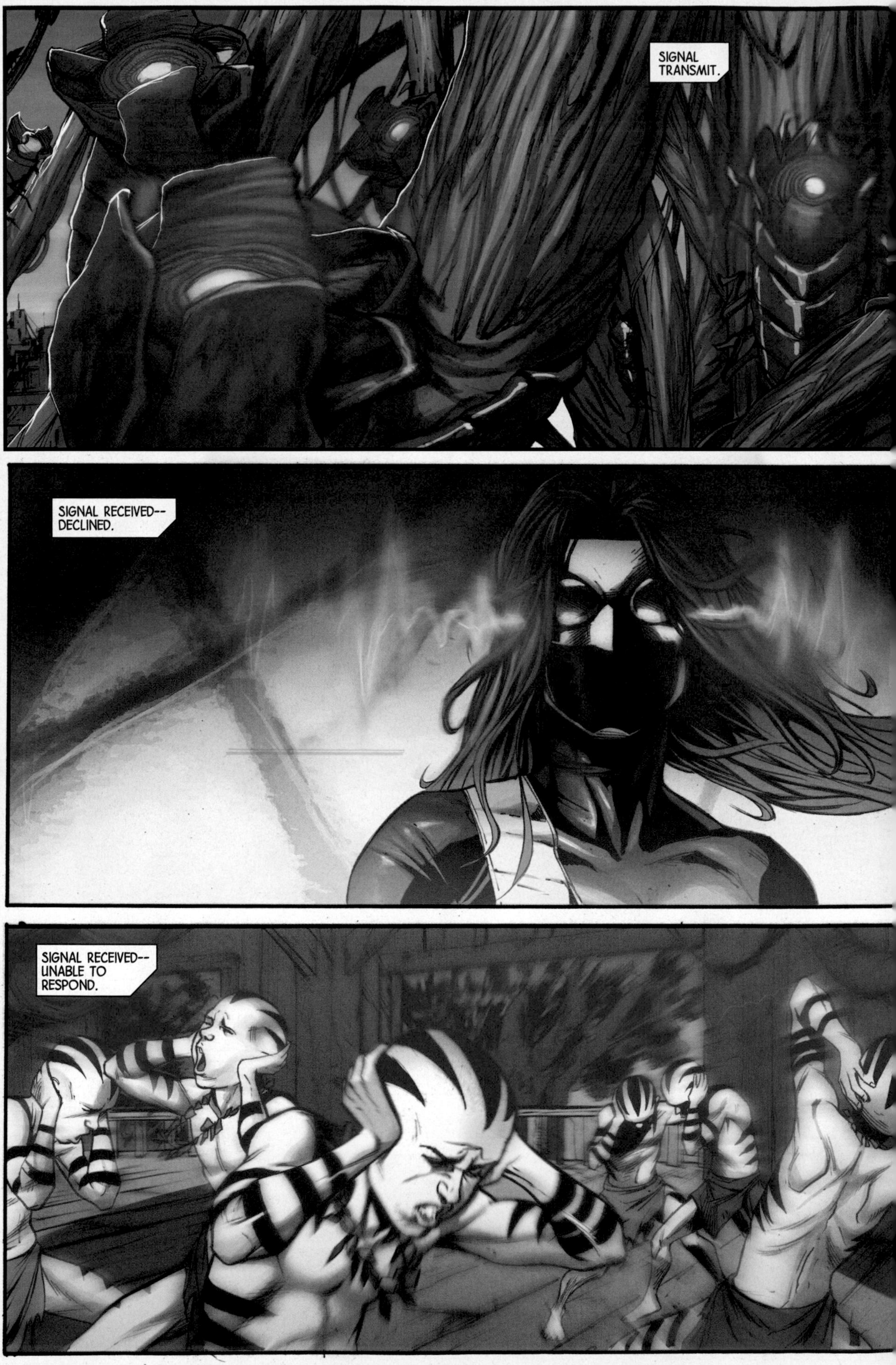
SIGNAL TRANSMIT.
SIGNAL RECEIVED-- DECLINED.
SIGNAL RECEIVED-- UNABLE TO RESPOND.

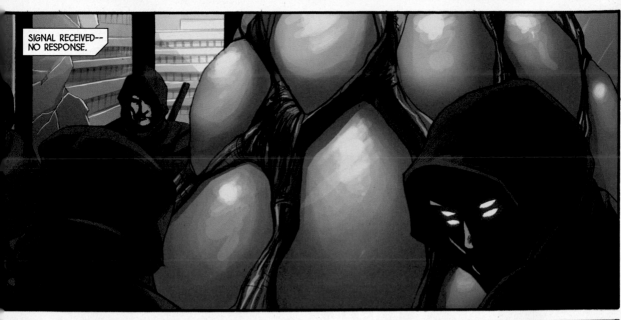

SIGNAL RECEIVED--
NO RESPONSE.

SIGNAL
RECEIVED--

ACCEPTED.

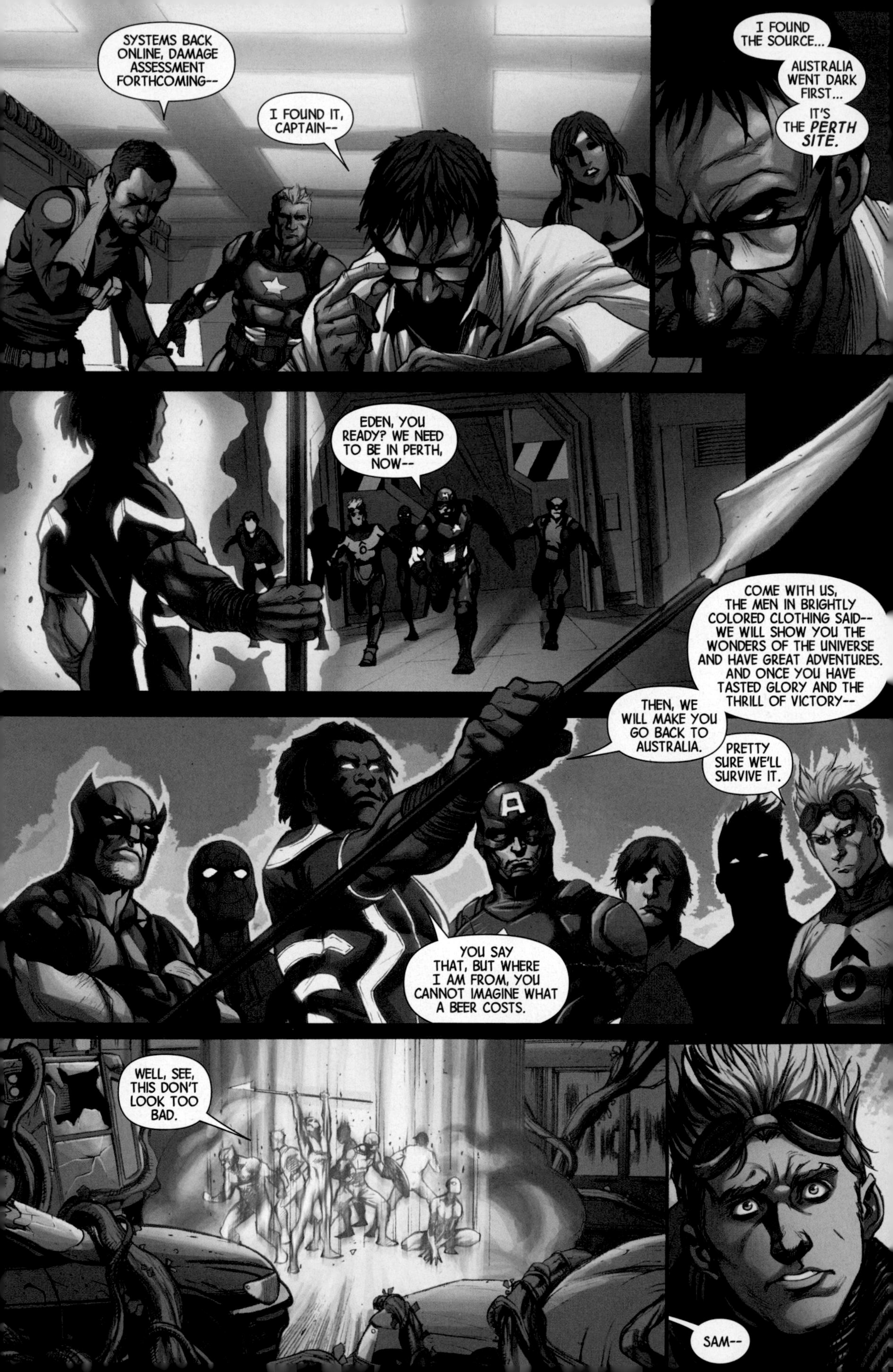

SYSTEMS BACK ONLINE, DAMAGE ASSESSMENT FORTHCOMING--
I FOUND IT, CAPTAIN--
I FOUND THE SOURCE...
AUSTRALIA WENT DARK FIRST...
IT'S THE PERTH SITE.
EDEN, YOU READY? WE NEED TO BE IN PERTH, NOW--
COME WITH US, THE MEN IN BRIGHTLY COLORED CLOTHING SAID-- WE WILL SHOW YOU THE WONDERS OF THE UNIVERSE AND HAVE GREAT ADVENTURES. AND ONCE YOU HAVE TASTED GLORY AND THE THRILL OF VICTORY--
THEN, WE WILL MAKE YOU GO BACK TO AUSTRALIA.
PRETTY SURE WE'LL SURVIVE IT.
YOU SAY THAT, BUT WHERE I AM FROM, YOU CANNOT IMAGINE WHAT A BEER COSTS.
WELL, SEE, THIS DON'T LOOK TOO BAD.
SAM--

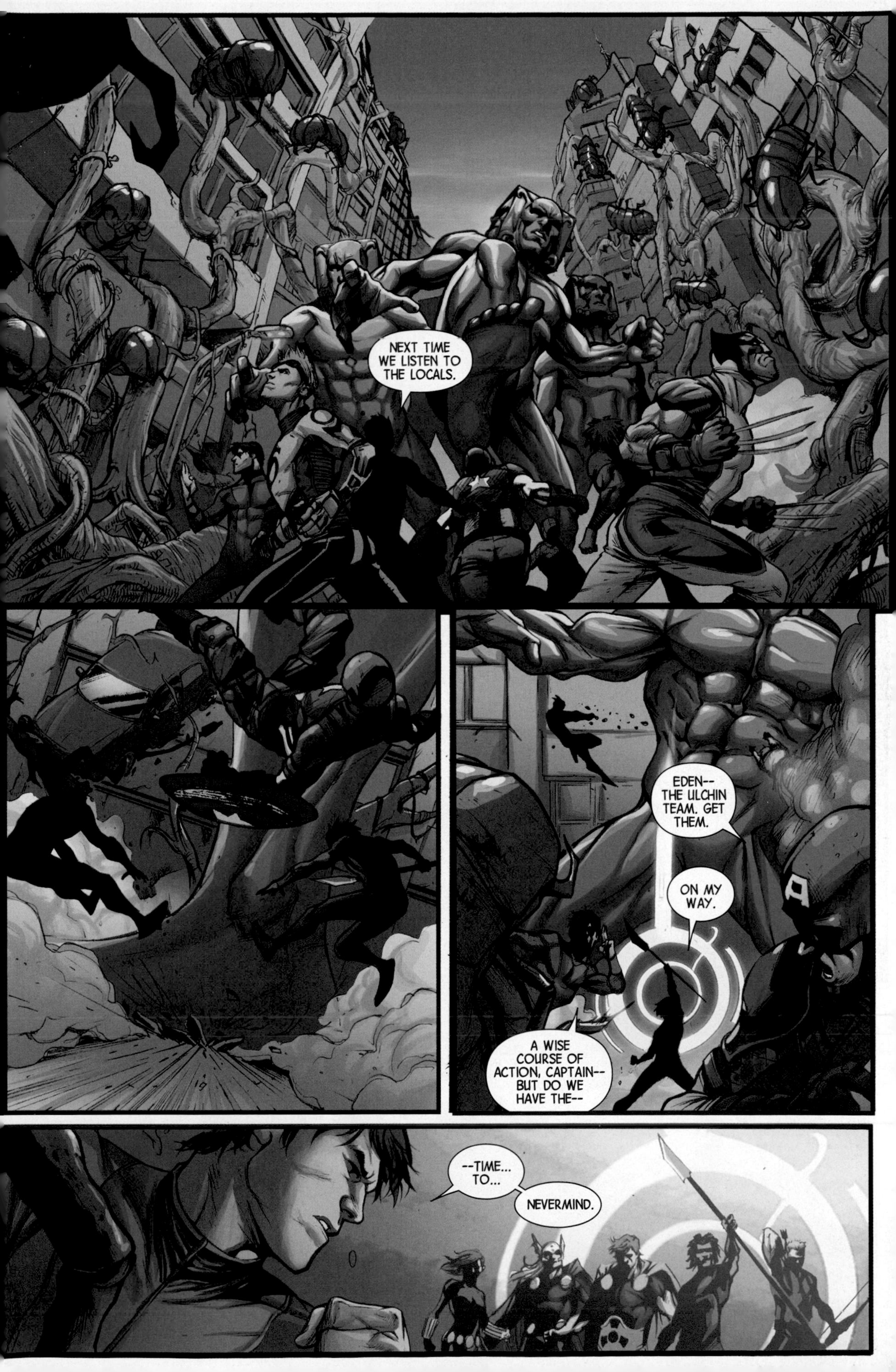
NEXT TIME WE LISTEN TO THE LOCALS.
EDEN-- THE ULCHIN TEAM. GET THEM.
ON MY WAY.
A WISE COURSE OF ACTION, CAPTAIN-- BUT DO WE HAVE THE--
--TIME... TO...
NEVERMIND.

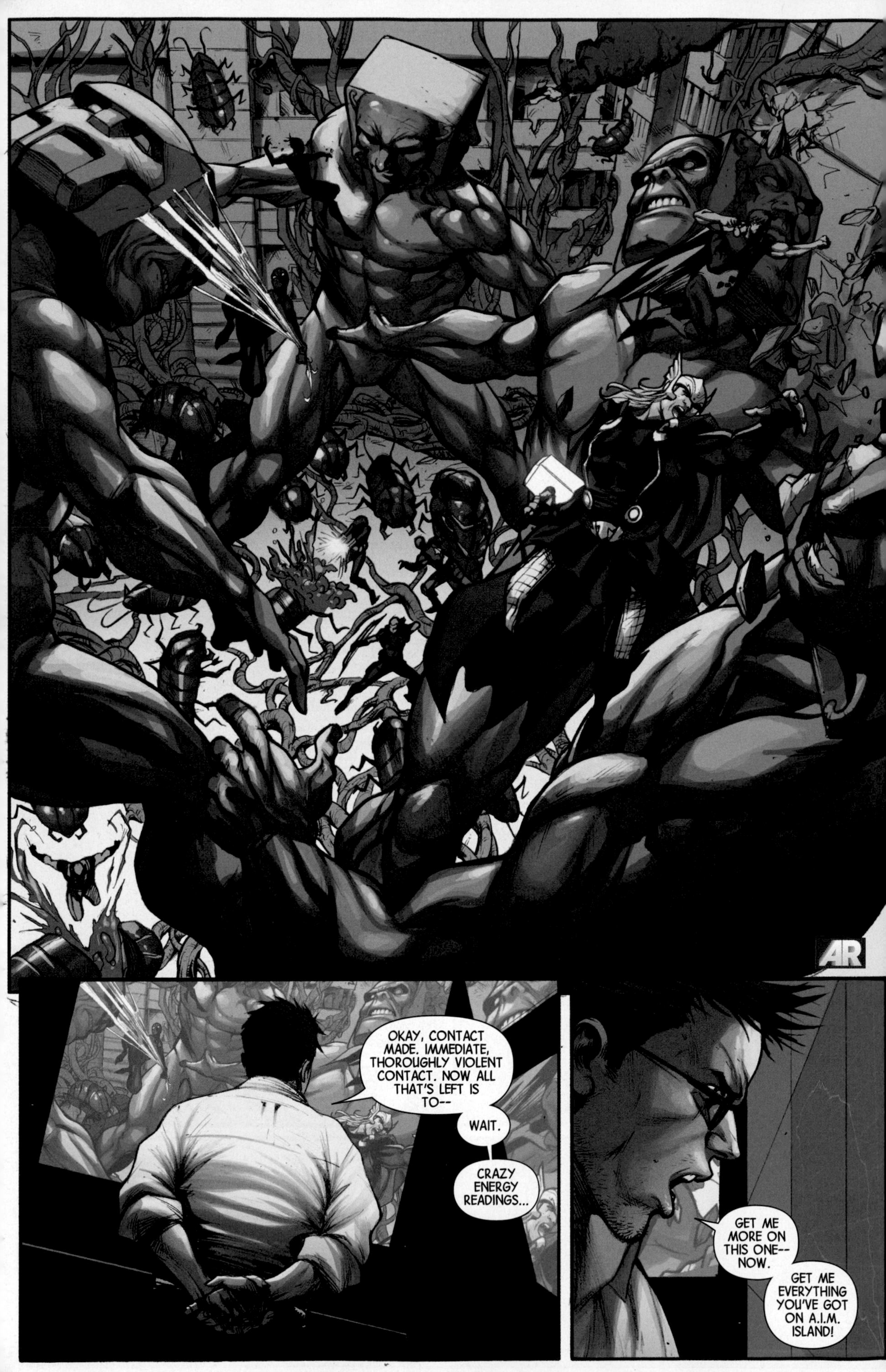

AR
OKAY, CONTACT MADE. IMMEDIATE, THOROUGHLY VIOLENT CONTACT. NOW ALL THAT'S LEFT IS TO--
WAIT.
CRAZY ENERGY READINGS...
GET ME MORE ON THIS ONE-- NOW.
GET ME EVERYTHING YOU'VE GOT ON A.I.M. ISLAND!

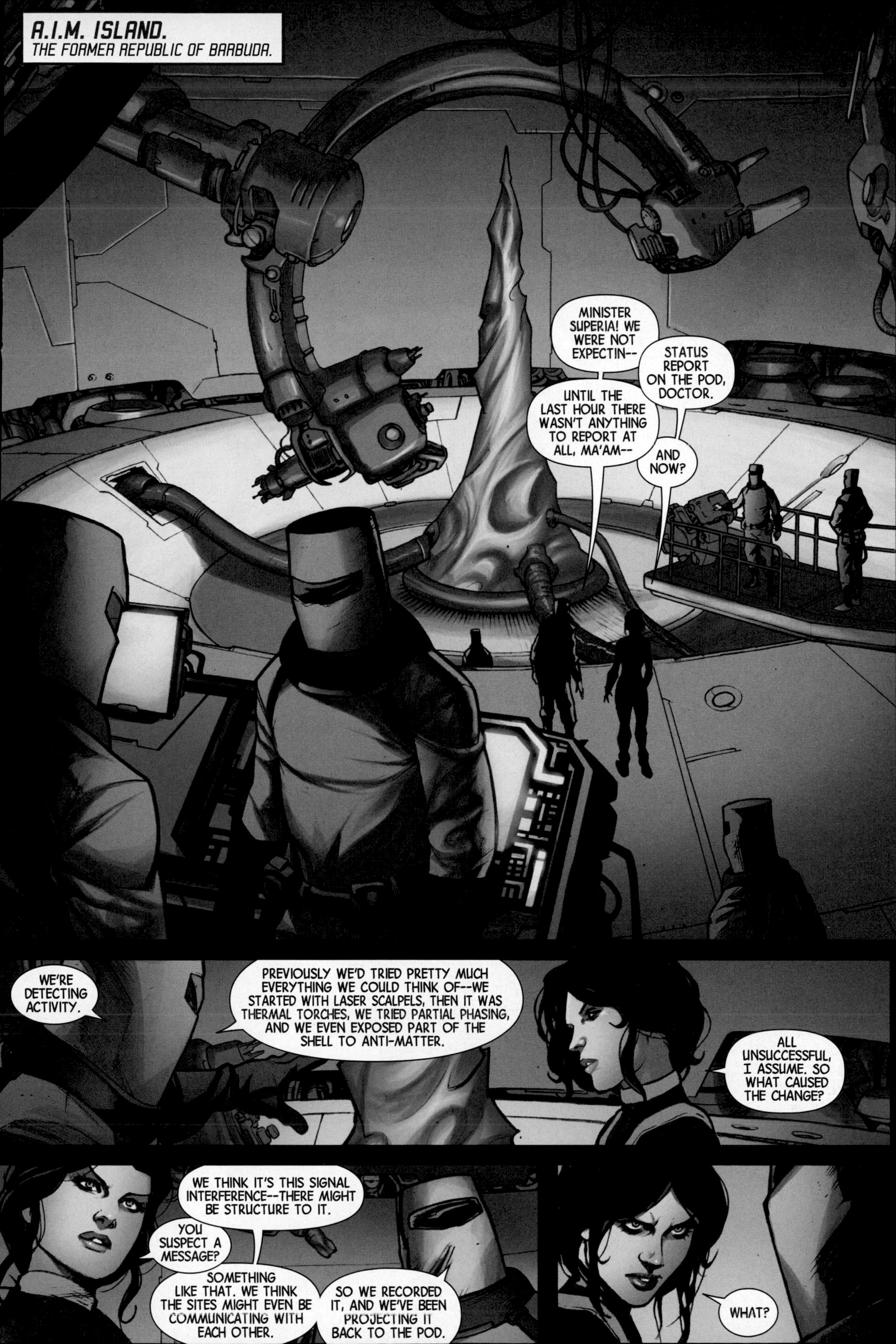
A.I.M. ISLAND.
THE FORMER REPUBLIC OF BARBUDA.
MINISTER SUPERIA! WE WERE NOT EXPECTIN--
STATUS REPORT ON THE POD, DOCTOR.
UNTIL THE LAST HOUR THERE WASN'T ANYTHING TO REPORT AT ALL, MA'AM--
AND NOW?
WE'RE DETECTING ACTIVITY.
PREVIOUSLY WE'D TRIED PRETTY MUCH EVERYTHING WE COULD THINK OF--WE STARTED WITH LASER SCALPELS, THEN IT WAS THERMAL TORCHES, WE TRIED PARTIAL PHASING, AND WE EVEN EXPOSED PART OF THE SHELL TO ANTI-MATTER.
ALL UNSUCCESSFUL, I ASSUME. SO WHAT CAUSED THE CHANGE?
WE THINK IT'S THIS SIGNAL INTERFERENCE--THERE MIGHT BE STRUCTURE TO IT.
YOU SUSPECT A MESSAGE?
SOMETHING LIKE THAT. WE THINK THE SITES MIGHT EVEN BE COMMUNICATING WITH EACH OTHER.
SO WE RECORDED IT, AND WE'VE BEEN PROJECTING IT BACK TO THE POD.
WHAT?

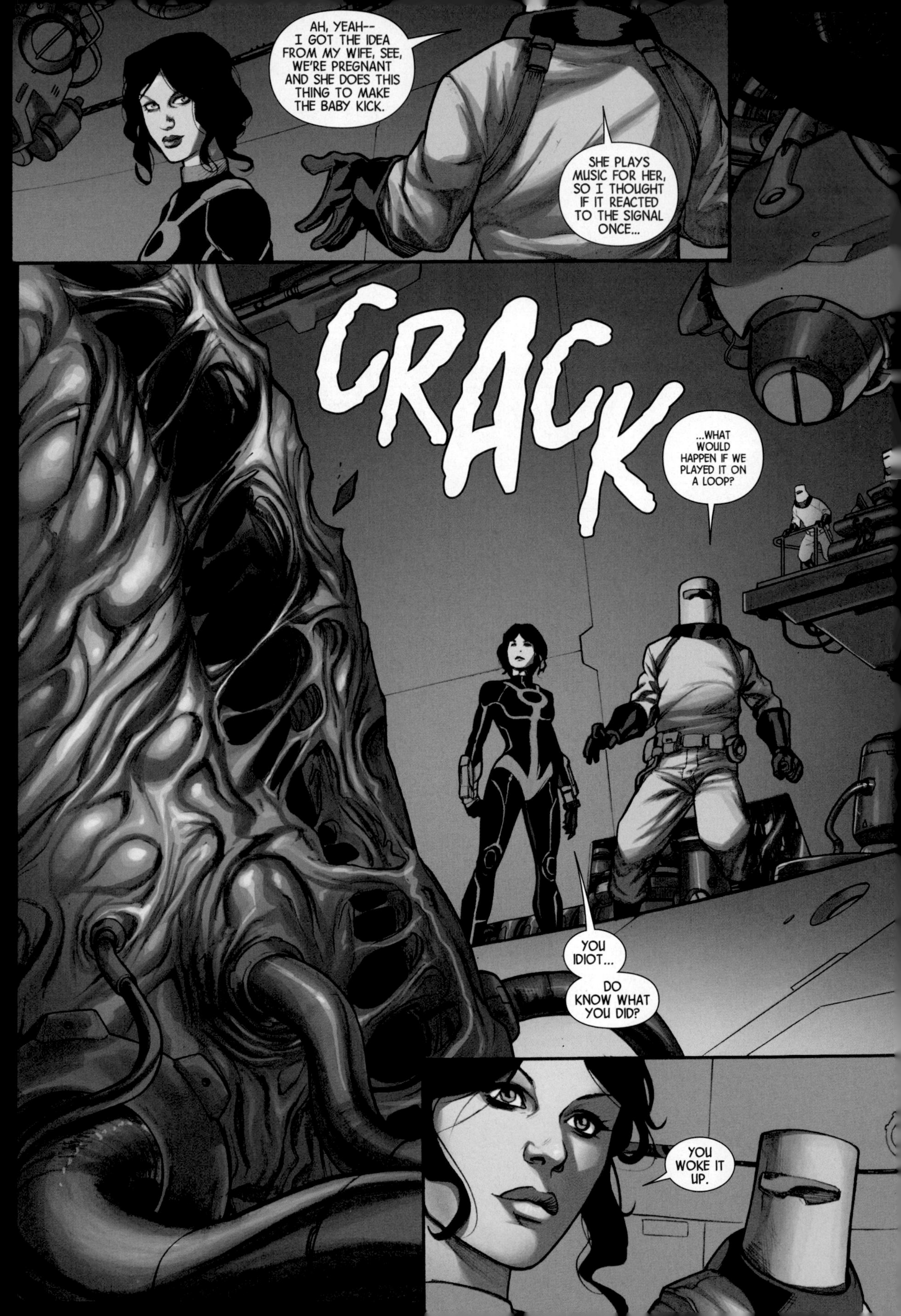
AH, YEAH-- I GOT THE IDEA FROM MY WIFE, SEE, WE'RE PREGNANT AND SHE DOES THIS THING TO MAKE THE BABY KICK.
SHE PLAYS MUSIC FOR HER, SO I THOUGHT IF IT REACTED TO THE SIGNAL ONCE...
CRACK
...WHAT WOULD HAPPEN IF WE PLAYED IT ON A LOOP?
YOU IDIOT...
DO KNOW WHAT YOU DID?
YOU WOKE IT UP.

"SENT AND RECEIVED"

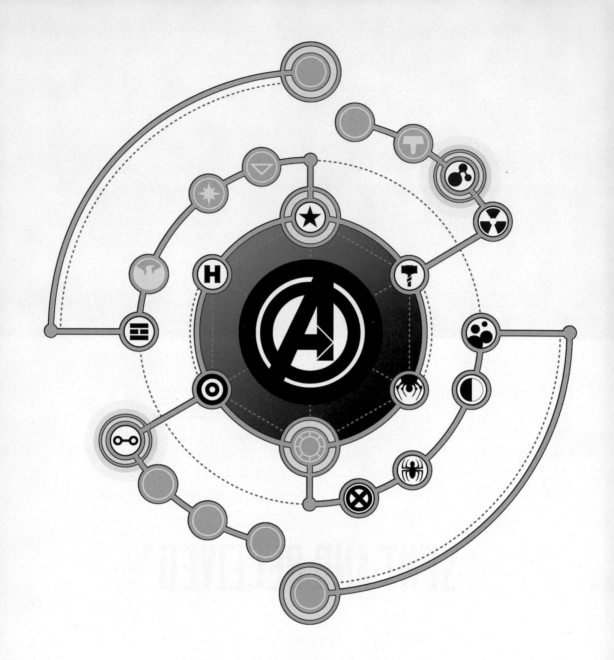

EARTH'S MIGHTIEST HEROES

CAPTAIN AMERICA · IRON MAN · THOR · HAWKEYE · BLACK WIDOW · HULK
WOLVERINE · SPIDER-MAN · CAPTAIN MARVEL · SPIDER-WOMAN
FALCON · SHANG-CHI · SUNSPOT · CANNONBALL · MANIFOLD
SMASHER · CAPTAIN UNIVERSE · HYPERION

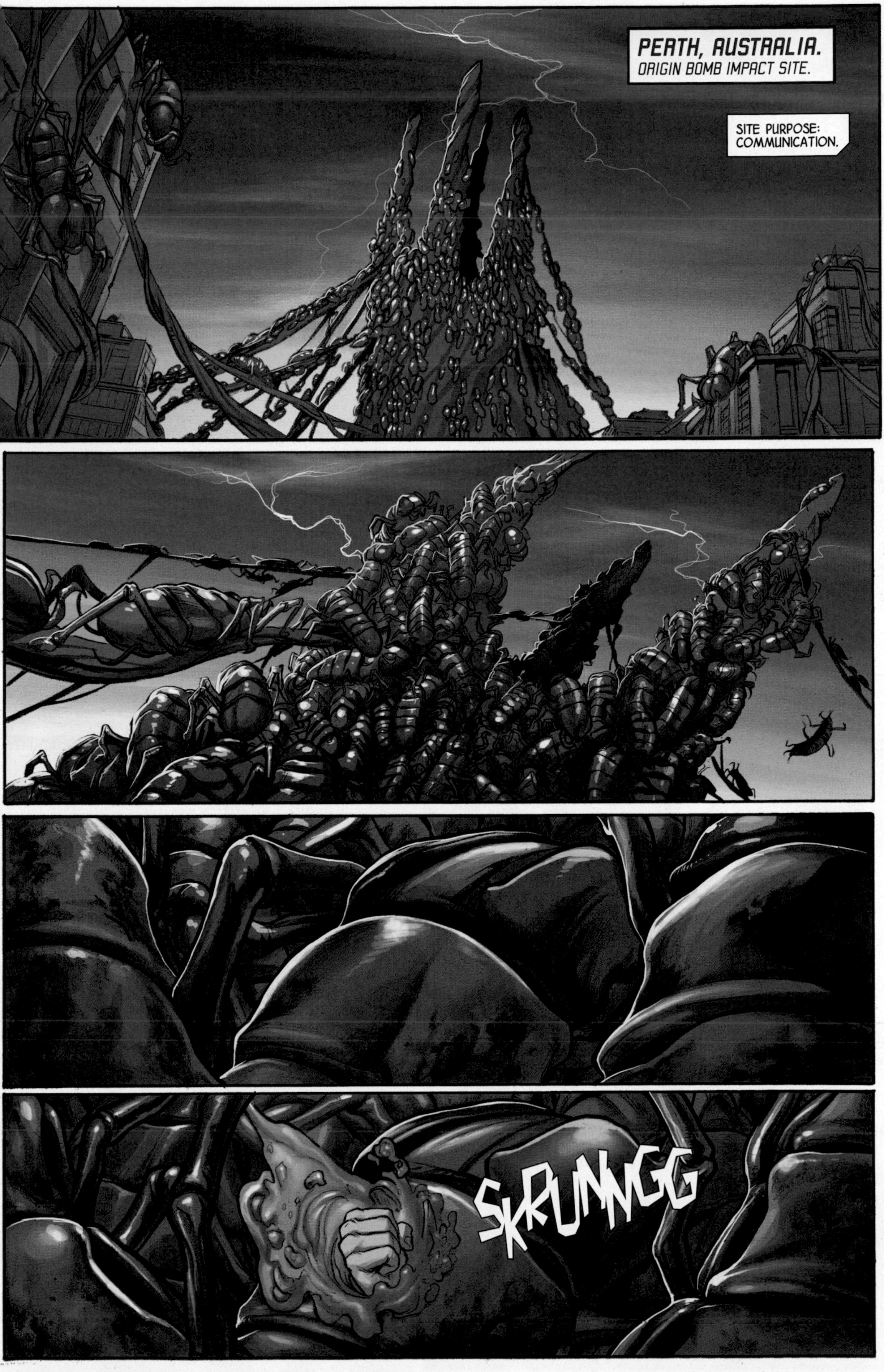
PERTH, AUSTRALIA.
ORIGIN BOMB IMPACT SITE.
SITE PURPOSE: COMMUNICATION.
SKRUNNGG

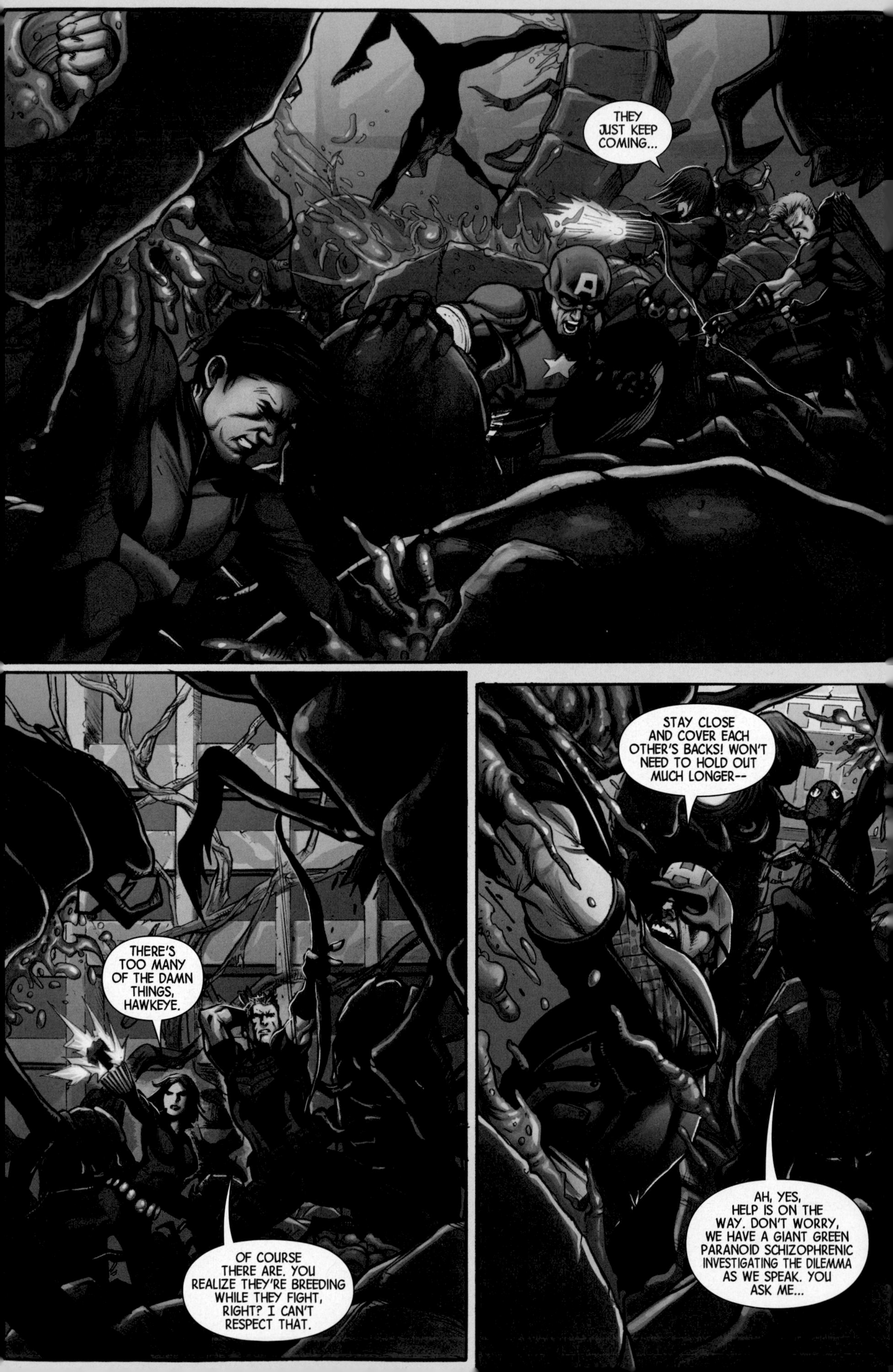
THEY JUST KEEP COMING...
THERE'S TOO MANY OF THE DAMN THINGS, HAWKEYE.
OF COURSE THERE ARE. YOU REALIZE THEY'RE BREEDING WHILE THEY FIGHT, RIGHT? I CAN'T RESPECT THAT.
STAY CLOSE AND COVER EACH OTHER'S BACKS! WON'T NEED TO HOLD OUT MUCH LONGER--
AH, YES, HELP IS ON THE WAY. DON'T WORRY, WE HAVE A GIANT GREEN PARANOID SCHIZOPHRENIC INVESTIGATING THE DILEMMA AS WE SPEAK. YOU ASK ME...

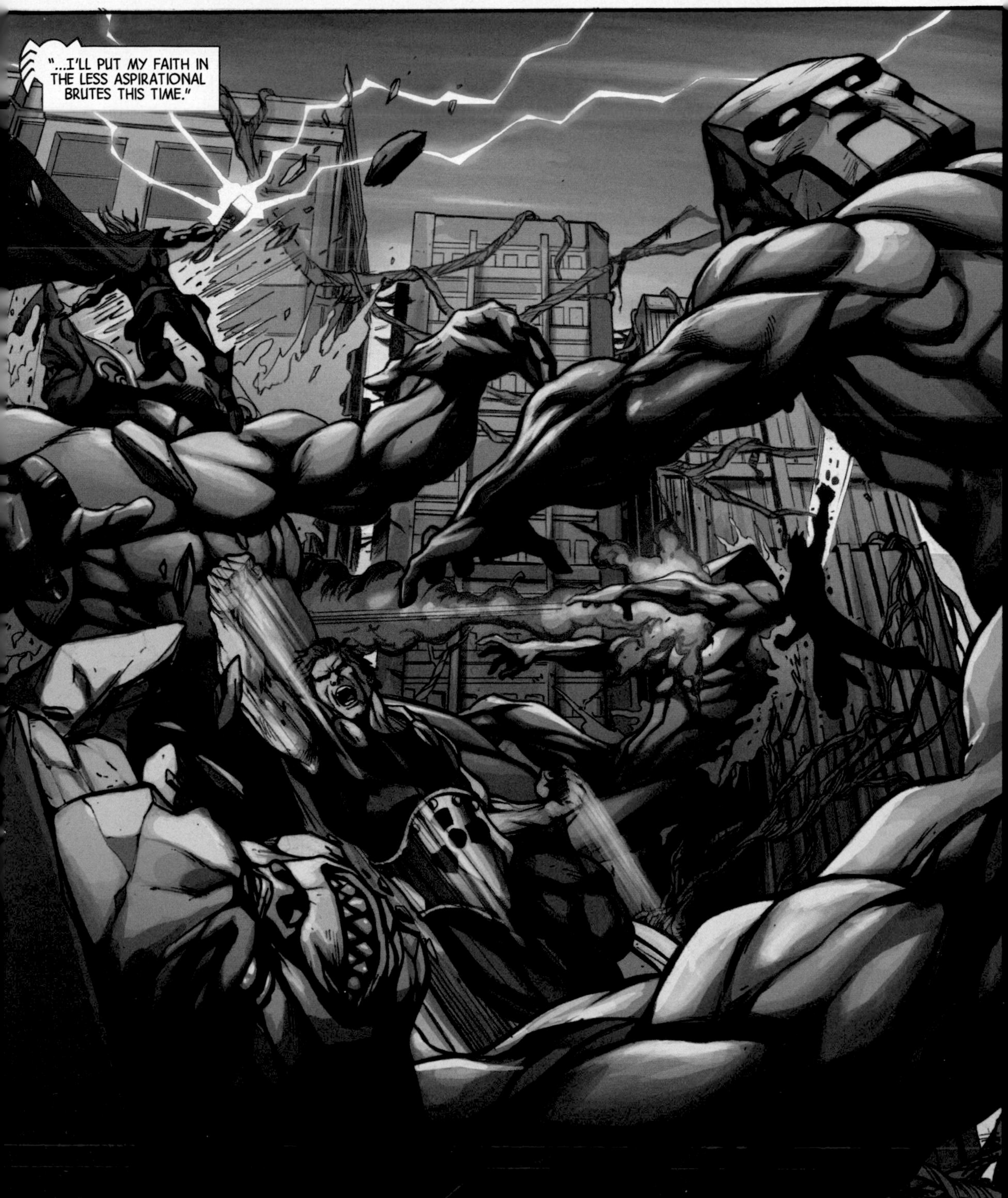
"...I'LL PUT MY FAITH IN THE LESS ASPIRATIONAL BRUTES THIS TIME."

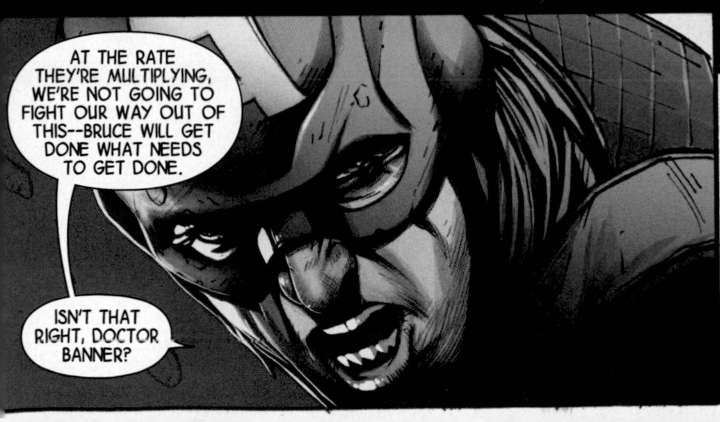
AT THE RATE THEY'RE MULTIPLYING, WE'RE NOT GOING TO FIGHT OUR WAY OUT OF THIS--BRUCE WILL GET DONE WHAT NEEDS TO GET DONE.
ISN'T THAT RIGHT, DOCTOR BANNER?

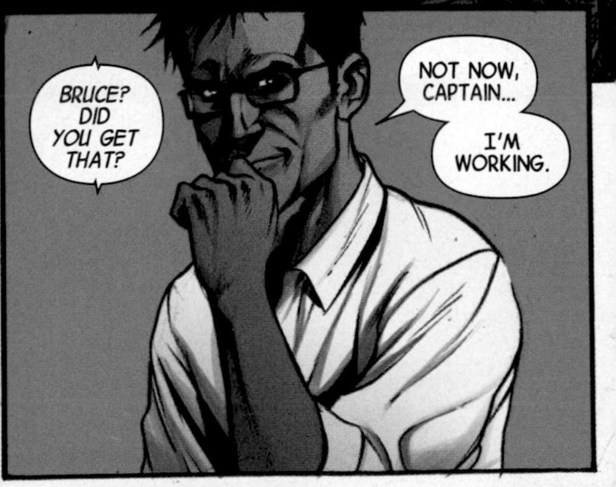
BRUCE? DID YOU GET THAT?
NOT NOW, CAPTAIN...
I'M WORKING.

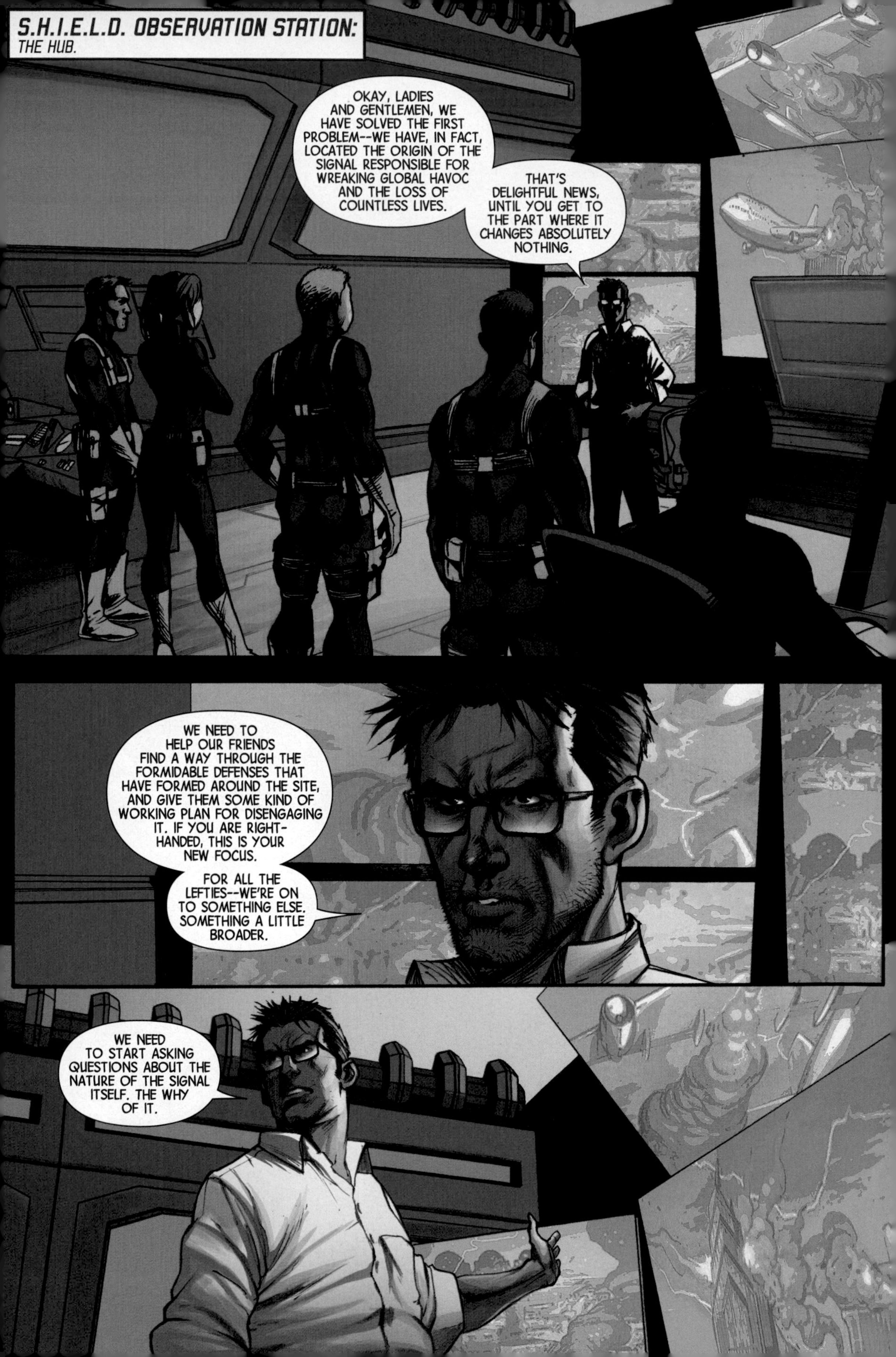
S.H.I.E.L.D. OBSERVATION STATION:
THE HUB.
OKAY, LADIES AND GENTLEMEN, WE HAVE SOLVED THE FIRST PROBLEM--WE HAVE, IN FACT, LOCATED THE ORIGIN OF THE SIGNAL RESPONSIBLE FOR WREAKING GLOBAL HAVOC AND THE LOSS OF COUNTLESS LIVES.
THAT'S DELIGHTFUL NEWS, UNTIL YOU GET TO THE PART WHERE IT CHANGES ABSOLUTELY NOTHING.
WE NEED TO HELP OUR FRIENDS FIND A WAY THROUGH THE FORMIDABLE DEFENSES THAT HAVE FORMED AROUND THE SITE, AND GIVE THEM SOME KIND OF WORKING PLAN FOR DISENGAGING IT. IF YOU ARE RIGHT-HANDED, THIS IS YOUR NEW FOCUS.
FOR ALL THE LEFTIES--WE'RE ON TO SOMETHING ELSE. SOMETHING A LITTLE BROADER.
WE NEED TO START ASKING QUESTIONS ABOUT THE NATURE OF THE SIGNAL ITSELF. THE WHY OF IT.

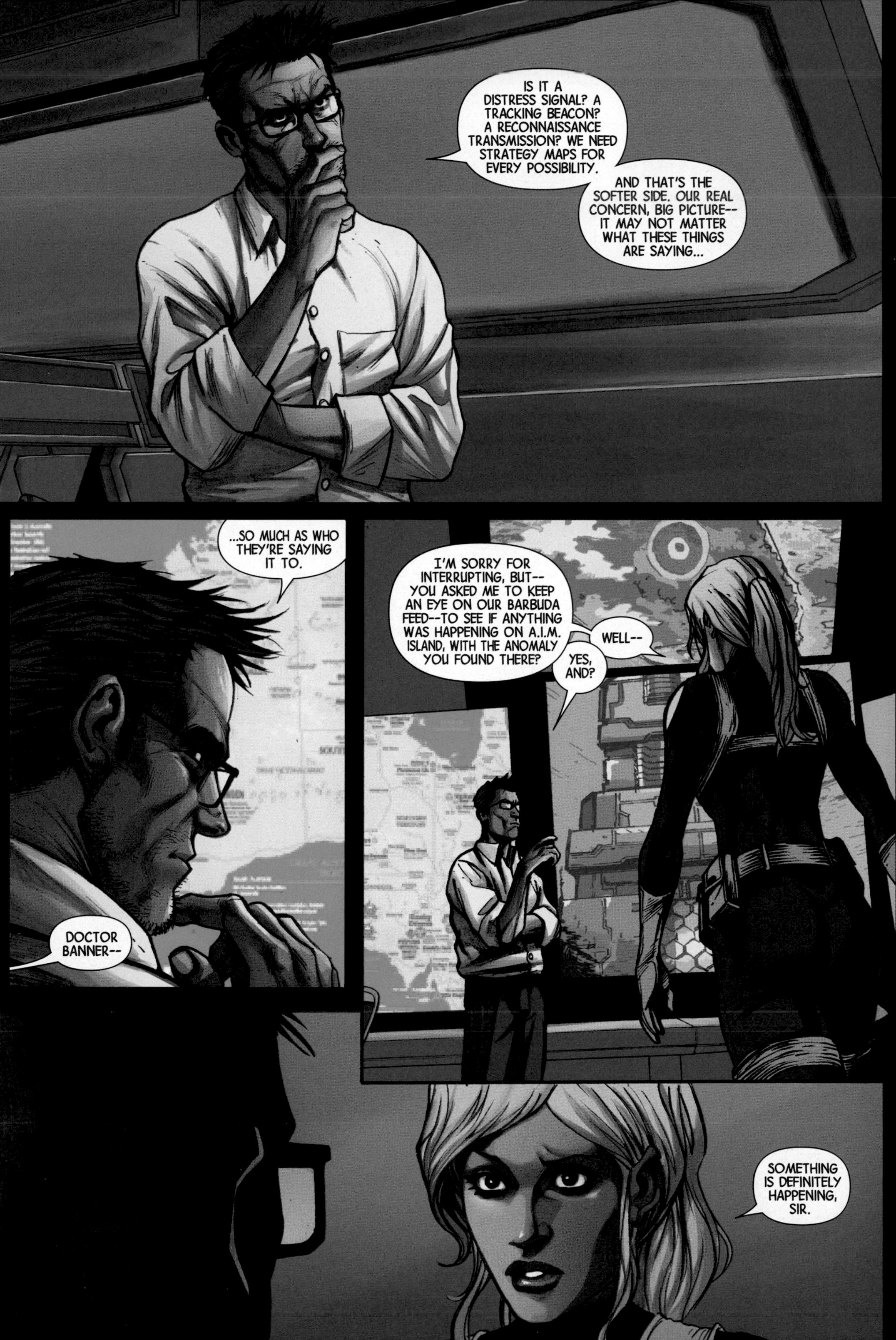
IS IT A DISTRESS SIGNAL? A TRACKING BEACON? A RECONNAISSANCE TRANSMISSION? WE NEED STRATEGY MAPS FOR EVERY POSSIBILITY.
AND THAT'S THE SOFTER SIDE. OUR REAL CONCERN, BIG PICTURE-- IT MAY NOT MATTER WHAT THESE THINGS ARE SAYING...
...SO MUCH AS WHO THEY'RE SAYING IT TO.
DOCTOR BANNER--
I'M SORRY FOR INTERRUPTING, BUT-- YOU ASKED ME TO KEEP AN EYE ON OUR BARBUDA FEED--TO SEE IF ANYTHING WAS HAPPENING ON A.I.M. ISLAND, WITH THE ANOMALY YOU FOUND THERE?
YES, AND?
WELL--
SOMETHING IS DEFINITELY HAPPENING, SIR.

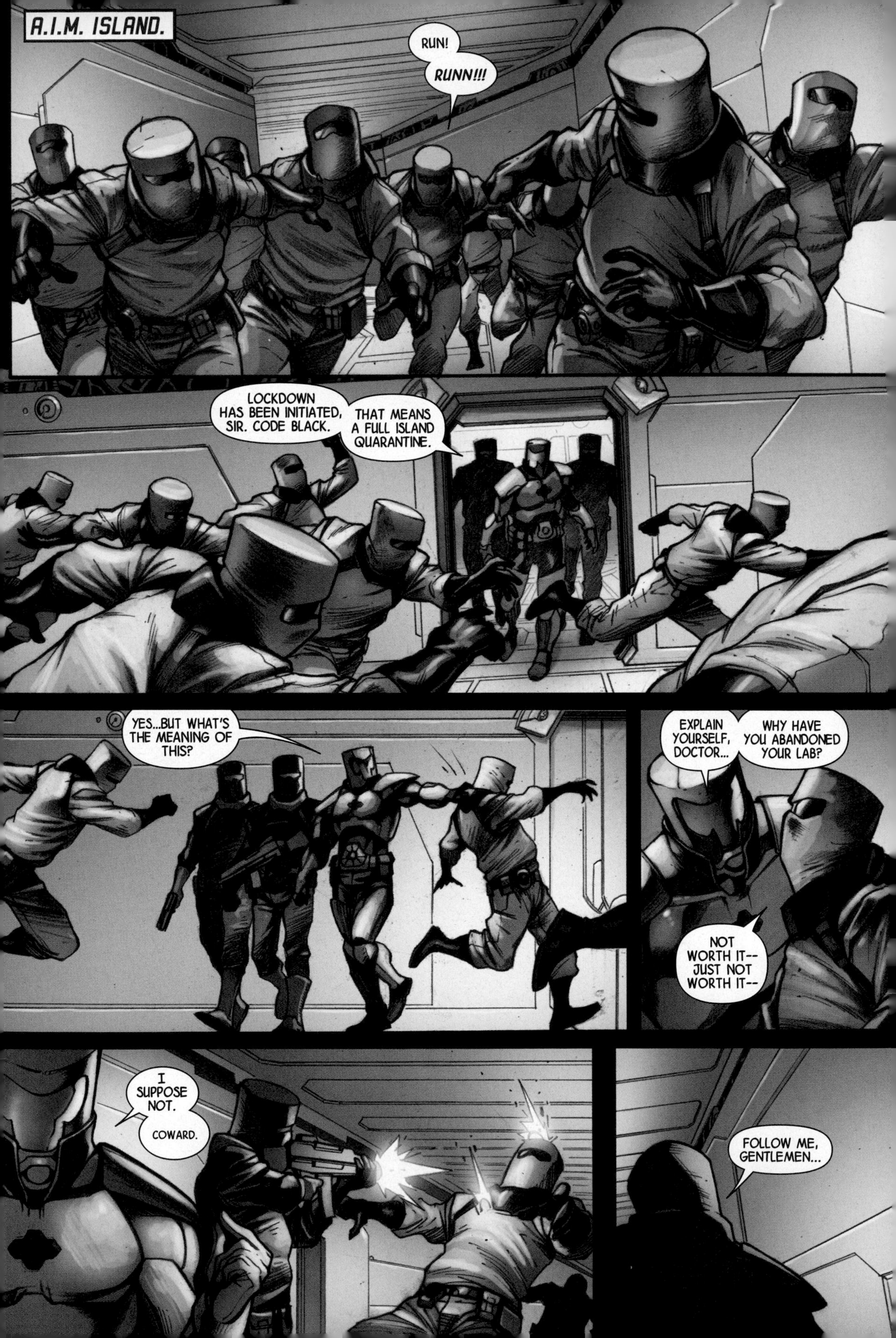
A.I.M. ISLAND.
RUN!
RUNN!!!
LOCKDOWN HAS BEEN INITIATED, SIR. CODE BLACK.
THAT MEANS A FULL ISLAND QUARANTINE.
YES...BUT WHAT'S THE MEANING OF THIS?
EXPLAIN YOURSELF, DOCTOR...
WHY HAVE YOU ABANDONED YOUR LAB?
NOT WORTH IT-- JUST NOT WORTH IT--
I SUPPOSE NOT.
COWARD.
FOLLOW ME, GENTLEMEN...

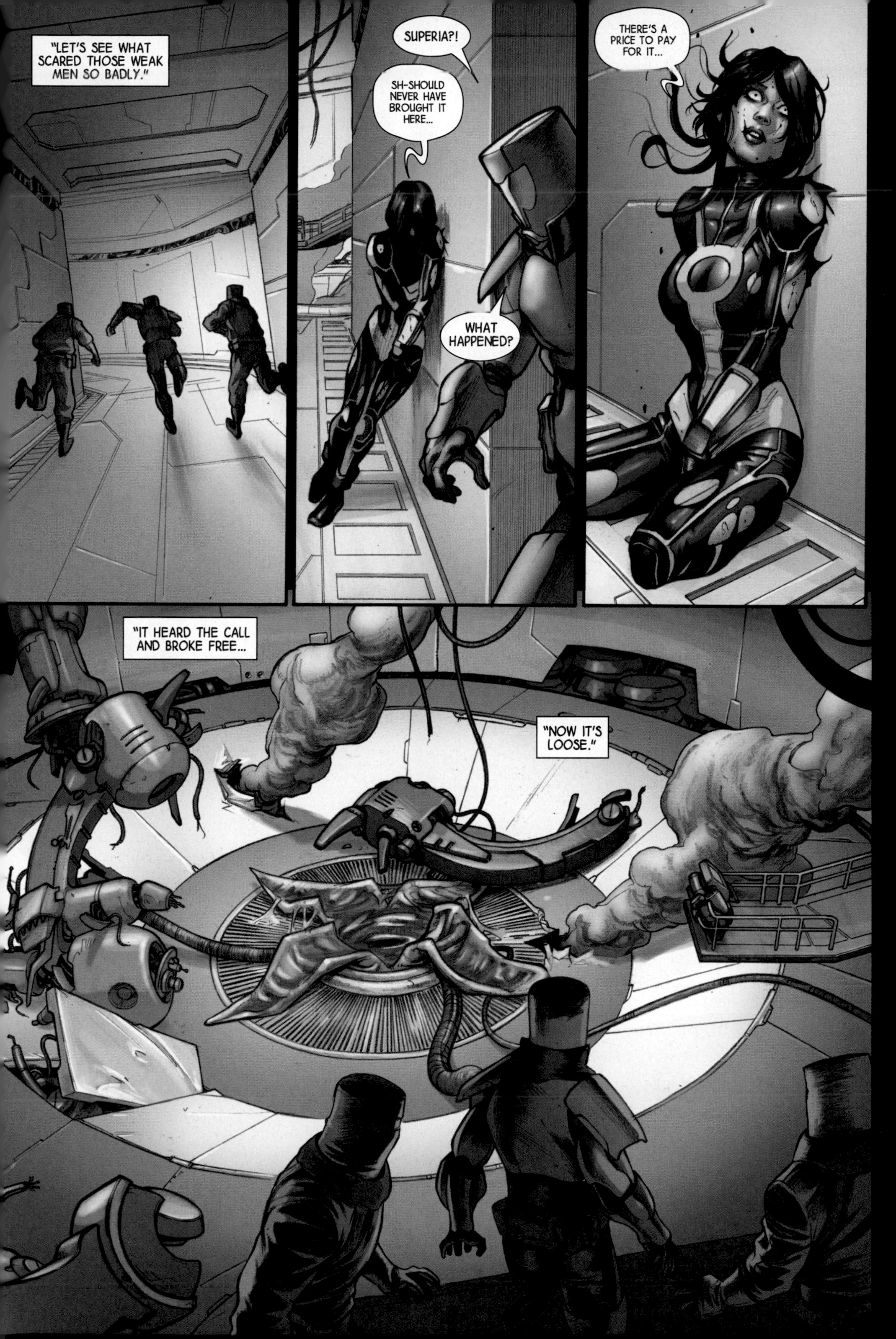
"LET'S SEE WHAT SCARED THOSE WEAK MEN SO BADLY."
SUPERIA?!
SH-SHOULD NEVER HAVE BROUGHT IT HERE...
WHAT HAPPENED?
THERE'S A PRICE TO PAY FOR IT...
"IT HEARD THE CALL AND BROKE FREE...
"NOW IT'S LOOSE."

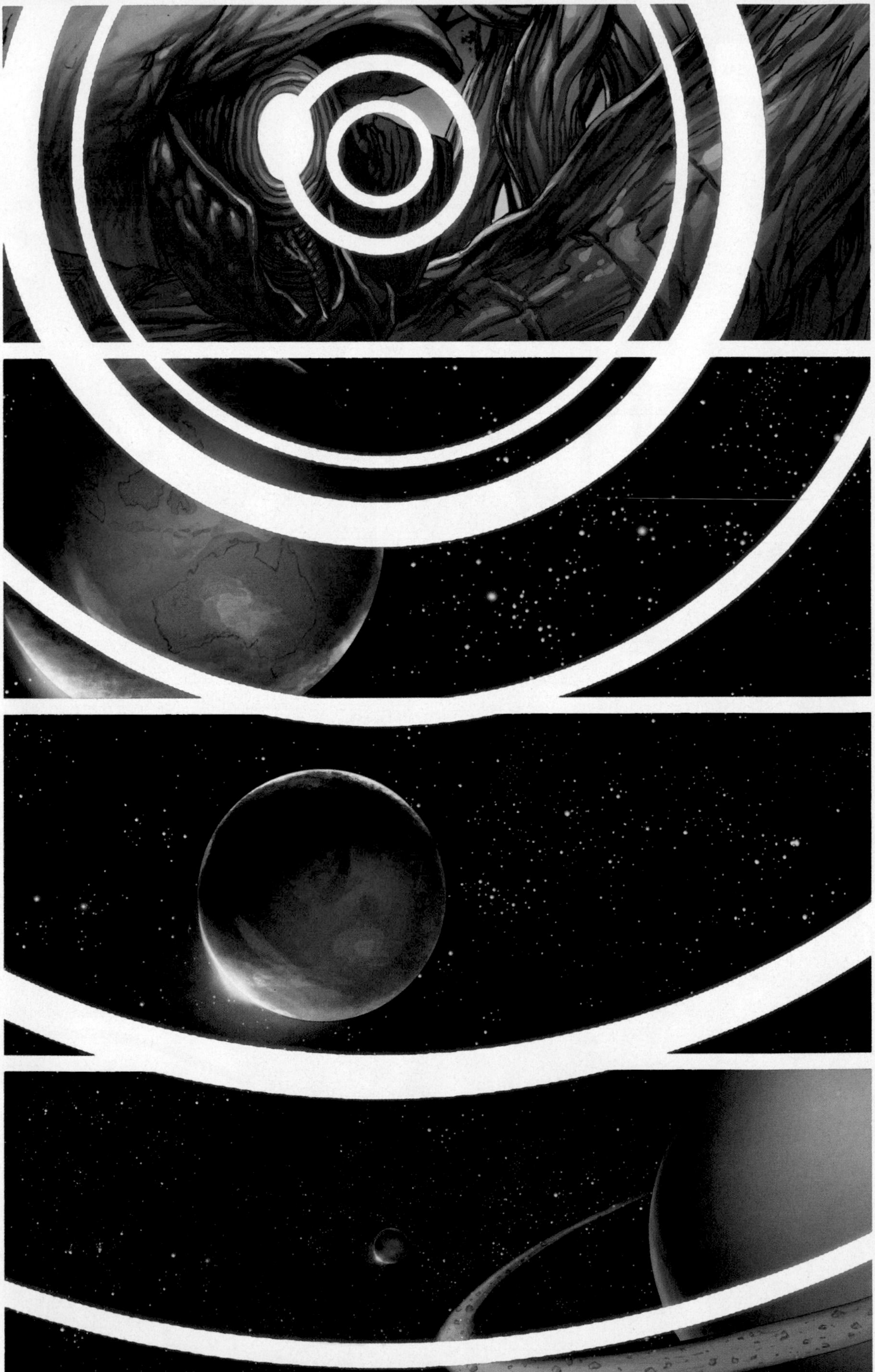

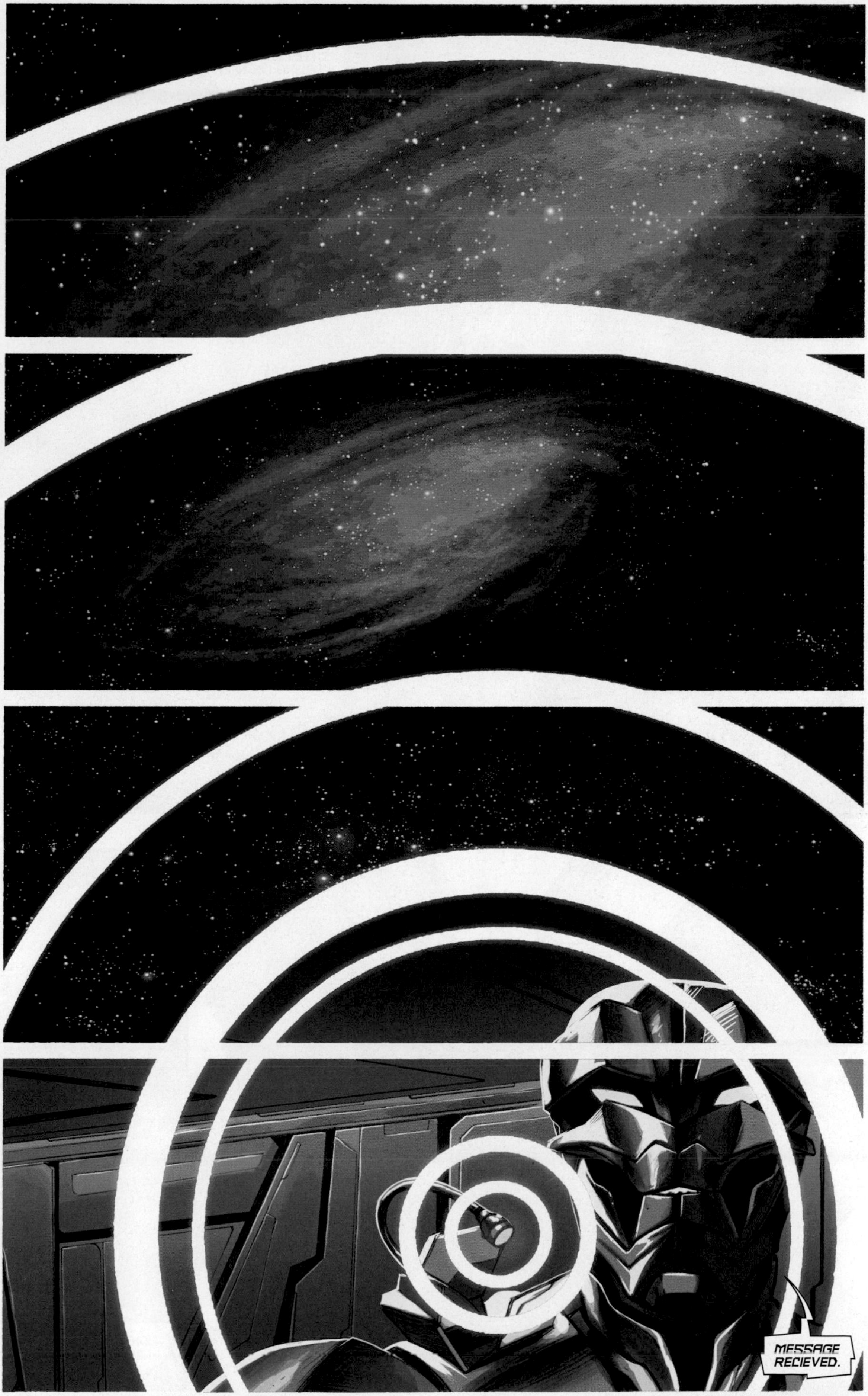
MESSAGE RECIEVED.

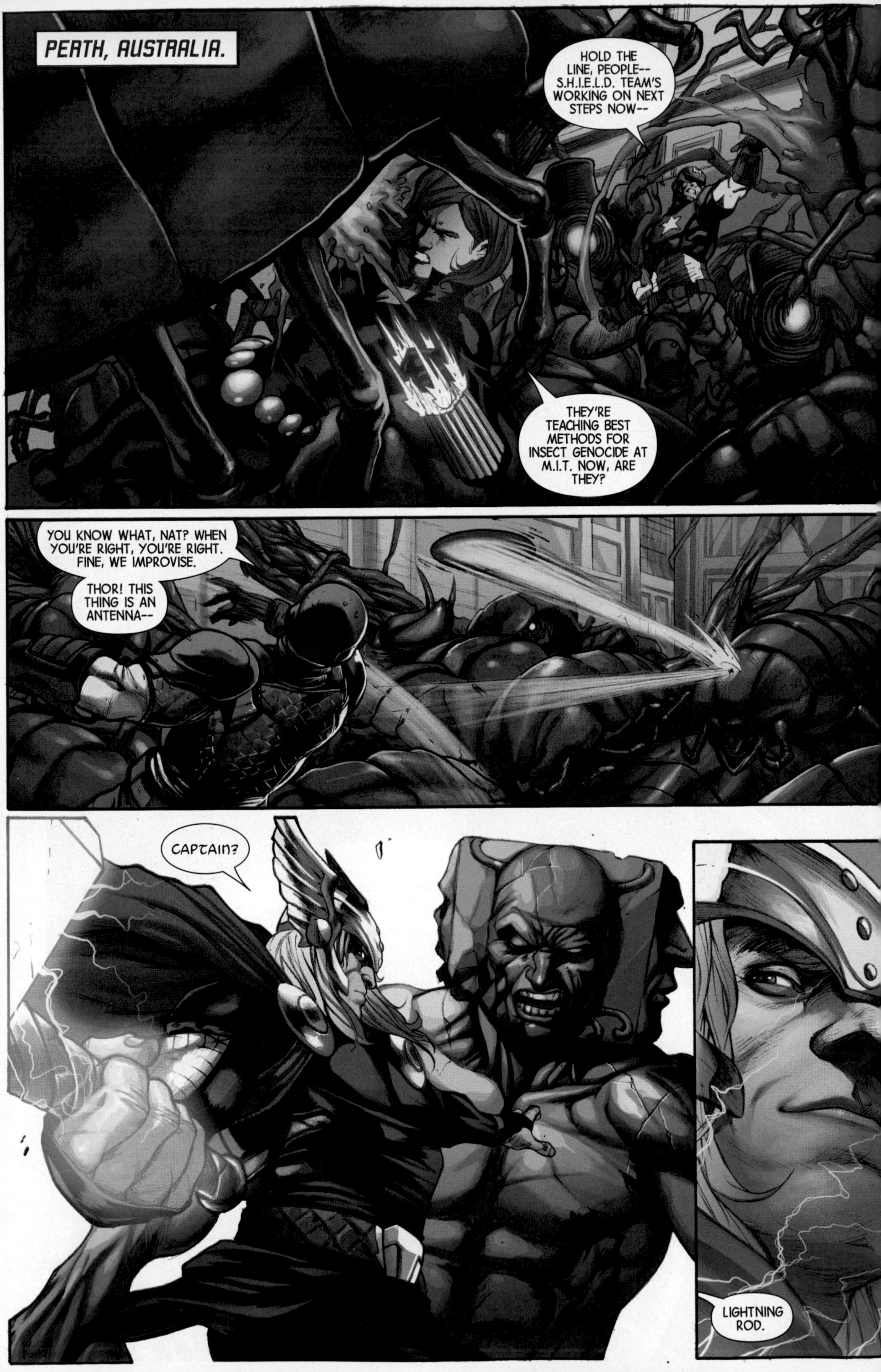
PERTH, AUSTRALIA.
HOLD THE LINE, PEOPLE-- S.H.I.E.L.D. TEAM'S WORKING ON NEXT STEPS NOW--
THEY'RE TEACHING BEST METHODS FOR INSECT GENOCIDE AT M.I.T. NOW, ARE THEY?
YOU KNOW WHAT, NAT? WHEN YOU'RE RIGHT, YOU'RE RIGHT. FINE, WE IMPROVISE.
THOR! THIS THING IS AN ANTENNA--
CAPTAIN?
LIGHTNING ROD.

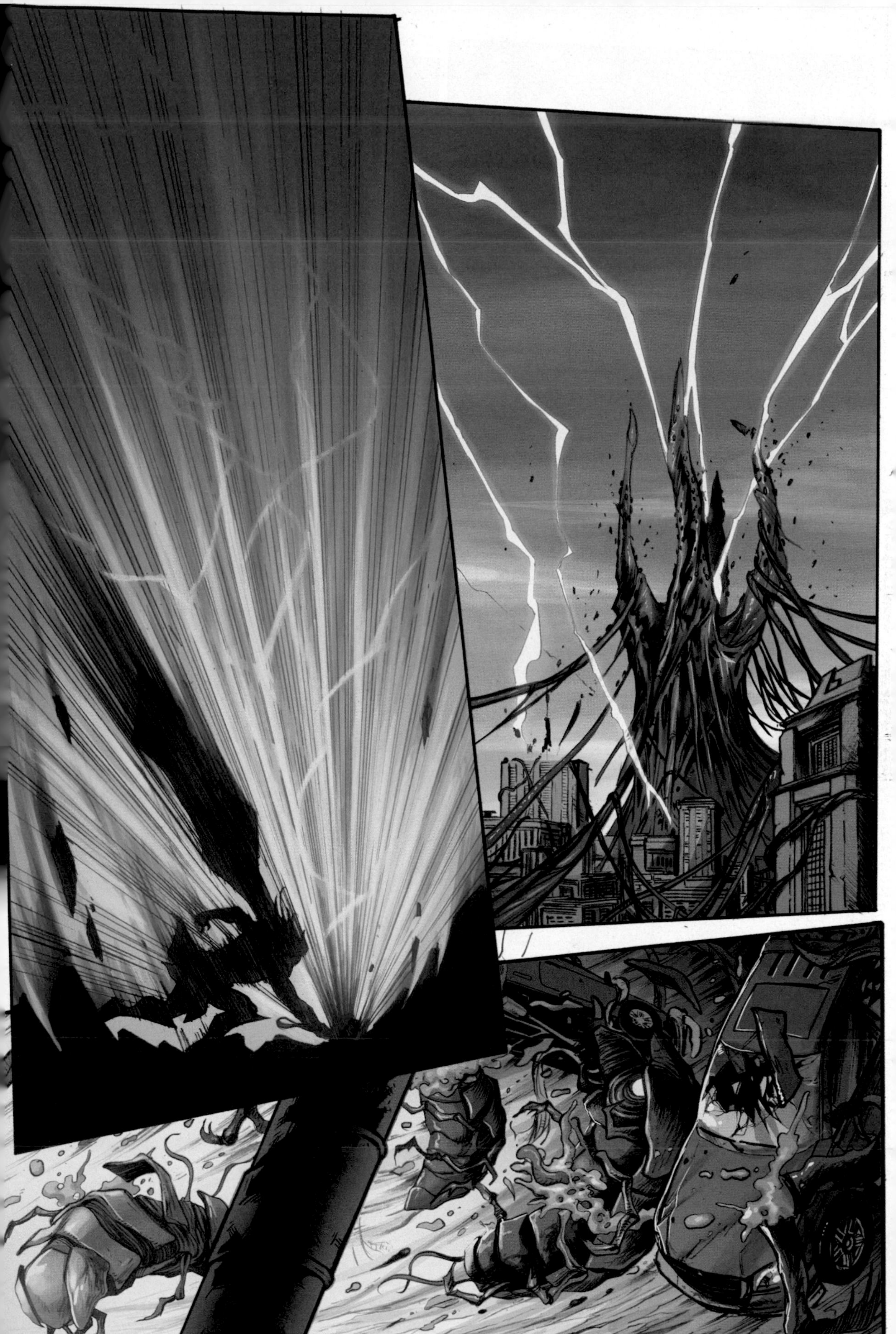

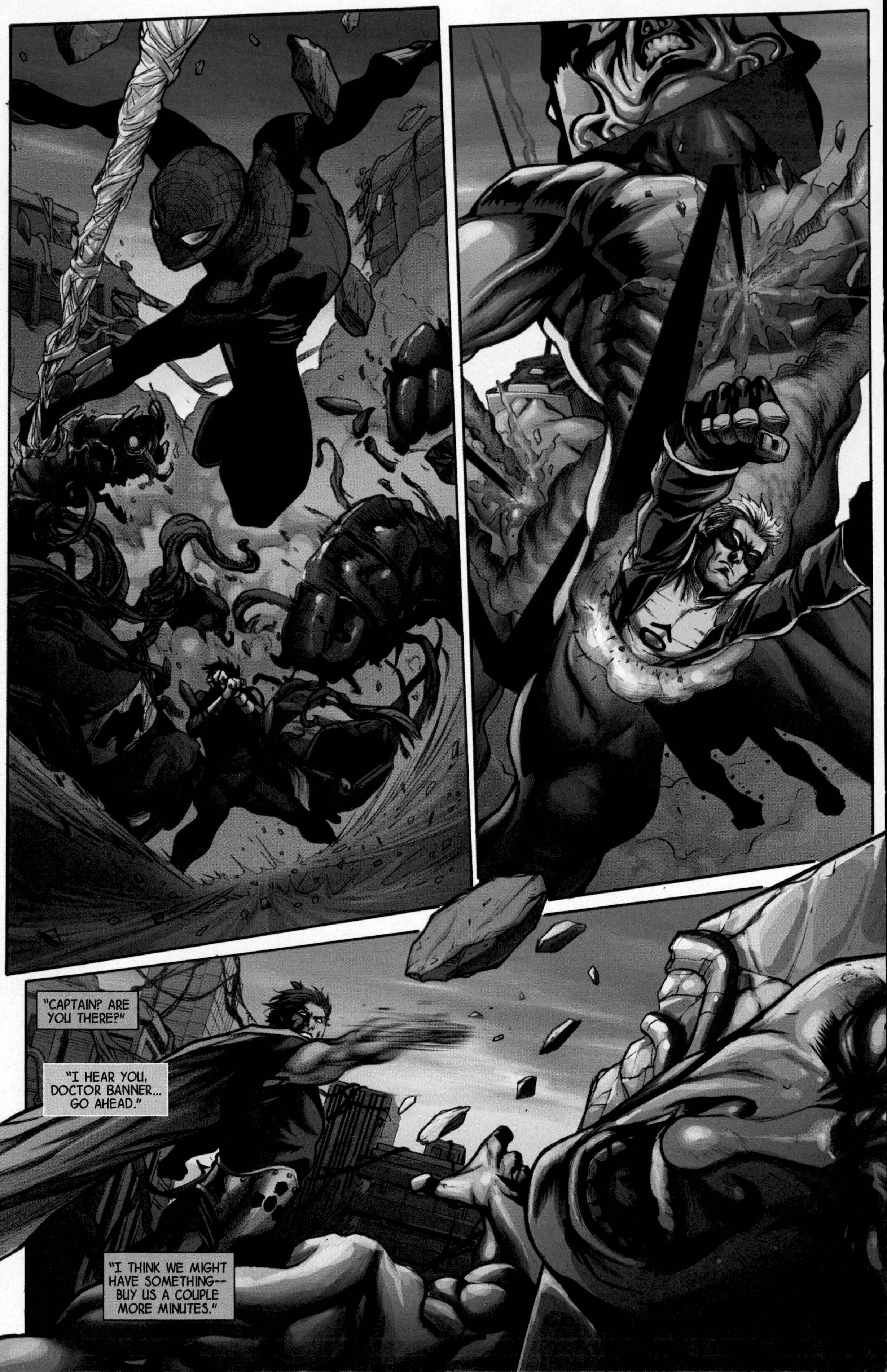
"CAPTAIN? ARE YOU THERE?"
"I HEAR YOU, DOCTOR BANNER... GO AHEAD."
"I THINK WE MIGHT HAVE SOMETHING-- BUY US A COUPLE MORE MINUTES."

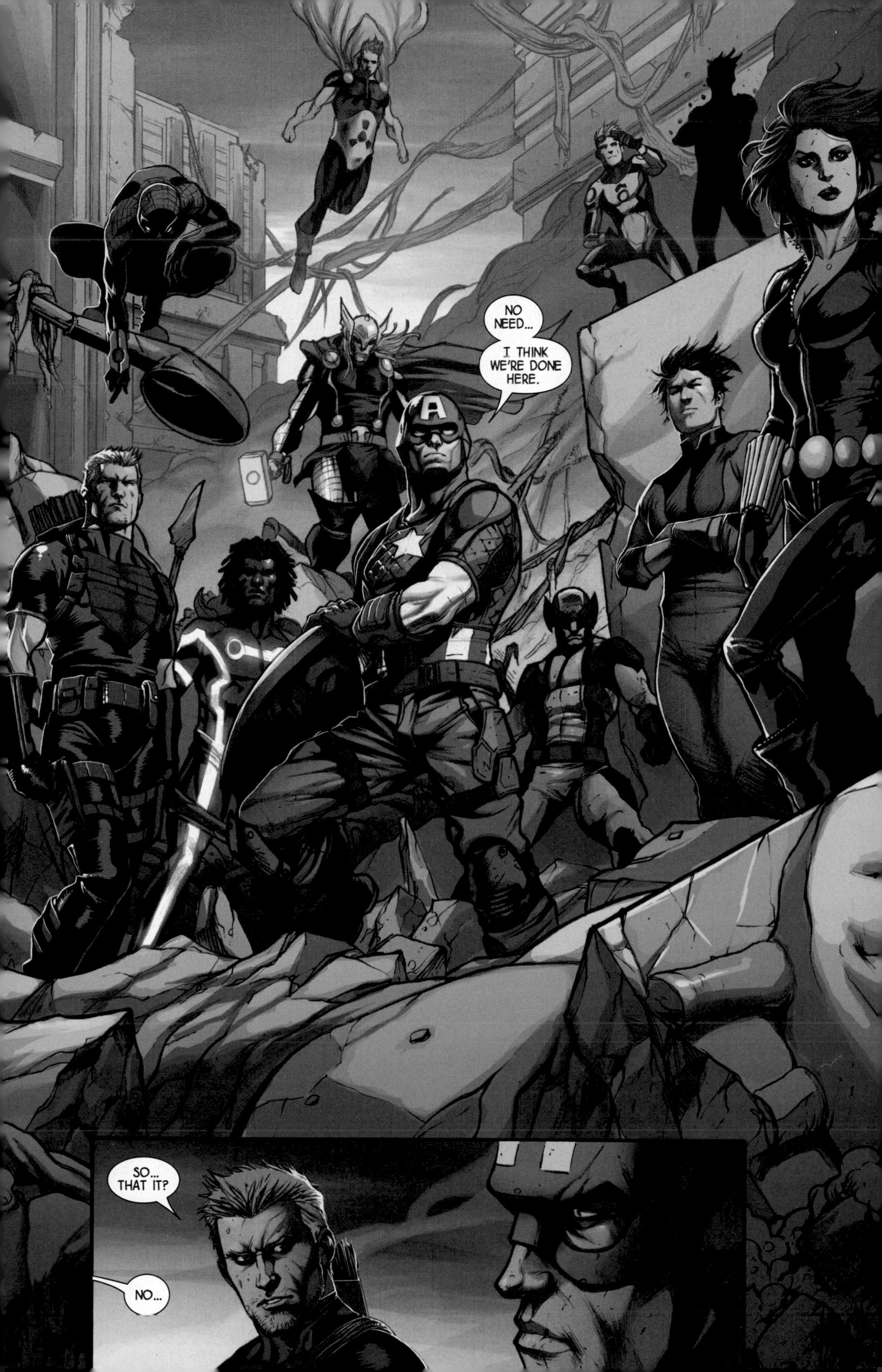
NO NEED...
I THINK WE'RE DONE HERE.
SO... THAT IT?
NO...

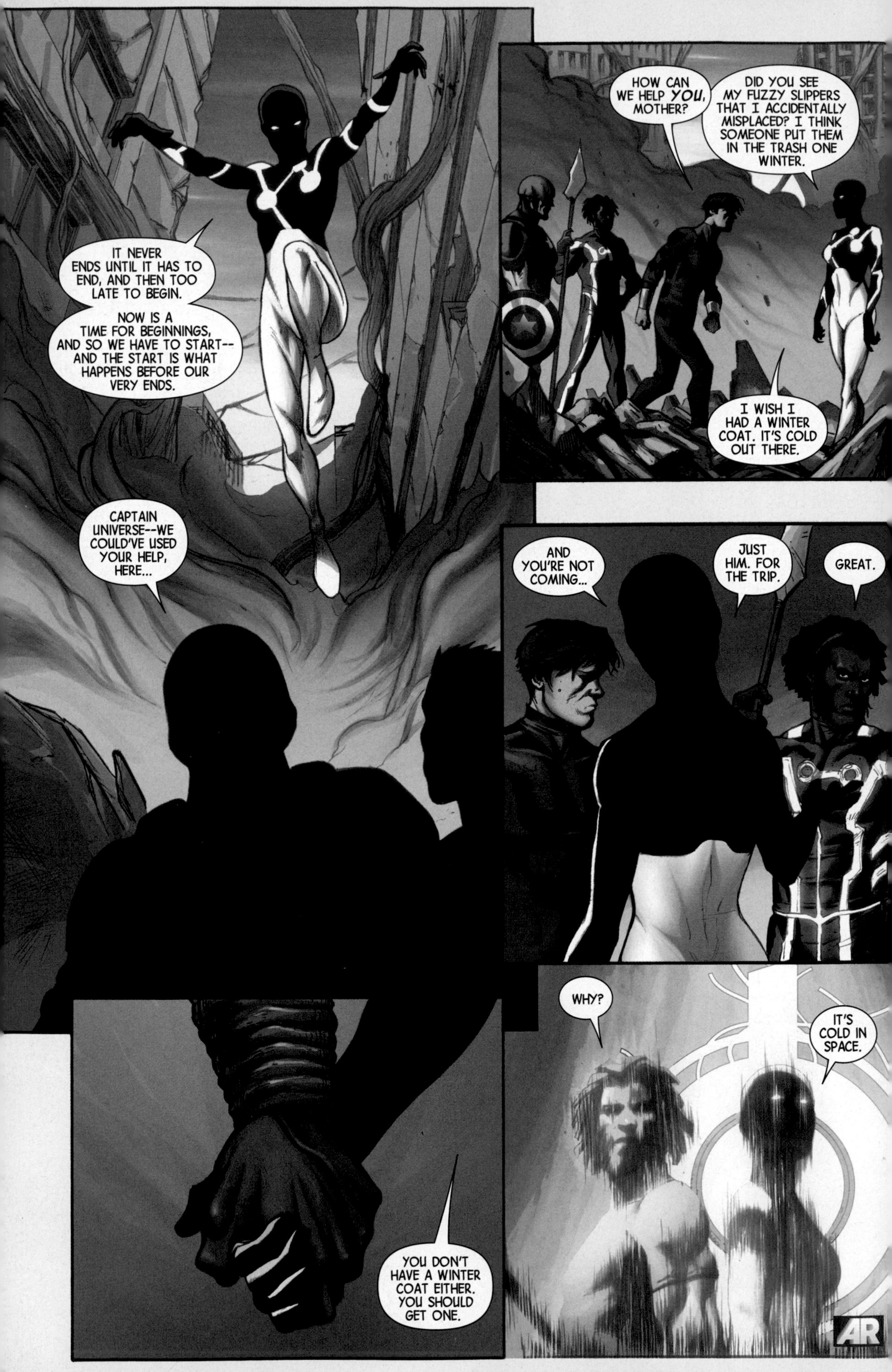
IT NEVER ENDS UNTIL IT HAS TO END, AND THEN TOO LATE TO BEGIN.
NOW IS A TIME FOR BEGINNINGS, AND SO WE HAVE TO START-- AND THE START IS WHAT HAPPENS BEFORE OUR VERY ENDS.
HOW CAN WE HELP *YOU*, MOTHER?
DID YOU SEE MY FUZZY SLIPPERS THAT I ACCIDENTALLY MISPLACED? I THINK SOMEONE PUT THEM IN THE TRASH ONE WINTER.
I WISH I HAD A WINTER COAT. IT'S COLD OUT THERE.
CAPTAIN UNIVERSE--WE COULD'VE USED YOUR HELP, HERE...
AND YOU'RE NOT COMING...
JUST HIM. FOR THE TRIP.
GREAT.
YOU DON'T HAVE A WINTER COAT EITHER. YOU SHOULD GET ONE.
WHY?
IT'S COLD IN SPACE.
AR

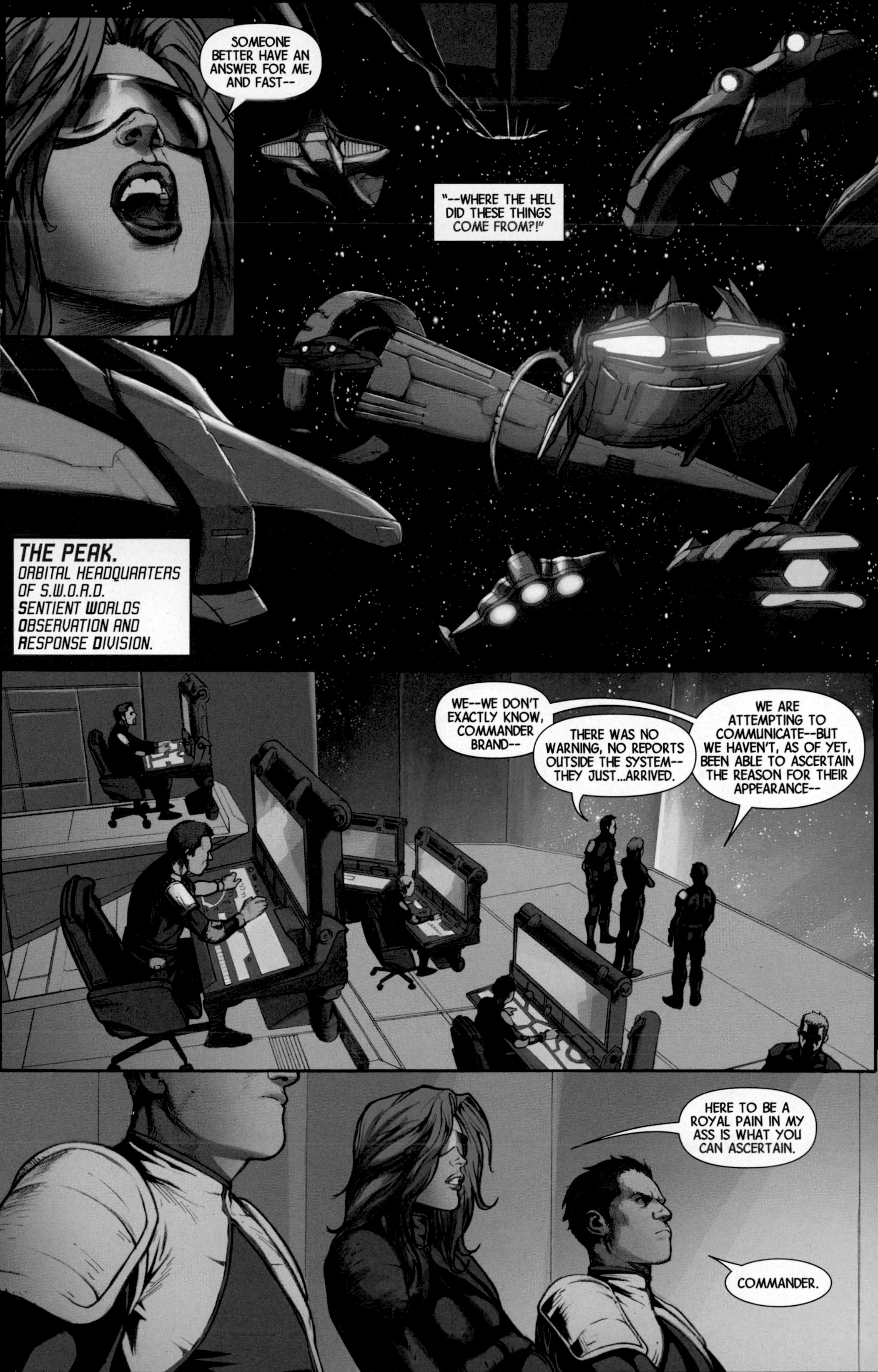
SOMEONE BETTER HAVE AN ANSWER FOR ME, AND FAST--
"--WHERE THE HELL DID THESE THINGS COME FROM?!"
THE PEAK. ORBITAL HEADQUARTERS OF S.W.O.R.D. SENTIENT WORLDS OBSERVATION AND RESPONSE DIVISION.
WE--WE DON'T EXACTLY KNOW, COMMANDER BRAND--
THERE WAS NO WARNING, NO REPORTS OUTSIDE THE SYSTEM--THEY JUST...ARRIVED.
WE ARE ATTEMPTING TO COMMUNICATE--BUT WE HAVEN'T, AS OF YET, BEEN ABLE TO ASCERTAIN THE REASON FOR THEIR APPEARANCE--
HERE TO BE A ROYAL PAIN IN MY ASS IS WHAT YOU CAN ASCERTAIN.
COMMANDER.

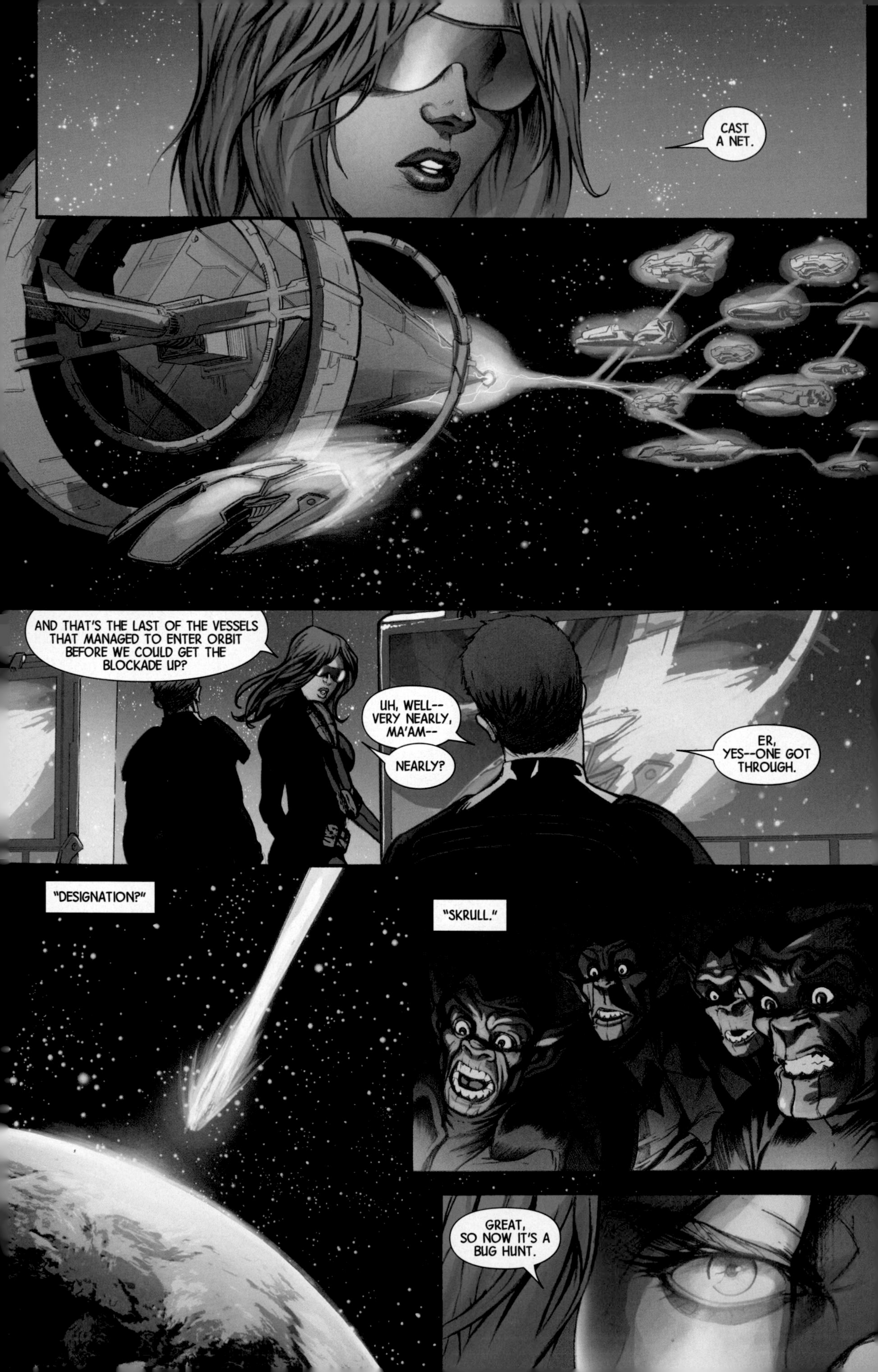
CAST A NET.
AND THAT'S THE LAST OF THE VESSELS THAT MANAGED TO ENTER ORBIT BEFORE WE COULD GET THE BLOCKADE UP?
UH, WELL-- VERY NEARLY, MA'AM--
NEARLY?
ER, YES--ONE GOT THROUGH.
"DESIGNATION?"
"SKRULL."
GREAT, SO NOW IT'S A BUG HUNT.

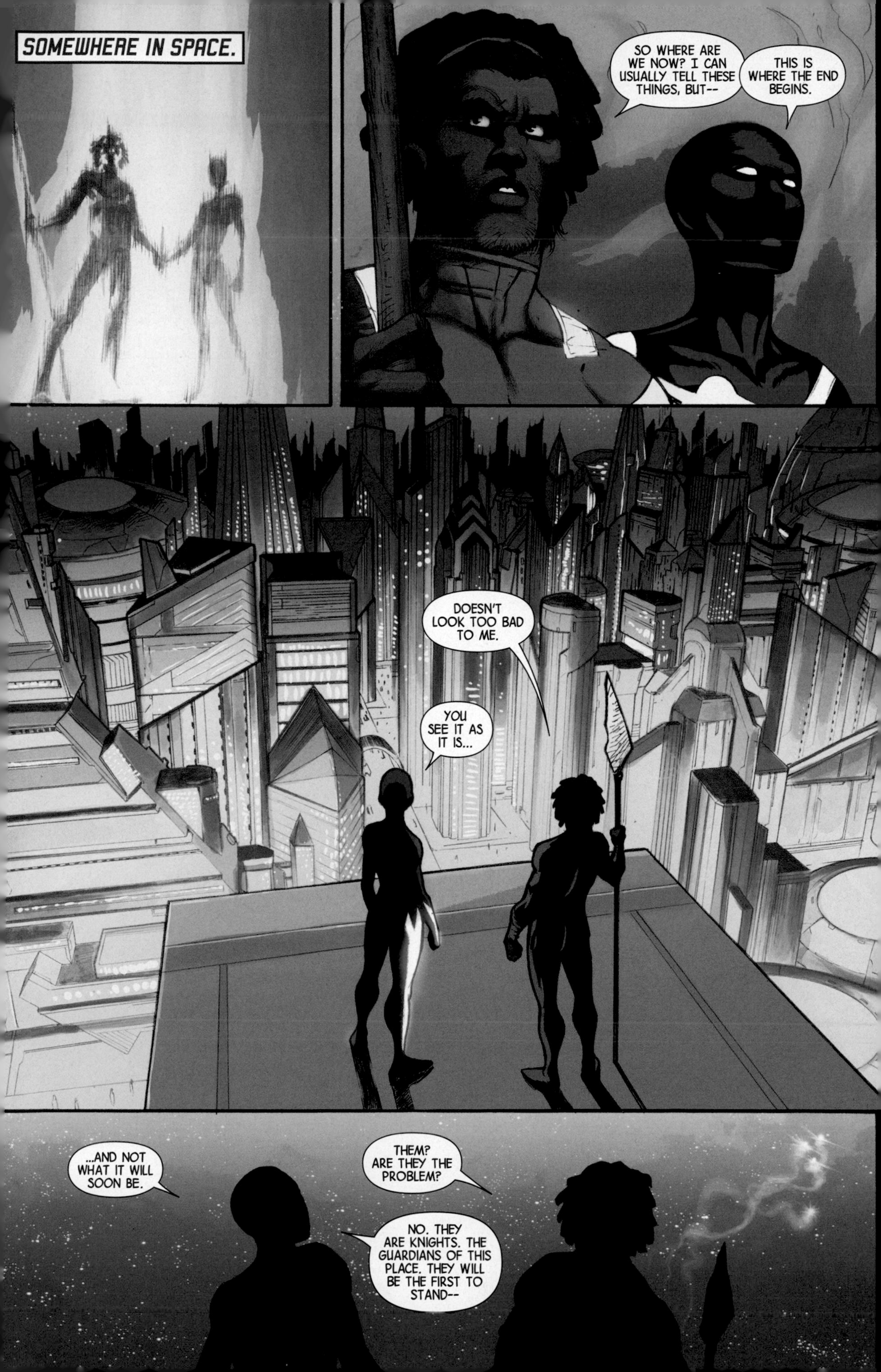
SOMEWHERE IN SPACE.
SO WHERE ARE WE NOW? I CAN USUALLY TELL THESE THINGS, BUT--
THIS IS WHERE THE END BEGINS.
DOESN'T LOOK TOO BAD TO ME.
YOU SEE IT AS IT IS...
...AND NOT WHAT IT WILL SOON BE.
THEM? ARE THEY THE PROBLEM?
NO. THEY ARE KNIGHTS. THE GUARDIANS OF THIS PLACE. THEY WILL BE THE FIRST TO STAND--

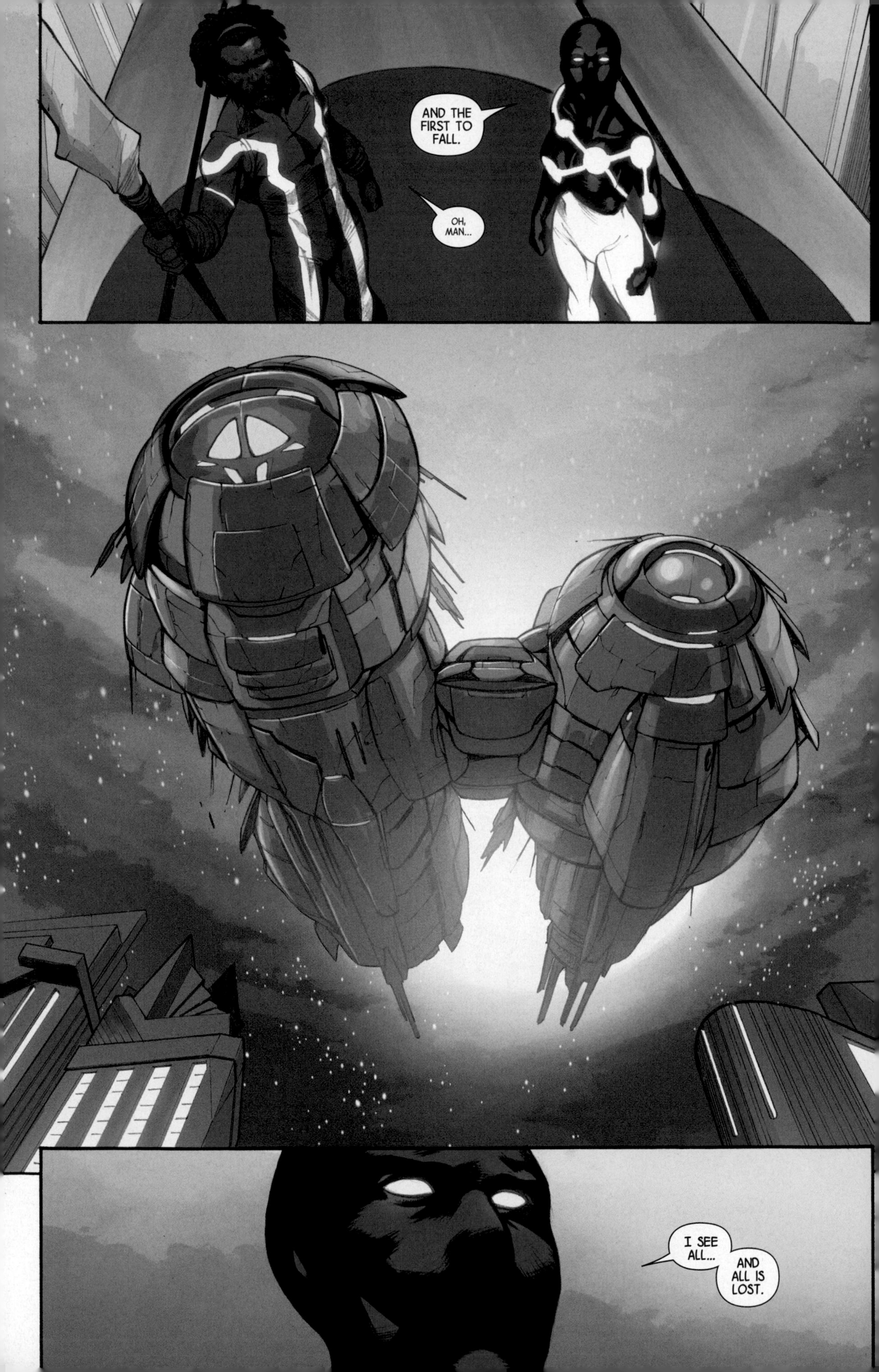
AND THE FIRST TO FALL.
OH, MAN...
I SEE ALL...
AND ALL IS LOST.

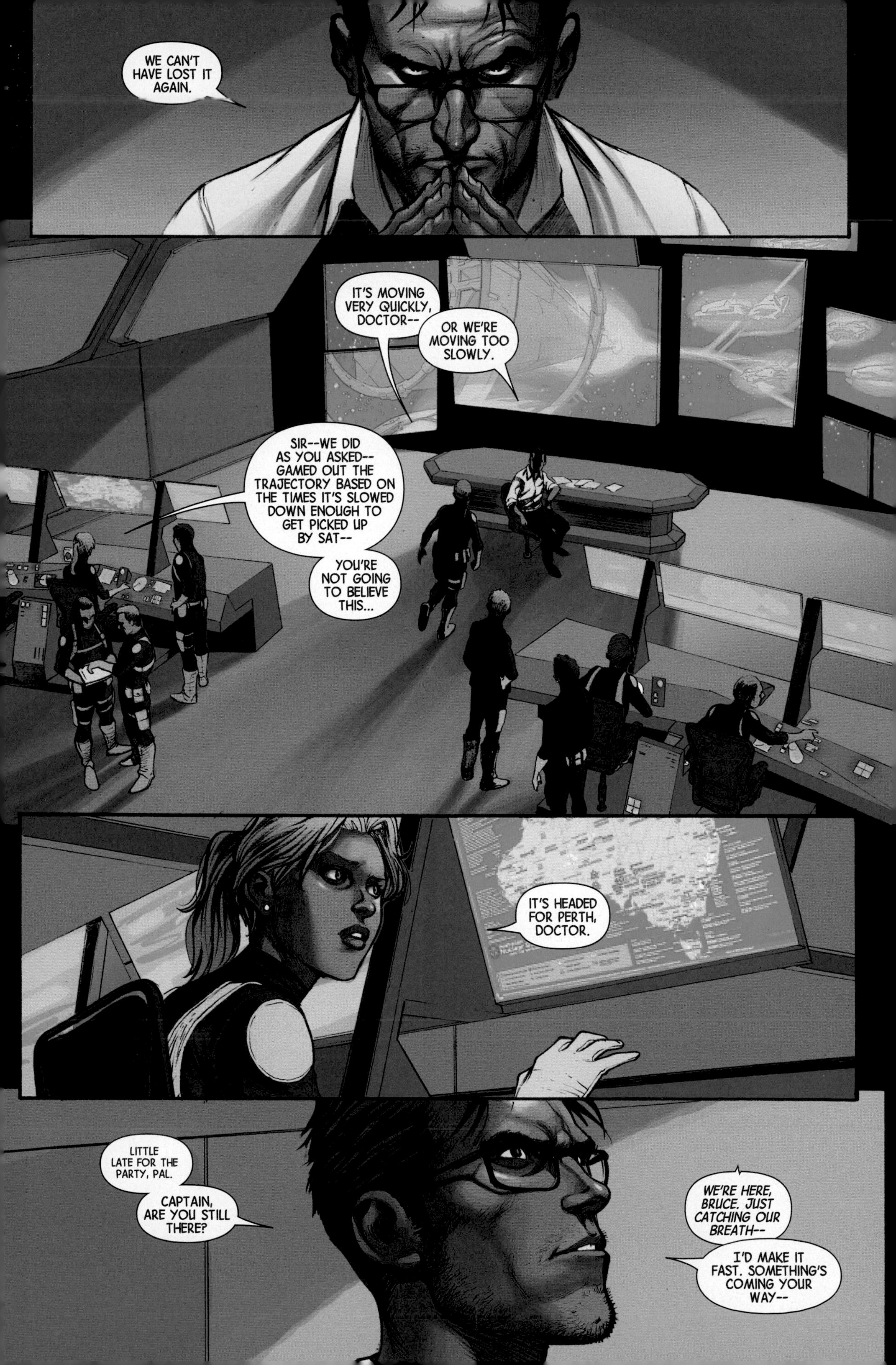
WE CAN'T HAVE LOST IT AGAIN.
IT'S MOVING VERY QUICKLY, DOCTOR--
OR WE'RE MOVING TOO SLOWLY.
SIR--WE DID AS YOU ASKED--GAMED OUT THE TRAJECTORY BASED ON THE TIMES IT'S SLOWED DOWN ENOUGH TO GET PICKED UP BY SAT--
YOU'RE NOT GOING TO BELIEVE THIS...
IT'S HEADED FOR PERTH, DOCTOR.
LITTLE LATE FOR THE PARTY, PAL.
CAPTAIN, ARE YOU STILL THERE?
WE'RE HERE, BRUCE. JUST CATCHING OUR BREATH--
I'D MAKE IT FAST. SOMETHING'S COMING YOUR WAY--

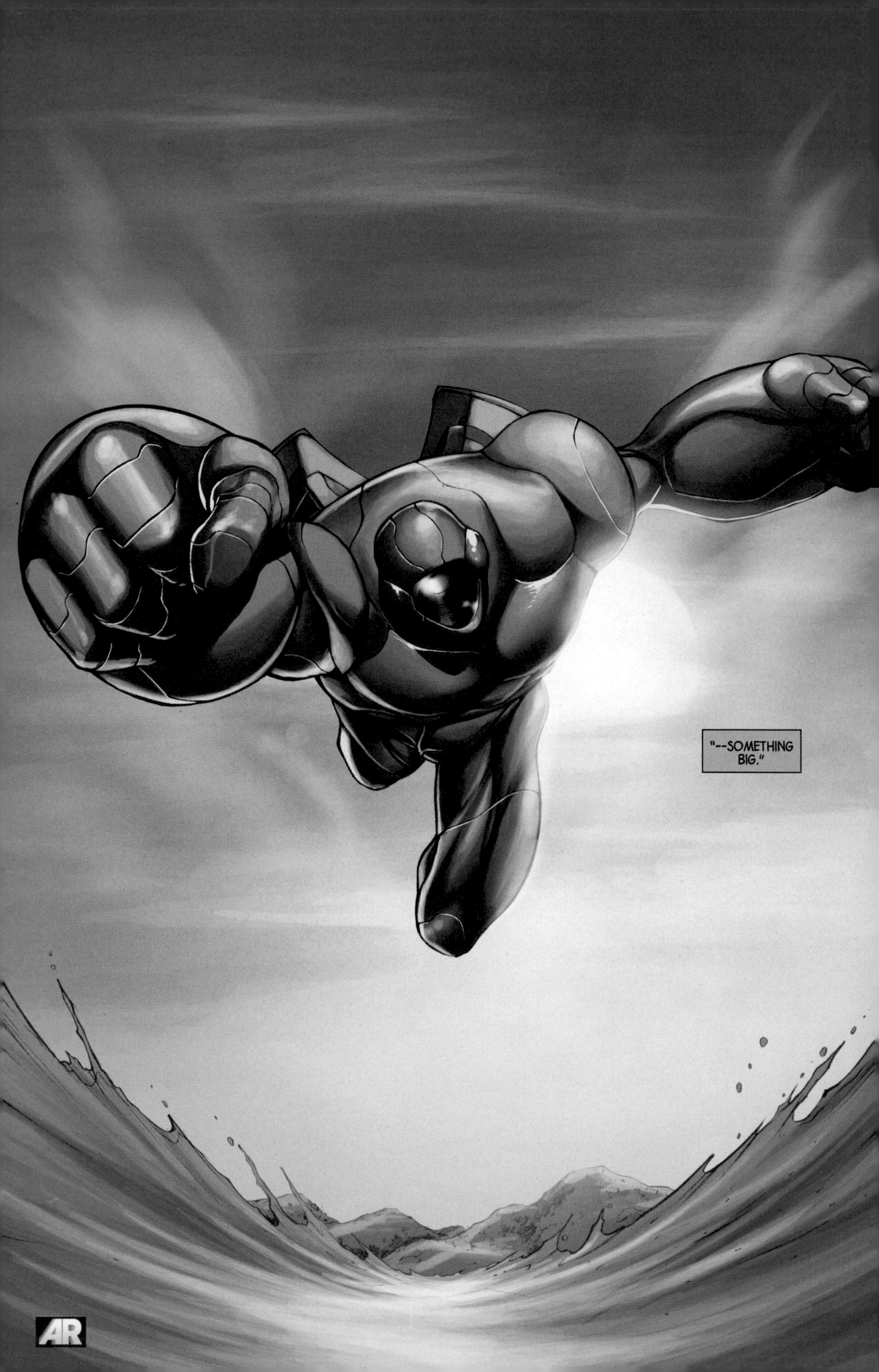
"--SOMETHING BIG."

"TO THE END"

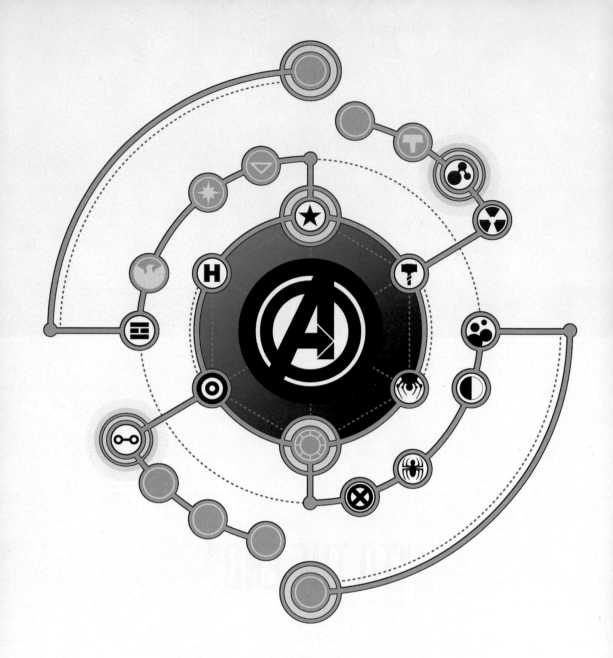

EARTH'S MIGHTIEST HEROES

CAPTAIN AMERICA · IRON MAN · THOR · HAWKEYE · BLACK WIDOW · HULK
WOLVERINE · SPIDER-MAN · CAPTAIN MARVEL · SPIDER-WOMAN
FALCON · SHANG-CHI · SUNSPOT · CANNONBALL · MANIFOLD
SMASHER · CAPTAIN UNIVERSE · HYPERION

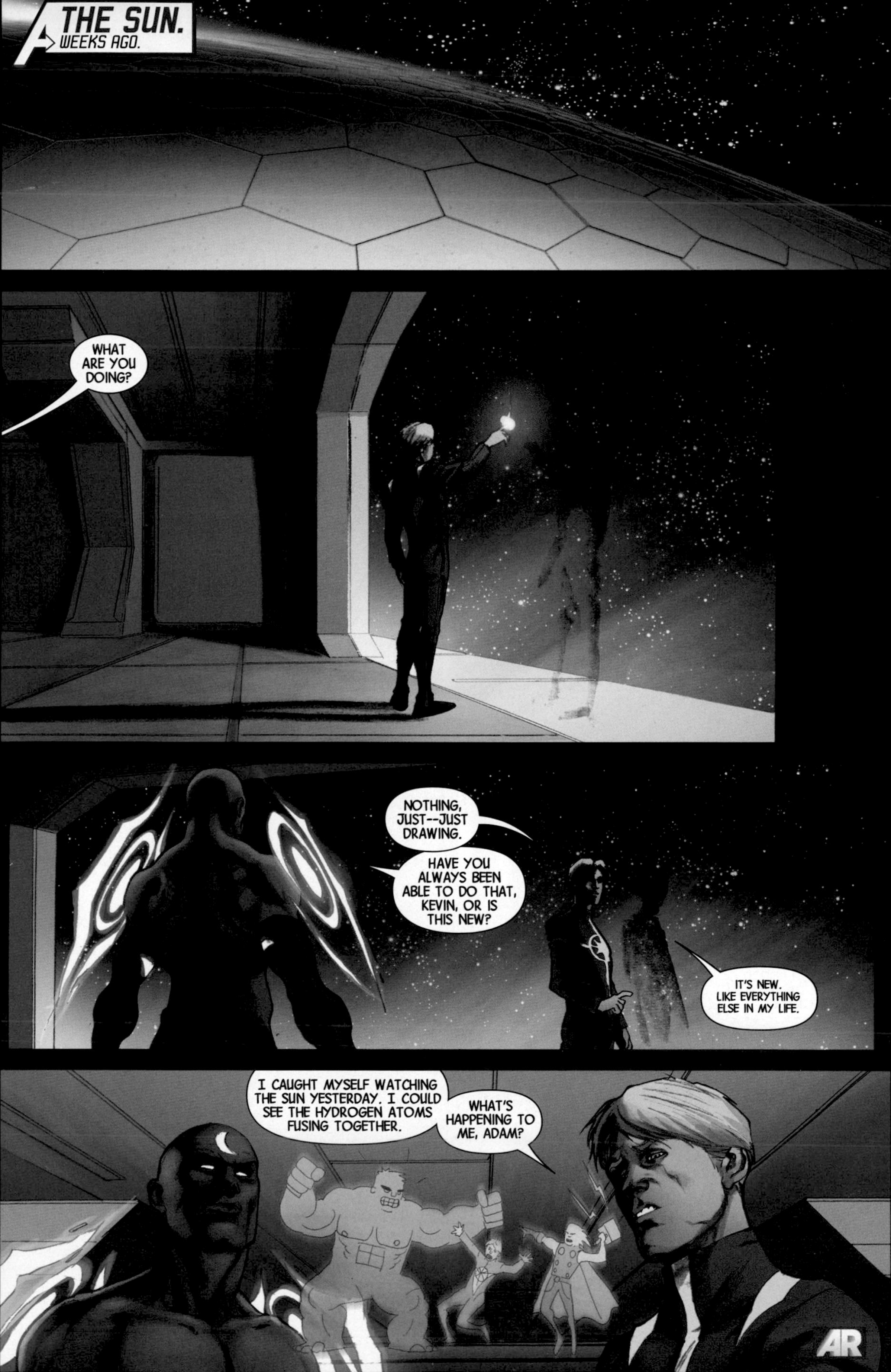
THE SUN.
WEEKS AGO.
WHAT ARE YOU DOING?
NOTHING, JUST--JUST DRAWING.
HAVE YOU ALWAYS BEEN ABLE TO DO THAT, KEVIN, OR IS THIS NEW?
IT'S NEW. LIKE EVERYTHING ELSE IN MY LIFE.
I CAUGHT MYSELF WATCHING THE SUN YESTERDAY. I COULD SEE THE HYDROGEN ATOMS FUSING TOGETHER.
WHAT'S HAPPENING TO ME, ADAM?
AR

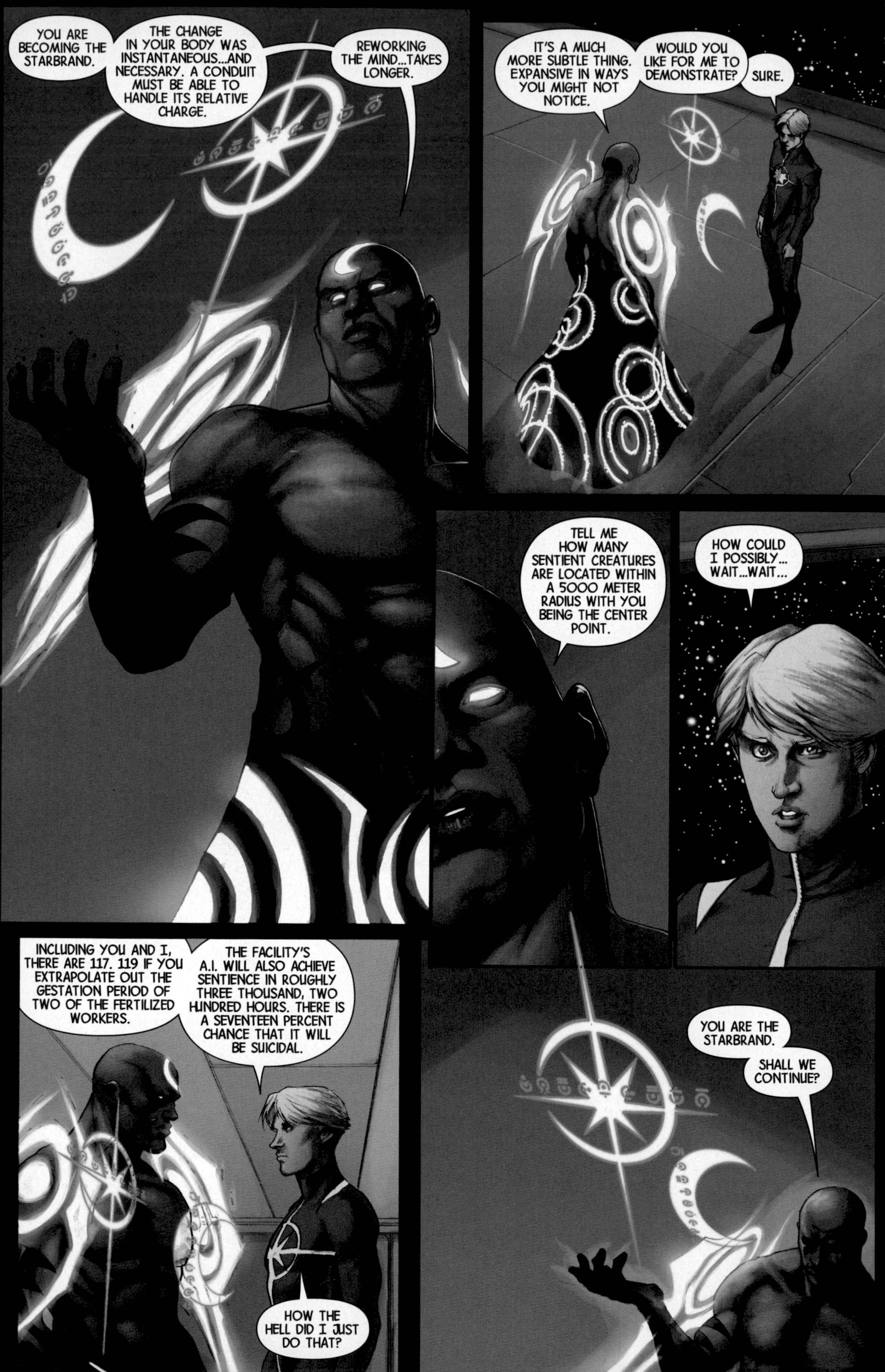
YOU ARE BECOMING THE STARBRAND.
THE CHANGE IN YOUR BODY WAS INSTANTANEOUS...AND NECESSARY. A CONDUIT MUST BE ABLE TO HANDLE ITS RELATIVE CHARGE.
REWORKING THE MIND...TAKES LONGER.
IT'S A MUCH MORE SUBTLE THING. EXPANSIVE IN WAYS YOU MIGHT NOT NOTICE.
WOULD YOU LIKE FOR ME TO DEMONSTRATE?
SURE.
TELL ME HOW MANY SENTIENT CREATURES ARE LOCATED WITHIN A 5000 METER RADIUS WITH YOU BEING THE CENTER POINT.
HOW COULD I POSSIBLY... WAIT...WAIT...
INCLUDING YOU AND I, THERE ARE 117. 119 IF YOU EXTRAPOLATE OUT THE GESTATION PERIOD OF TWO OF THE FERTILIZED WORKERS.
THE FACILITY'S A.I. WILL ALSO ACHIEVE SENTIENCE IN ROUGHLY THREE THOUSAND, TWO HUNDRED HOURS. THERE IS A SEVENTEEN PERCENT CHANCE THAT IT WILL BE SUICIDAL.
HOW THE HELL DID I JUST DO THAT?
YOU ARE THE STARBRAND.
SHALL WE CONTINUE?

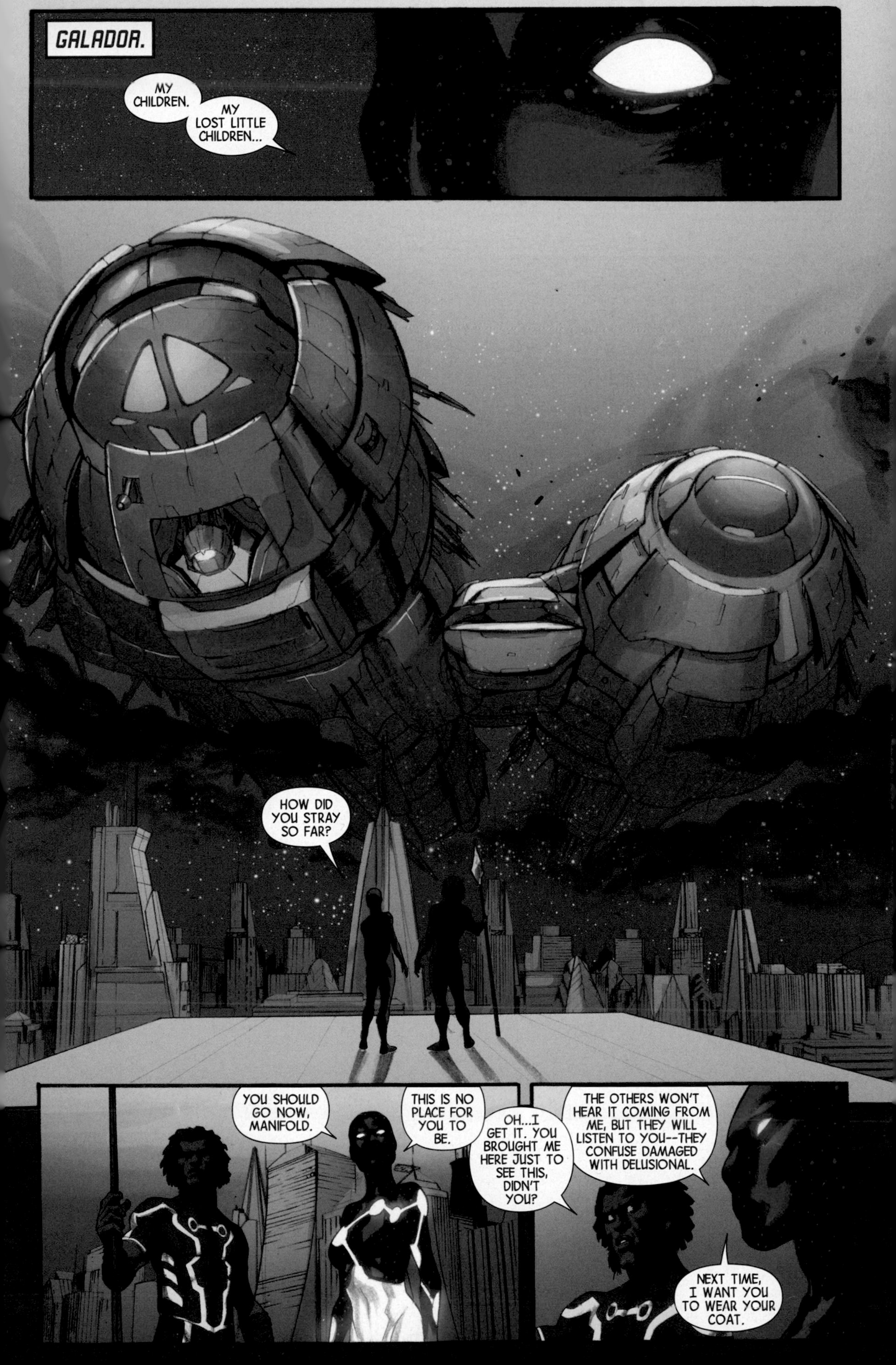
GALADOR.
MY CHILDREN.
MY LOST LITTLE CHILDREN...
HOW DID YOU STRAY SO FAR?
YOU SHOULD GO NOW, MANIFOLD.
THIS IS NO PLACE FOR YOU TO BE.
OH...I GET IT. YOU BROUGHT ME HERE JUST TO SEE THIS, DIDN'T YOU?
THE OTHERS WON'T HEAR IT COMING FROM ME, BUT THEY WILL LISTEN TO YOU--THEY CONFUSE DAMAGED WITH DELUSIONAL.
NEXT TIME, I WANT YOU TO WEAR YOUR COAT.

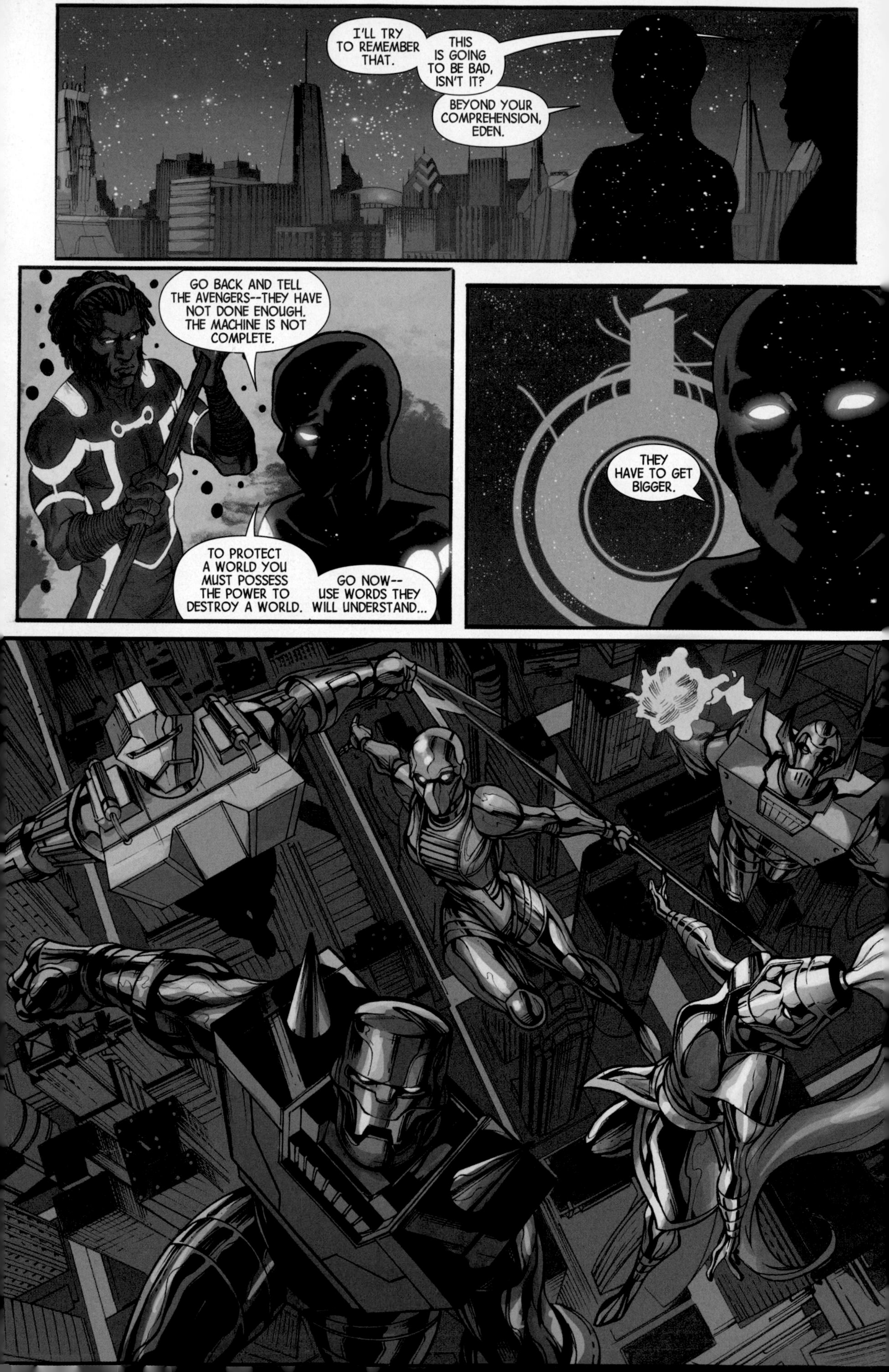
I'LL TRY TO REMEMBER THAT.
THIS IS GOING TO BE BAD, ISN'T IT?
BEYOND YOUR COMPREHENSION, EDEN.
GO BACK AND TELL THE AVENGERS--THEY HAVE NOT DONE ENOUGH. THE MACHINE IS NOT COMPLETE.
TO PROTECT A WORLD YOU MUST POSSESS THE POWER TO DESTROY A WORLD.
GO NOW-- USE WORDS THEY WILL UNDERSTAND...
THEY HAVE TO GET BIGGER.

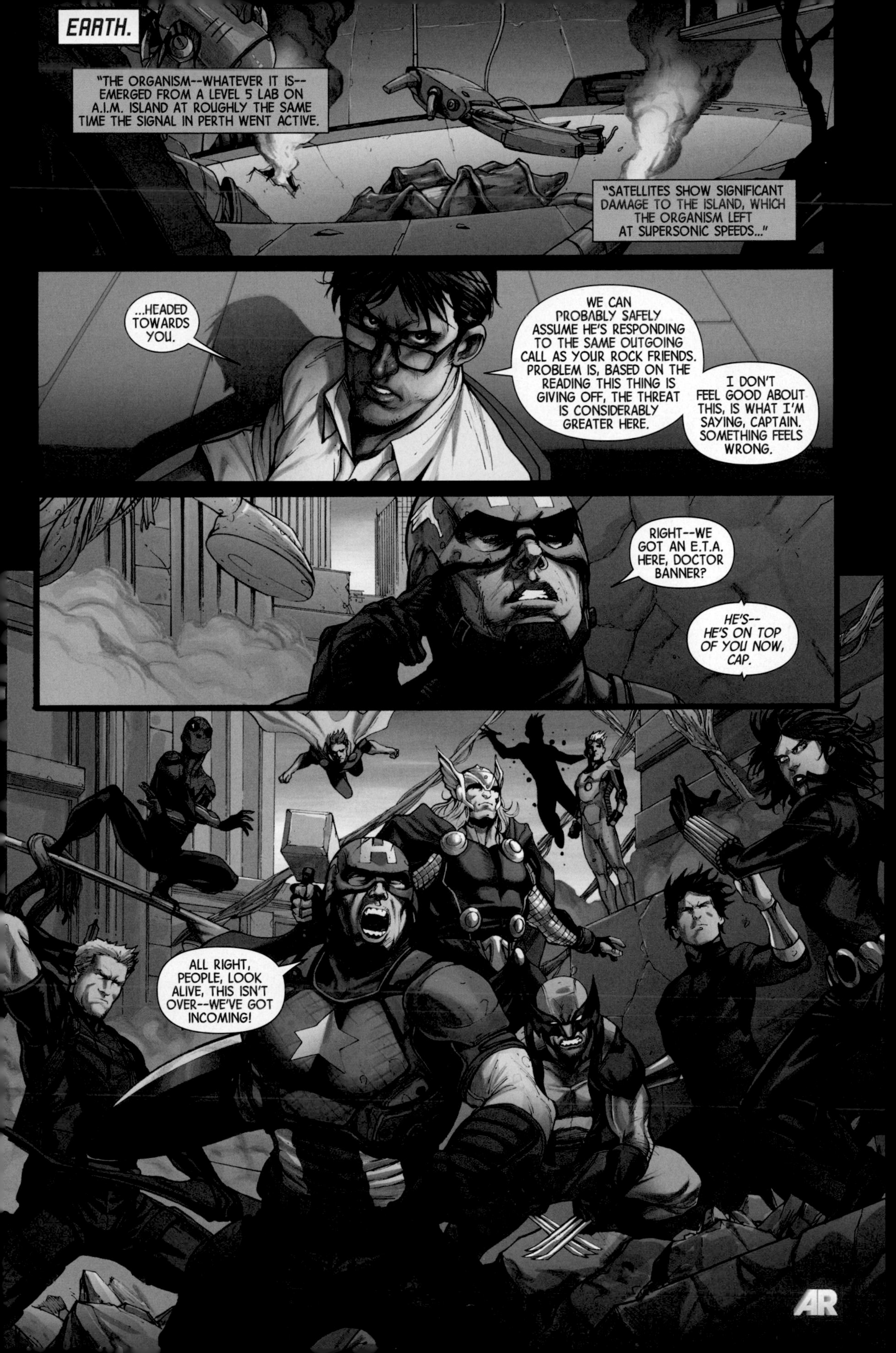
EARTH.
"THE ORGANISM--WHATEVER IT IS--EMERGED FROM A LEVEL 5 LAB ON A.I.M. ISLAND AT ROUGHLY THE SAME TIME THE SIGNAL IN PERTH WENT ACTIVE.
"SATELLITES SHOW SIGNIFICANT DAMAGE TO THE ISLAND, WHICH THE ORGANISM LEFT AT SUPERSONIC SPEEDS..."
...HEADED TOWARDS YOU.
WE CAN PROBABLY SAFELY ASSUME HE'S RESPONDING TO THE SAME OUTGOING CALL AS YOUR ROCK FRIENDS. PROBLEM IS, BASED ON THE READING THIS THING IS GIVING OFF, THE THREAT IS CONSIDERABLY GREATER HERE.
I DON'T FEEL GOOD ABOUT THIS, IS WHAT I'M SAYING, CAPTAIN. SOMETHING FEELS WRONG.
RIGHT--WE GOT AN E.T.A. HERE, DOCTOR BANNER?
HE'S-- HE'S ON TOP OF YOU NOW, CAP.
ALL RIGHT, PEOPLE, LOOK ALIVE, THIS ISN'T OVER--WE'VE GOT INCOMING!
AR

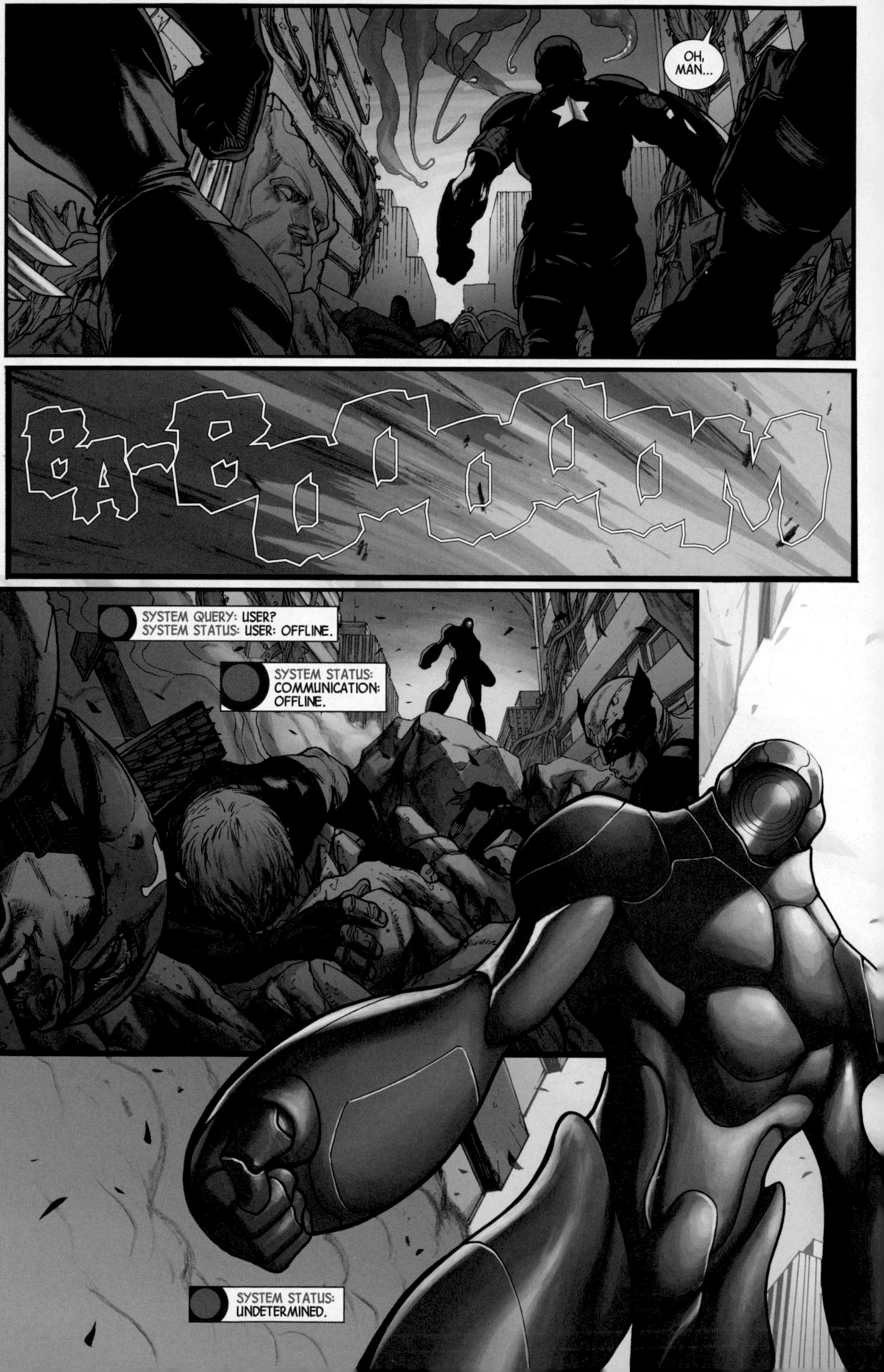
OH, MAN...
BA-BOOOOOM
SYSTEM QUERY: USER?
SYSTEM STATUS: USER: OFFLINE.
SYSTEM STATUS: COMMUNICATION: OFFLINE.
SYSTEM STATUS: UNDETERMINED.

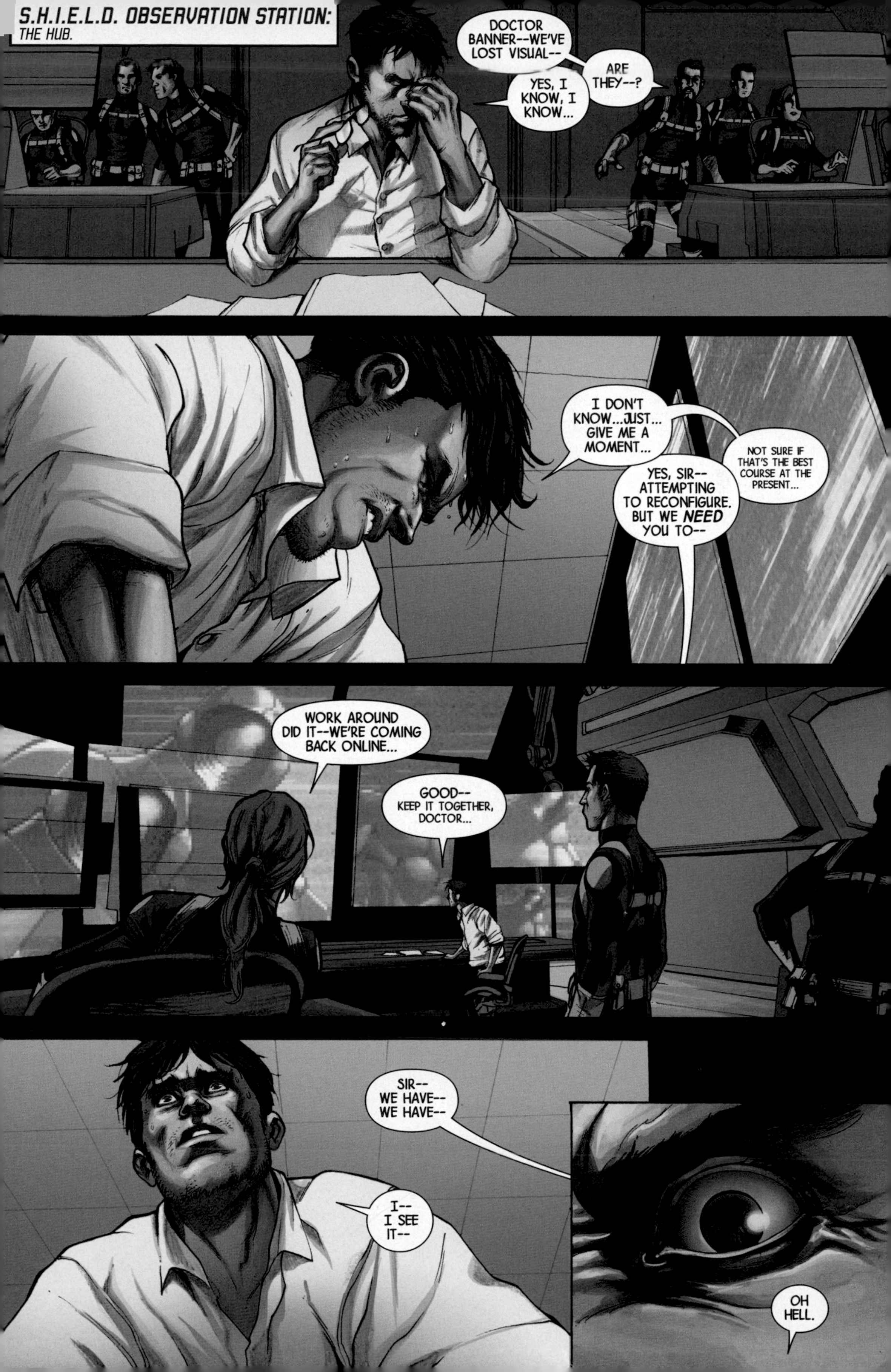
S.H.I.E.L.D. OBSERVATION STATION:
THE HUB.
DOCTOR BANNER--WE'VE LOST VISUAL--
ARE THEY--?
YES, I KNOW, I KNOW...
I DON'T KNOW...JUST... GIVE ME A MOMENT...
NOT SURE IF THAT'S THE BEST COURSE AT THE PRESENT...
YES, SIR--ATTEMPTING TO RECONFIGURE. BUT WE NEED YOU TO--
WORK AROUND DID IT--WE'RE COMING BACK ONLINE...
GOOD-- KEEP IT TOGETHER, DOCTOR...
SIR-- WE HAVE-- WE HAVE--
I-- I SEE IT--
OH HELL.

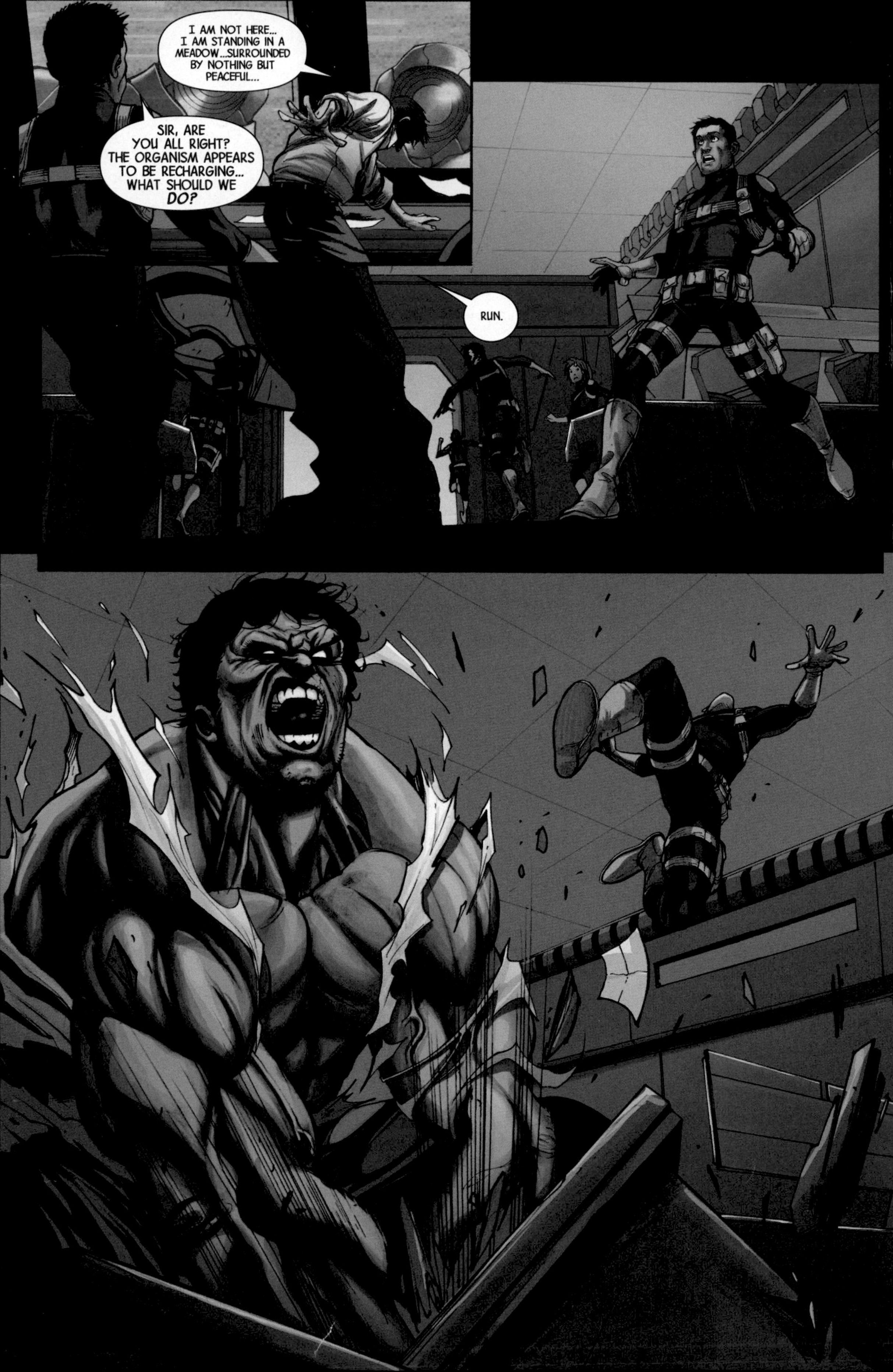
I AM NOT HERE... I AM STANDING IN A MEADOW...SURROUNDED BY NOTHING BUT PEACEFUL...
SIR, ARE YOU ALL RIGHT? THE ORGANISM APPEARS TO BE RECHARGING... WHAT SHOULD WE *DO?*
RUN.

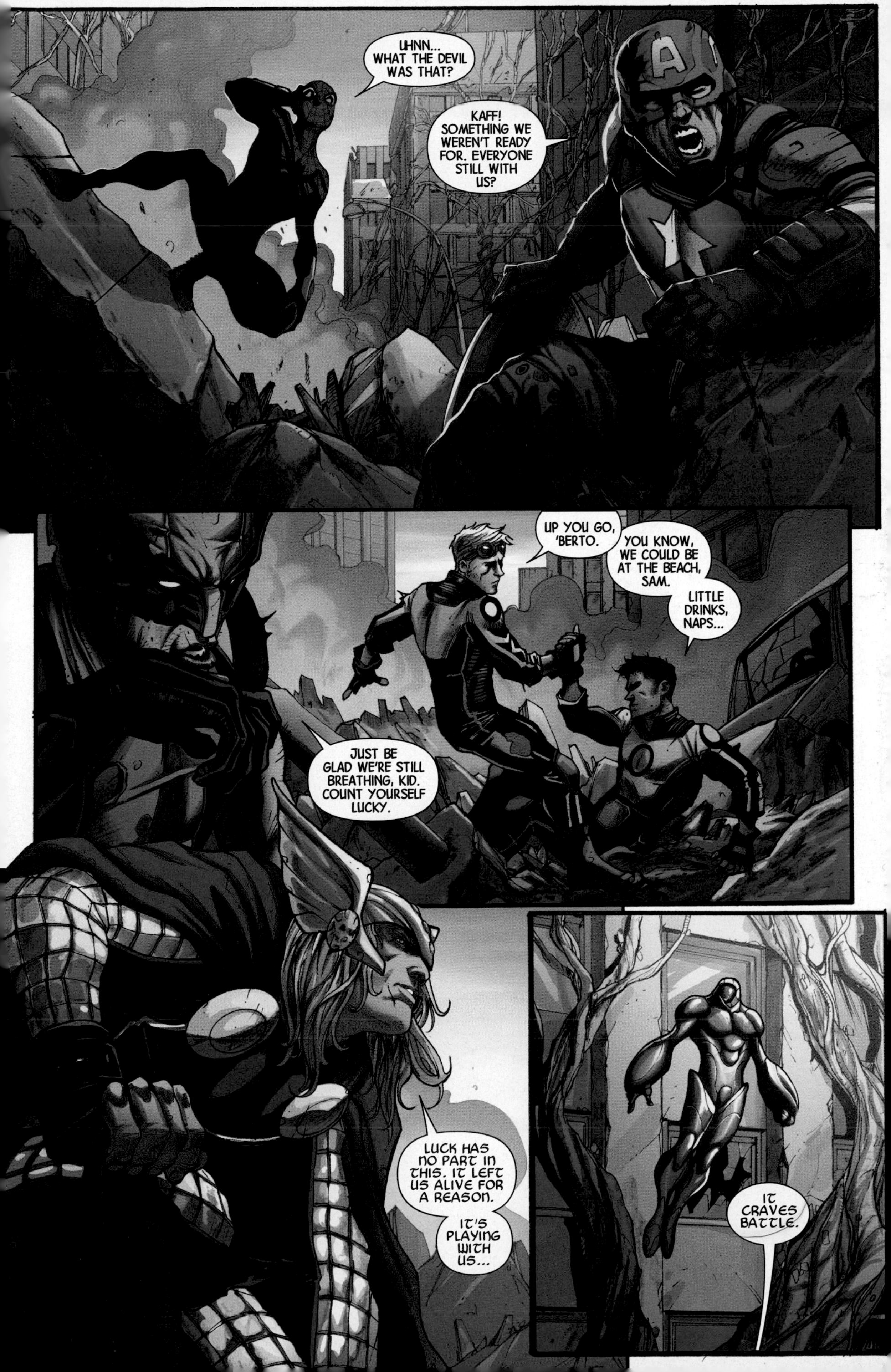
UHNN... WHAT THE DEVIL WAS THAT?
KAFF! SOMETHING WE WEREN'T READY FOR. EVERYONE STILL WITH US?
UP YOU GO, 'BERTO.
YOU KNOW, WE COULD BE AT THE BEACH, SAM.
LITTLE DRINKS, NAPS...
JUST BE GLAD WE'RE STILL BREATHING, KID. COUNT YOURSELF LUCKY.
LUCK HAS NO PART IN THIS. IT LEFT US ALIVE FOR A REASON.
IT'S PLAYING WITH US...
IT CRAVES BATTLE.

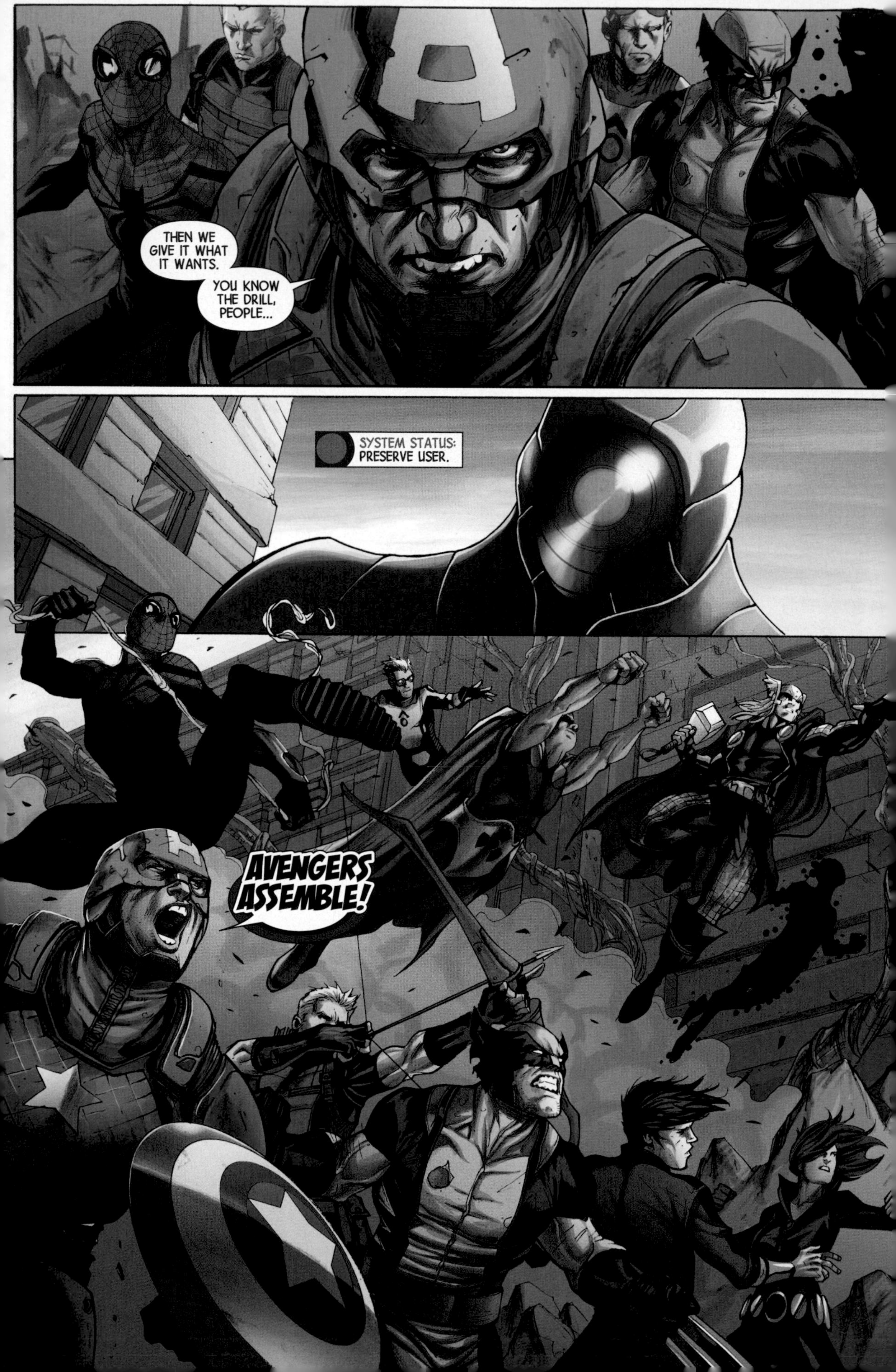
THEN WE GIVE IT WHAT IT WANTS.
YOU KNOW THE DRILL, PEOPLE...
SYSTEM STATUS: PRESERVE USER.
AVENGERS ASSEMBLE!

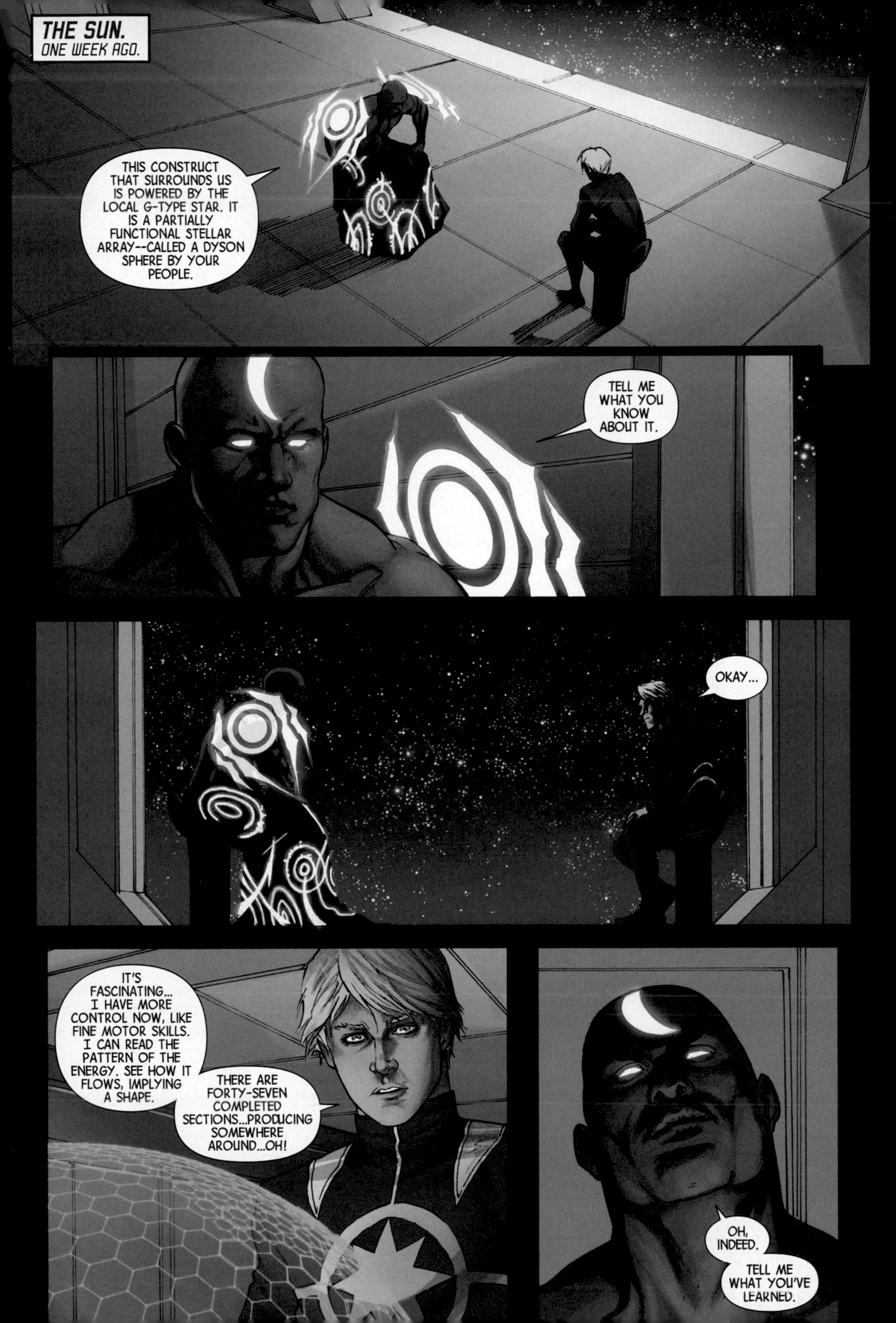
THE SUN.
ONE WEEK AGO.
THIS CONSTRUCT THAT SURROUNDS US IS POWERED BY THE LOCAL G-TYPE STAR. IT IS A PARTIALLY FUNCTIONAL STELLAR ARRAY--CALLED A DYSON SPHERE BY YOUR PEOPLE.
TELL ME WHAT YOU KNOW ABOUT IT.
OKAY...
IT'S FASCINATING... I HAVE MORE CONTROL NOW, LIKE FINE MOTOR SKILLS. I CAN READ THE PATTERN OF THE ENERGY. SEE HOW IT FLOWS, IMPLYING A SHAPE.
THERE ARE FORTY-SEVEN COMPLETED SECTIONS...PRODUCING SOMEWHERE AROUND...OH!
OH, INDEED.
TELL ME WHAT YOU'VE LEARNED.

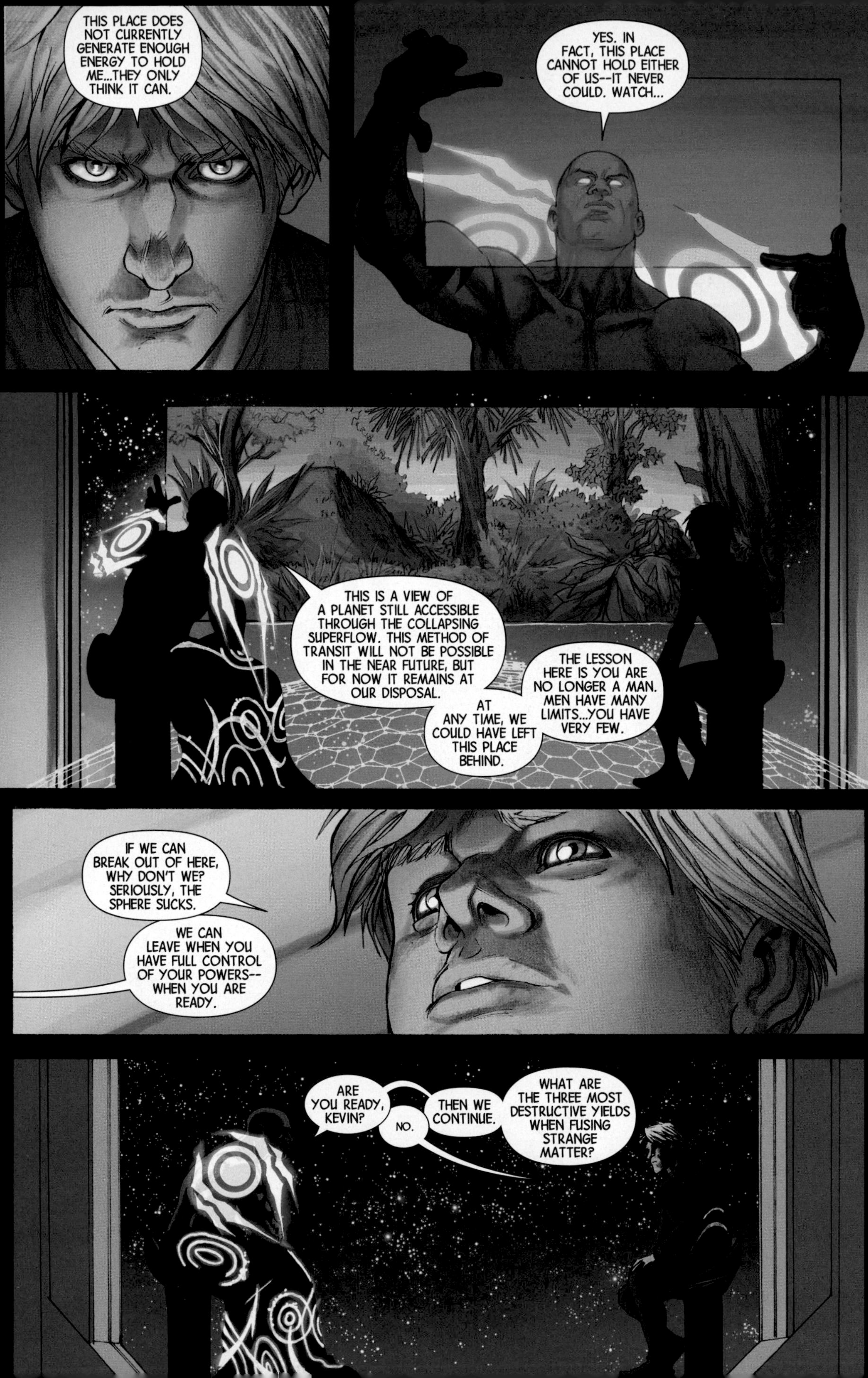
THIS PLACE DOES NOT CURRENTLY GENERATE ENOUGH ENERGY TO HOLD ME...THEY ONLY THINK IT CAN.
YES. IN FACT, THIS PLACE CANNOT HOLD EITHER OF US--IT NEVER COULD. WATCH...
THIS IS A VIEW OF A PLANET STILL ACCESSIBLE THROUGH THE COLLAPSING SUPERFLOW. THIS METHOD OF TRANSIT WILL NOT BE POSSIBLE IN THE NEAR FUTURE, BUT FOR NOW IT REMAINS AT OUR DISPOSAL.
AT ANY TIME, WE COULD HAVE LEFT THIS PLACE BEHIND.
THE LESSON HERE IS YOU ARE NO LONGER A MAN. MEN HAVE MANY LIMITS...YOU HAVE VERY FEW.
IF WE CAN BREAK OUT OF HERE, WHY DON'T WE? SERIOUSLY, THE SPHERE SUCKS.
WE CAN LEAVE WHEN YOU HAVE FULL CONTROL OF YOUR POWERS--WHEN YOU ARE READY.
ARE YOU READY, KEVIN?
NO.
THEN WE CONTINUE.
WHAT ARE THE THREE MOST DESTRUCTIVE YIELDS WHEN FUSING STRANGE MATTER?

PERTH.

SYSTEM STATUS: ENGAGED.

SYSTEM TARGET: ENHANCED.
SYSTEM STATUS: UPGRADE.

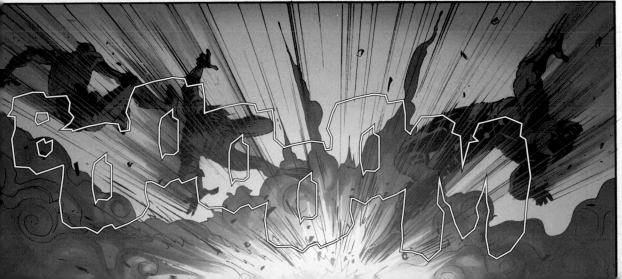

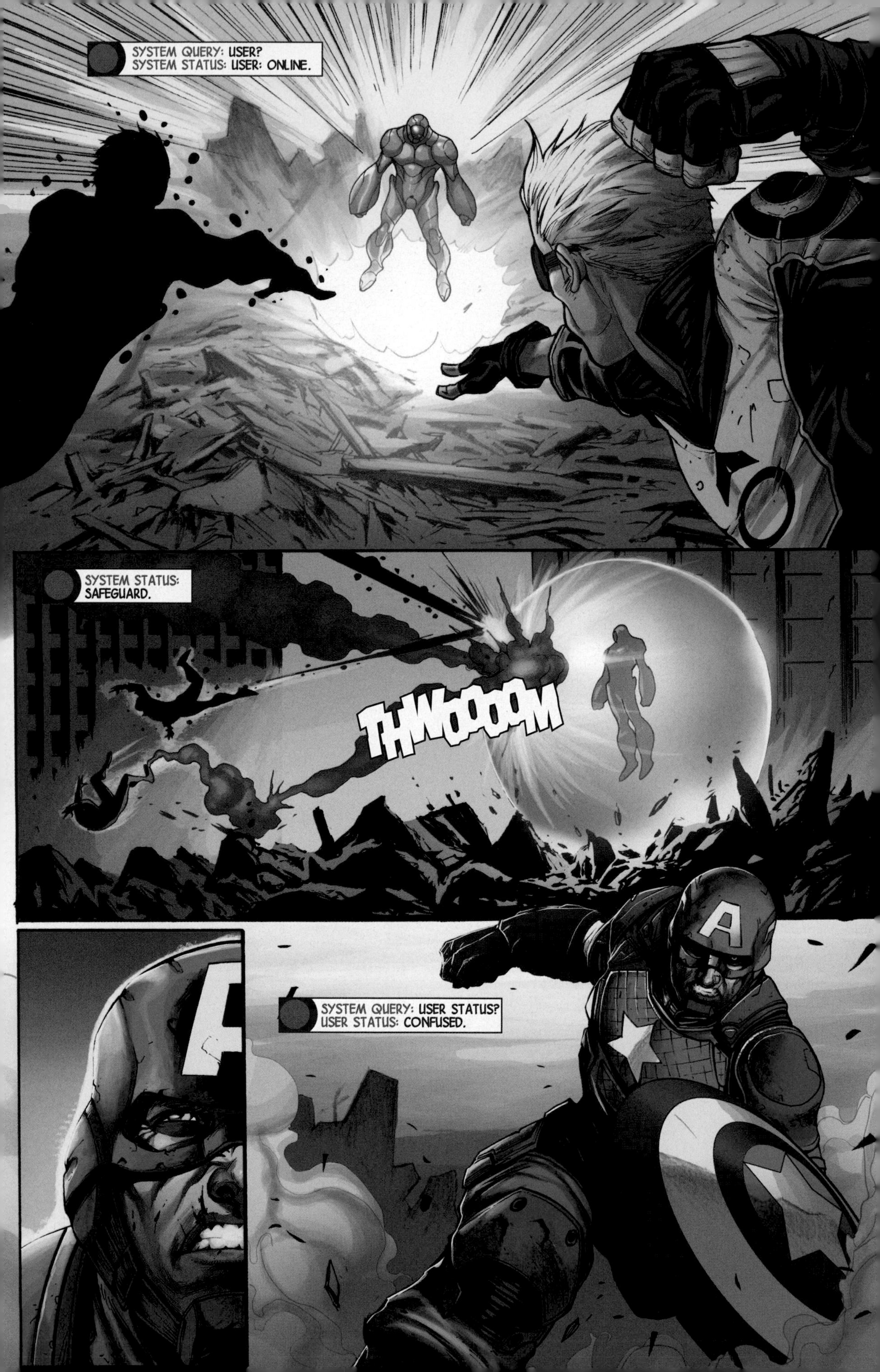
SYSTEM QUERY: USER?
SYSTEM STATUS: USER: ONLINE.
SYSTEM STATUS:
SAFEGUARD.
THWOOOOM
SYSTEM QUERY: USER STATUS?
USER STATUS: CONFUSED.

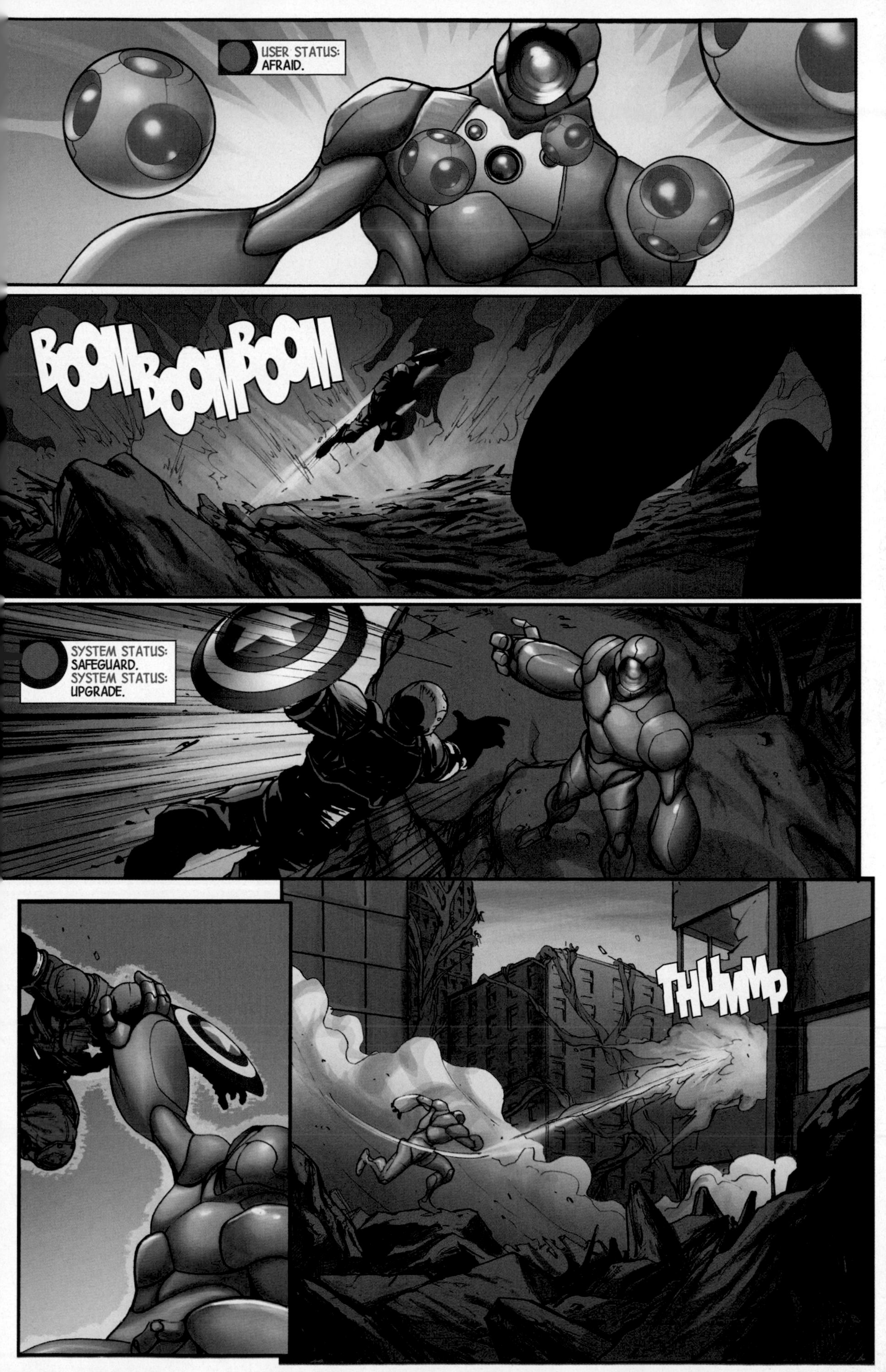
USER STATUS:
AFRAID.
BOOMBOOMBOOM
SYSTEM STATUS:
SAFEGUARD.
SYSTEM STATUS:
UPGRADE.
THUMMP

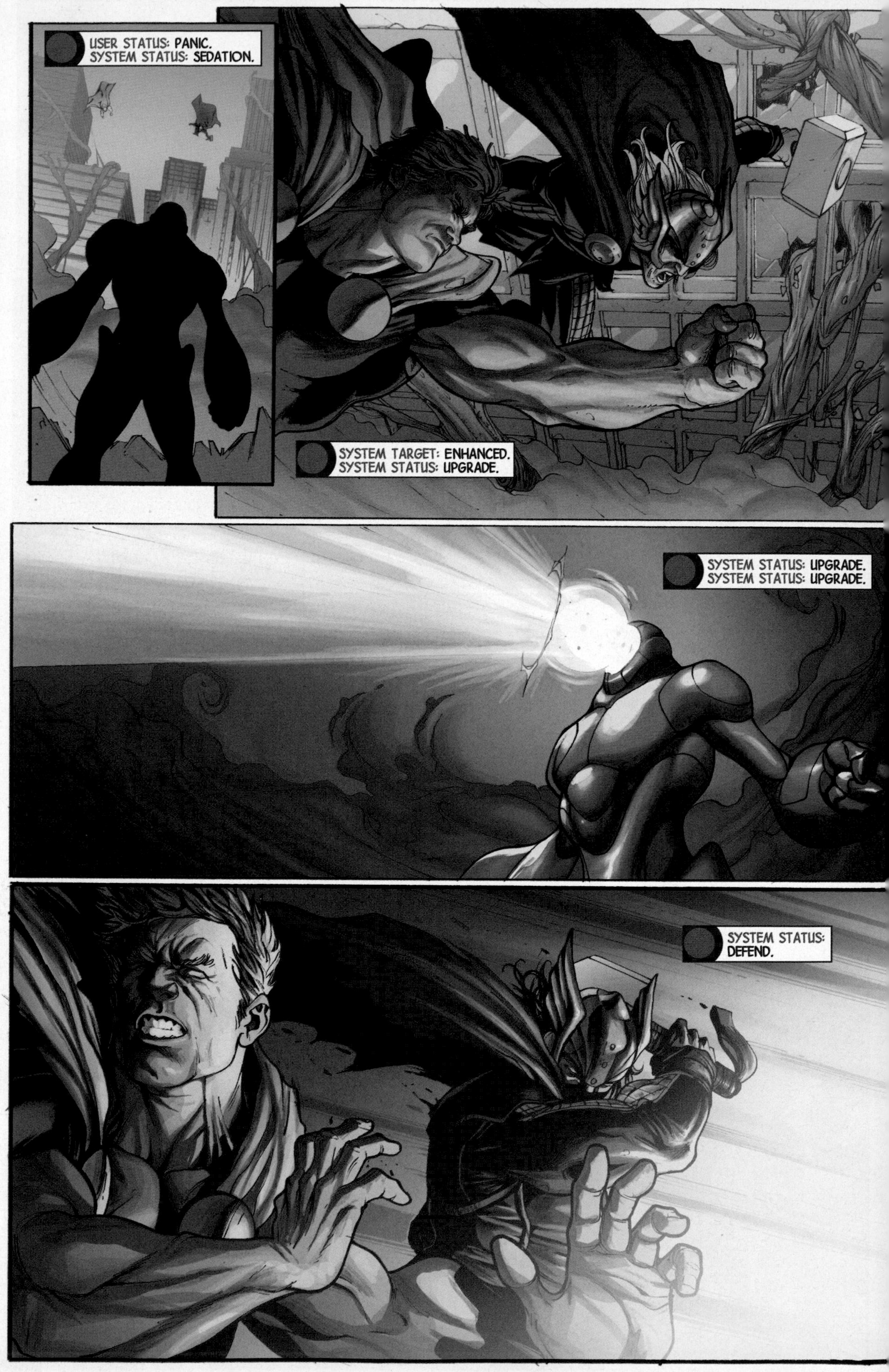
USER STATUS: PANIC.
SYSTEM STATUS: SEDATION.
SYSTEM TARGET: ENHANCED.
SYSTEM STATUS: UPGRADE.
SYSTEM STATUS: UPGRADE.
SYSTEM STATUS: UPGRADE.
SYSTEM STATUS:
DEFEND.

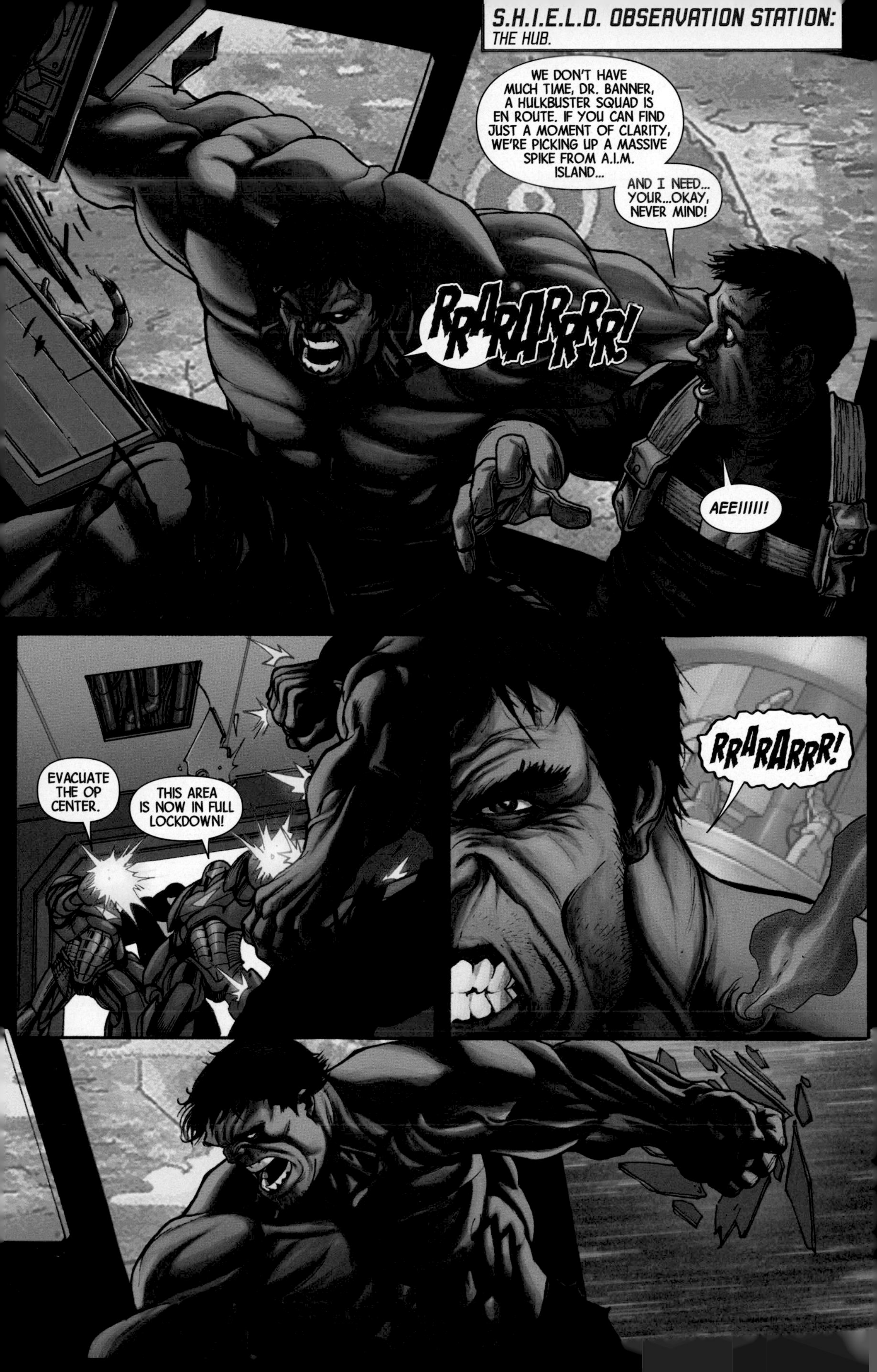
S.H.I.E.L.D. OBSERVATION STATION:
THE HUB.
WE DON'T HAVE MUCH TIME, DR. BANNER, A HULKBUSTER SQUAD IS EN ROUTE. IF YOU CAN FIND JUST A MOMENT OF CLARITY, WE'RE PICKING UP A MASSIVE SPIKE FROM A.I.M. ISLAND...
AND I NEED... YOUR...OKAY, NEVER MIND!
RRARARRRR!
AEEIIIII!
EVACUATE THE OP CENTER.
THIS AREA IS NOW IN FULL LOCKDOWN!
RRARARRR!

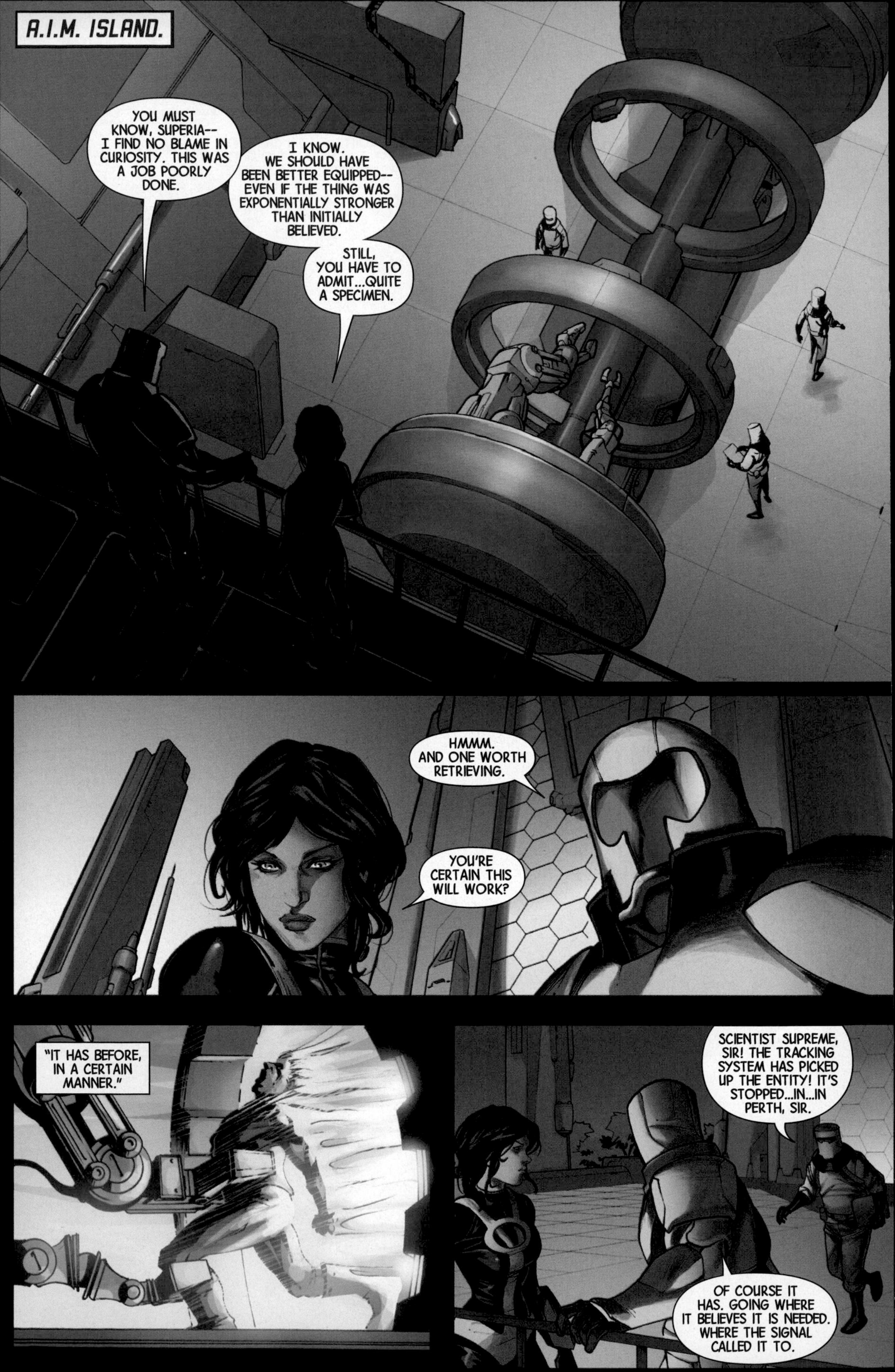
A.I.M. ISLAND.
YOU MUST KNOW, SUPERIA-- I FIND NO BLAME IN CURIOSITY. THIS WAS A JOB POORLY DONE.
I KNOW. WE SHOULD HAVE BEEN BETTER EQUIPPED-- EVEN IF THE THING WAS EXPONENTIALLY STRONGER THAN INITIALLY BELIEVED.
STILL, YOU HAVE TO ADMIT...QUITE A SPECIMEN.
HMMM. AND ONE WORTH RETRIEVING.
YOU'RE CERTAIN THIS WILL WORK?
"IT HAS BEFORE, IN A CERTAIN MANNER."
SCIENTIST SUPREME, SIR! THE TRACKING SYSTEM HAS PICKED UP THE ENTITY! IT'S STOPPED...IN...IN PERTH, SIR.
OF COURSE IT HAS. GOING WHERE IT BELIEVES IT IS NEEDED. WHERE THE SIGNAL CALLED IT TO.

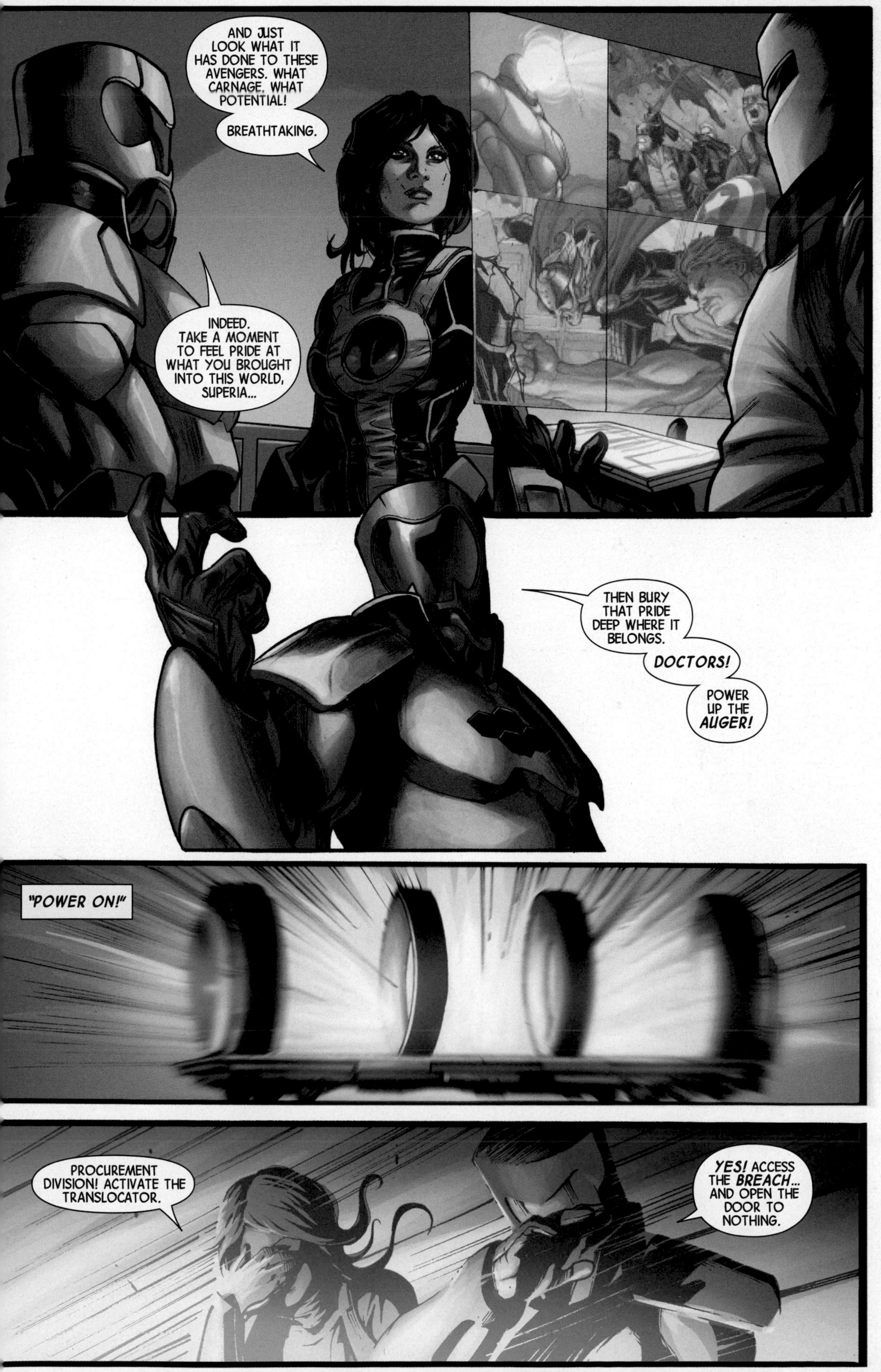
AND JUST LOOK WHAT IT HAS DONE TO THESE AVENGERS. WHAT CARNAGE. WHAT POTENTIAL!
BREATHTAKING.
INDEED. TAKE A MOMENT TO FEEL PRIDE AT WHAT YOU BROUGHT INTO THIS WORLD, SUPERIA...
THEN BURY THAT PRIDE DEEP WHERE IT BELONGS.
DOCTORS!
POWER UP THE AUGER!
"POWER ON!"
PROCUREMENT DIVISION! ACTIVATE THE TRANSLOCATOR.
YES! ACCESS THE BREACH... AND OPEN THE DOOR TO NOTHING.

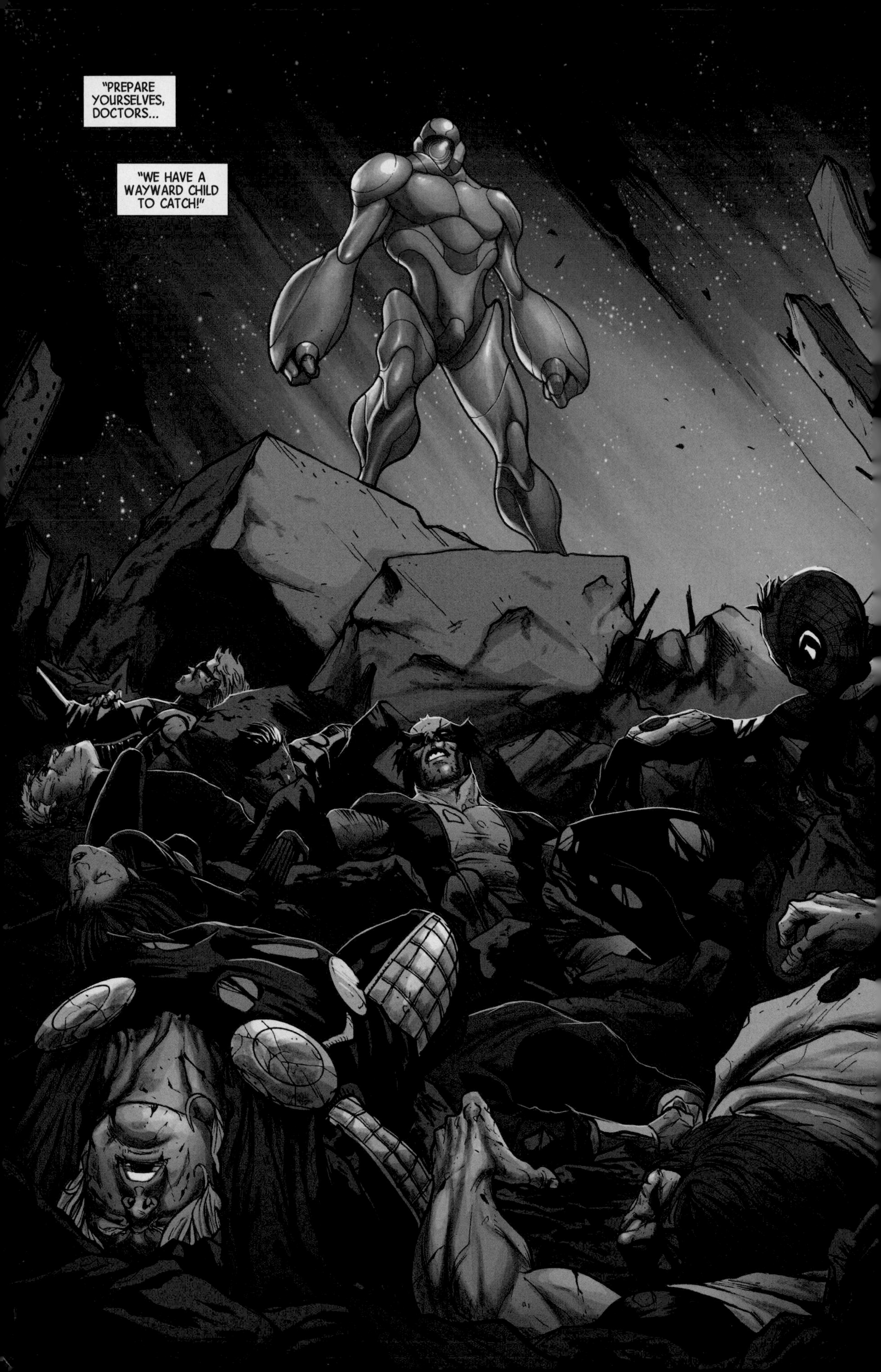
"PREPARE YOURSELVES, DOCTORS...
"WE HAVE A WAYWARD CHILD TO CATCH!"

"...TO THE LIGHT"

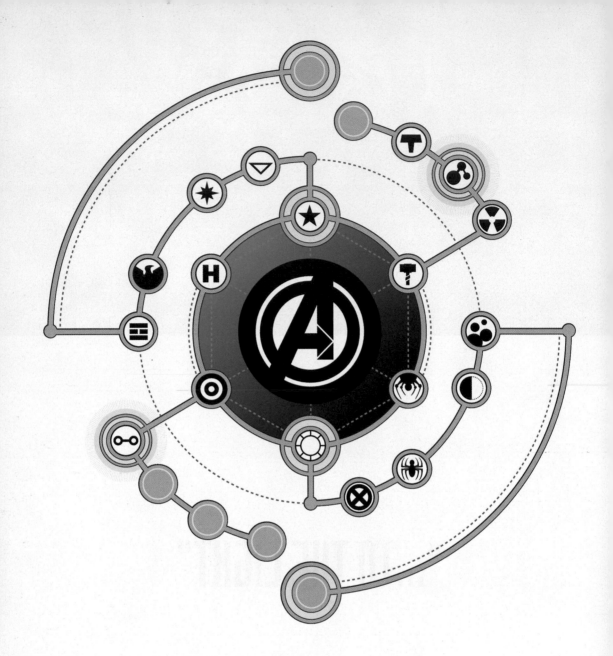

EARTH'S MIGHTIEST HEROES

CAPTAIN AMERICA · IRON MAN · THOR · HAWKEYE · BLACK WIDOW · HULK
WOLVERINE · SPIDER-MAN · CAPTAIN MARVEL · SPIDER-WOMAN
FALCON · SHANG-CHI · SUNSPOT · CANNONBALL · MANIFOLD
SMASHER · CAPTAIN UNIVERSE · HYPERION

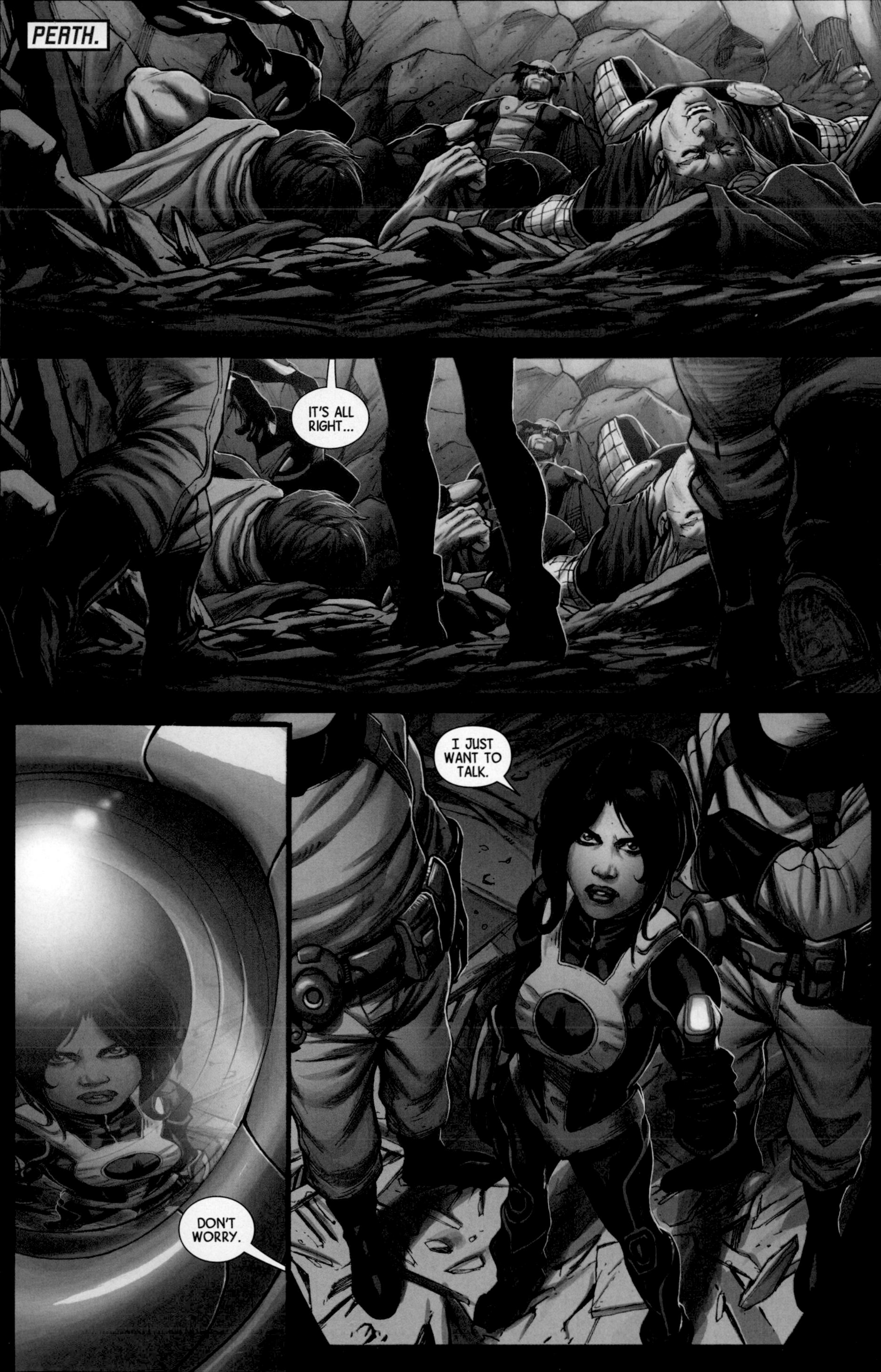
PERTH.
IT'S ALL RIGHT...
DON'T WORRY.
I JUST WANT TO TALK.

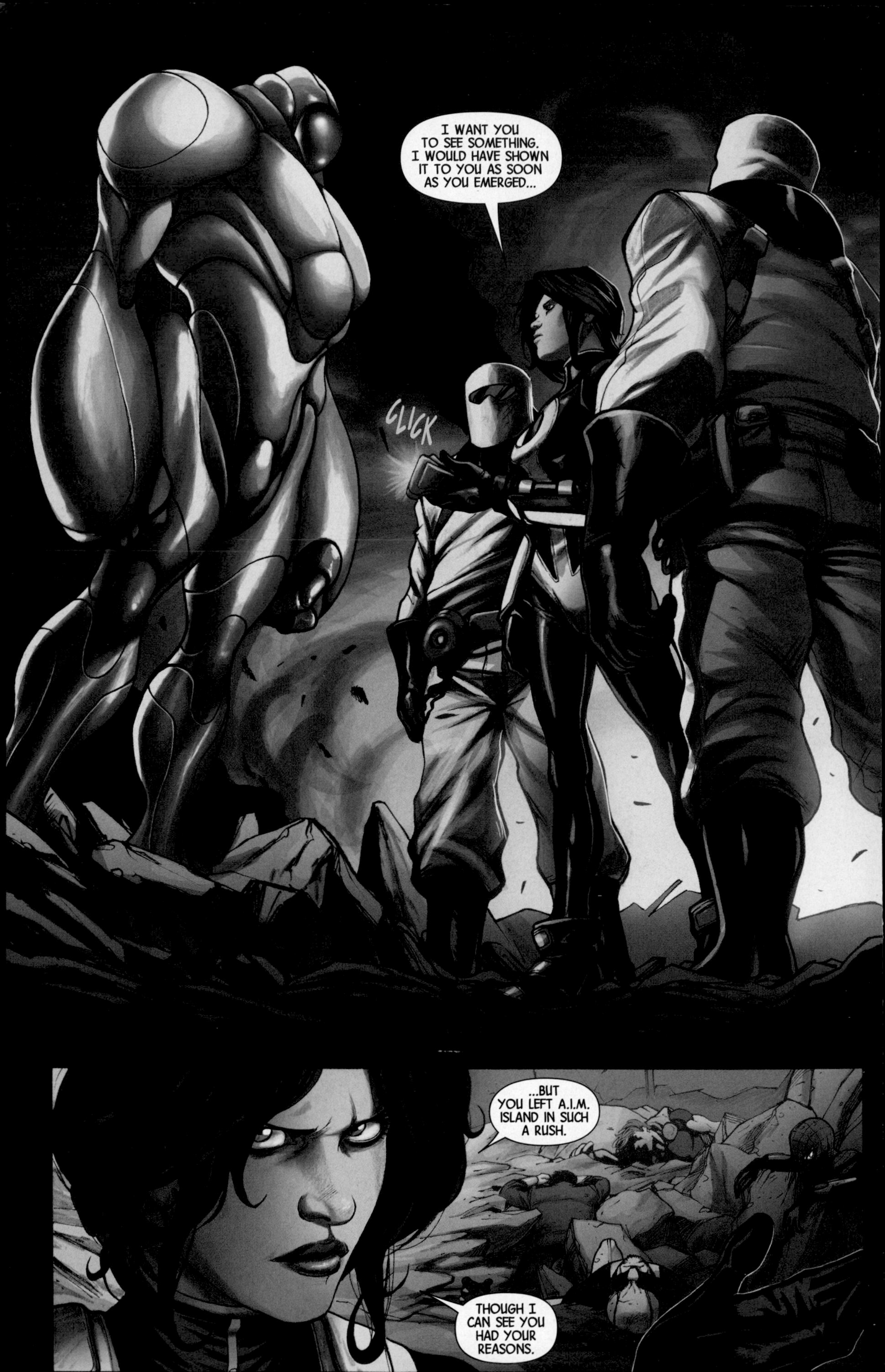
I WANT YOU TO SEE SOMETHING. I WOULD HAVE SHOWN IT TO YOU AS SOON AS YOU EMERGED...
CLICK
...BUT YOU LEFT A.I.M. ISLAND IN SUCH A RUSH.
THOUGH I CAN SEE YOU HAD YOUR REASONS.

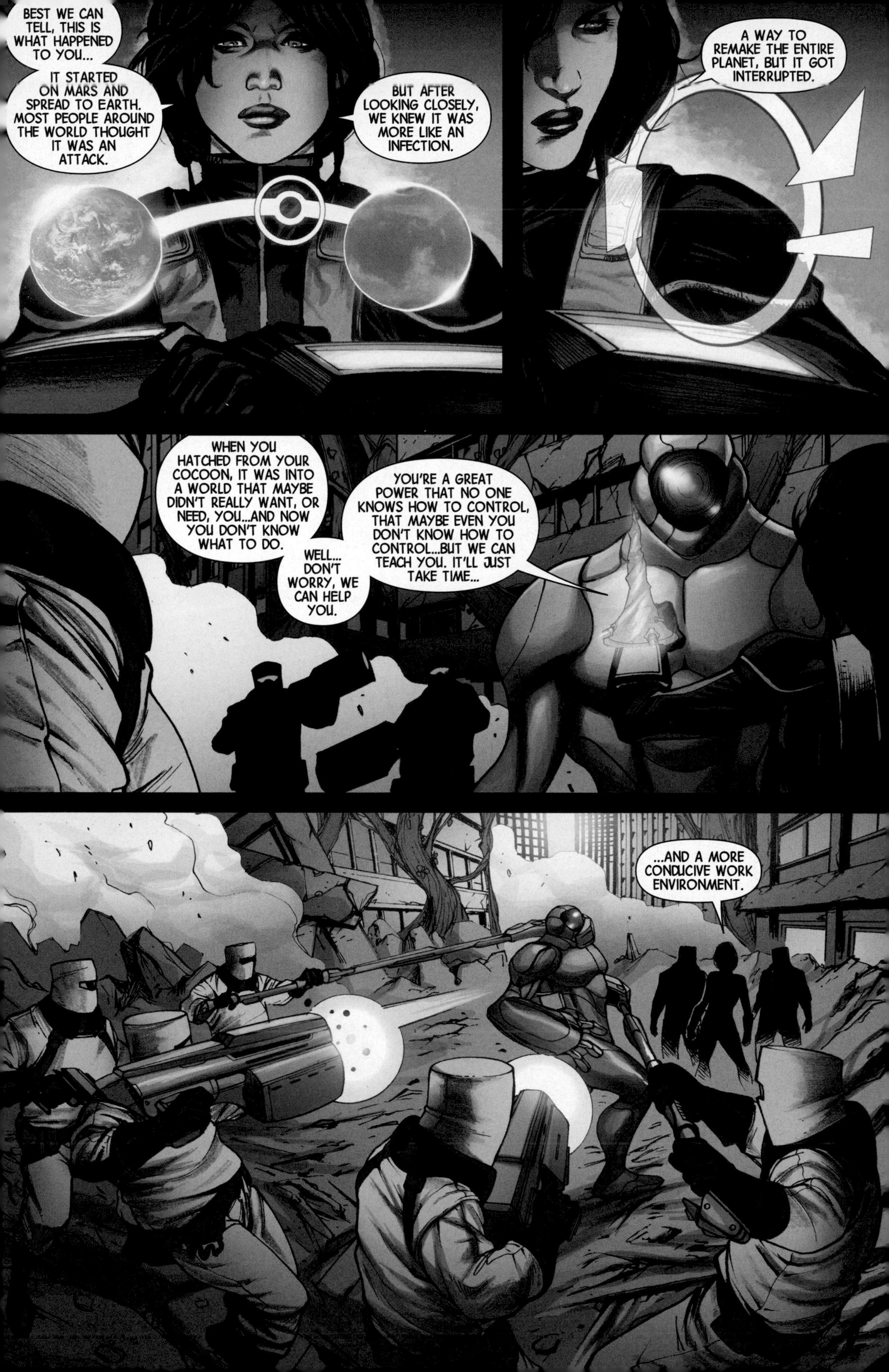
BEST WE CAN TELL, THIS IS WHAT HAPPENED TO YOU...
IT STARTED ON MARS AND SPREAD TO EARTH. MOST PEOPLE AROUND THE WORLD THOUGHT IT WAS AN ATTACK.
BUT AFTER LOOKING CLOSELY, WE KNEW IT WAS MORE LIKE AN INFECTION.
A WAY TO REMAKE THE ENTIRE PLANET, BUT IT GOT INTERRUPTED.
WHEN YOU HATCHED FROM YOUR COCOON, IT WAS INTO A WORLD THAT MAYBE DIDN'T REALLY WANT, OR NEED, YOU...AND NOW YOU DON'T KNOW WHAT TO DO.
WELL... DON'T WORRY, WE CAN HELP YOU.
YOU'RE A GREAT POWER THAT NO ONE KNOWS HOW TO CONTROL, THAT MAYBE EVEN YOU DON'T KNOW HOW TO CONTROL...BUT WE CAN TEACH YOU. IT'LL JUST TAKE TIME...
...AND A MORE CONDUCIVE WORK ENVIRONMENT.

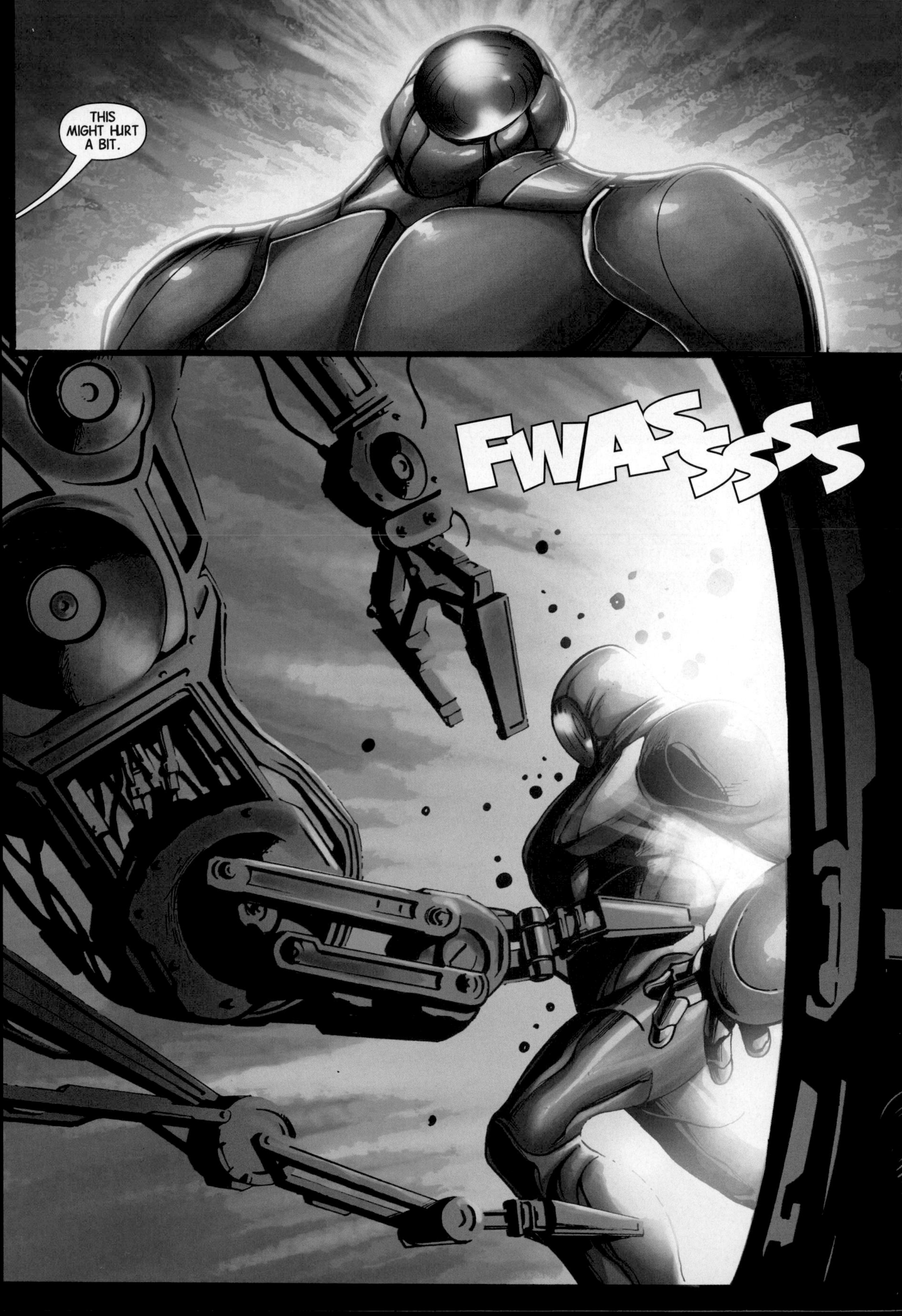
THIS MIGHT HURT A BIT.
FWASSSSS

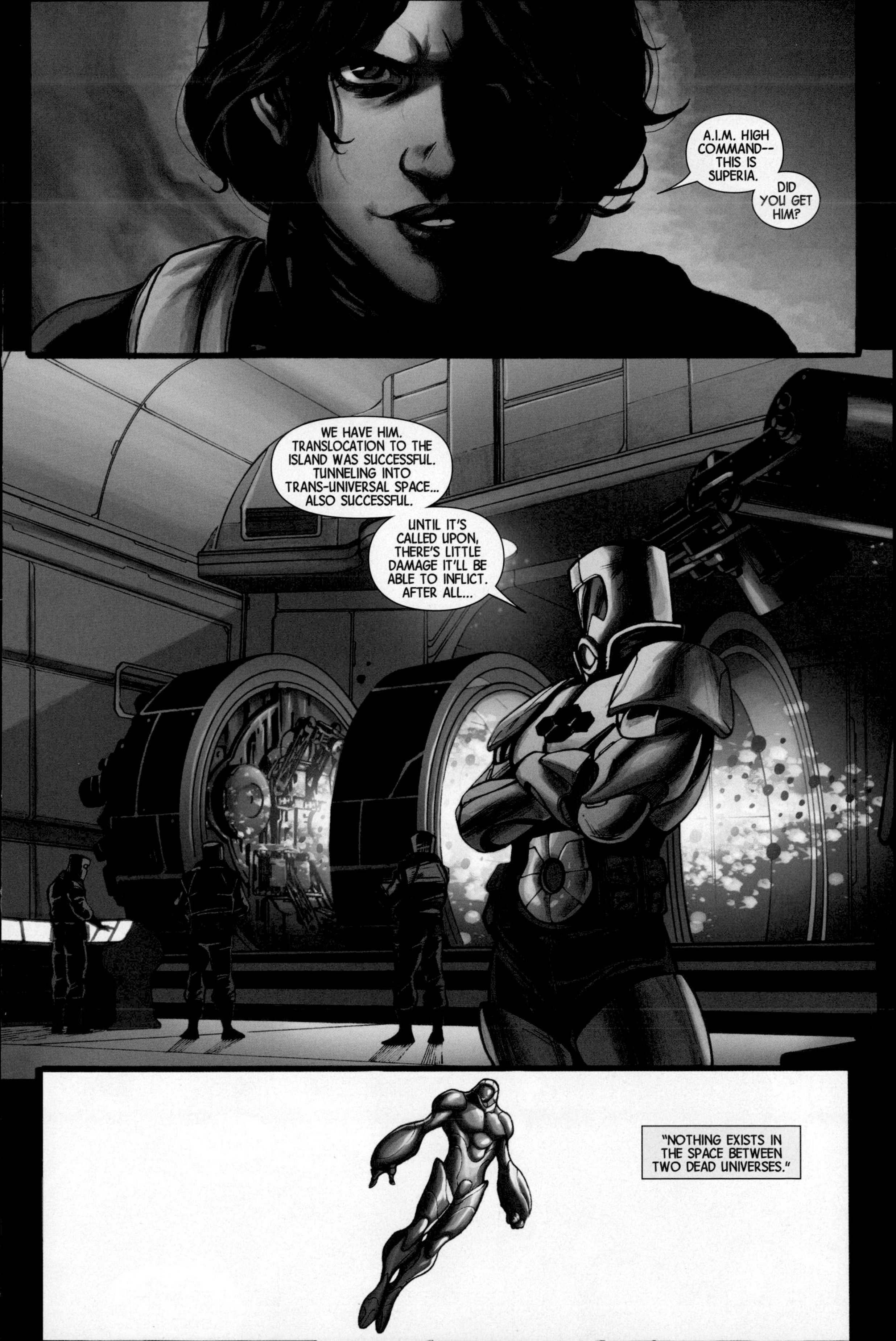
A.I.M. HIGH COMMAND-- THIS IS SUPERIA.
DID YOU GET HIM?
WE HAVE HIM. TRANSLOCATION TO THE ISLAND WAS SUCCESSFUL. TUNNELING INTO TRANS-UNIVERSAL SPACE... ALSO SUCCESSFUL.
UNTIL IT'S CALLED UPON, THERE'S LITTLE DAMAGE IT'LL BE ABLE TO INFLICT. AFTER ALL...
"NOTHING EXISTS IN THE SPACE BETWEEN TWO DEAD UNIVERSES."

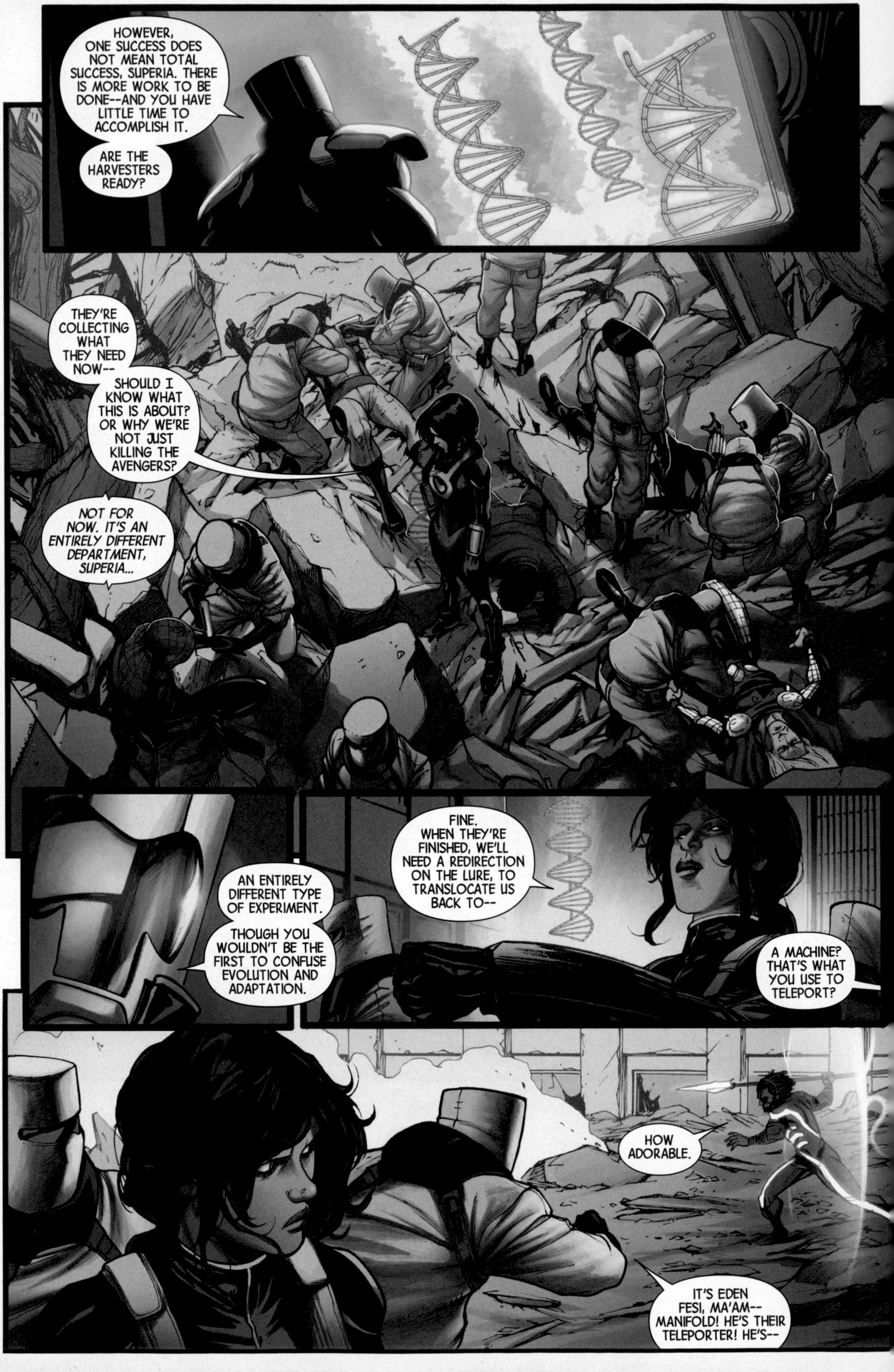
HOWEVER, ONE SUCCESS DOES NOT MEAN TOTAL SUCCESS, SUPERIA. THERE IS MORE WORK TO BE DONE--AND YOU HAVE LITTLE TIME TO ACCOMPLISH IT.
ARE THE HARVESTERS READY?
THEY'RE COLLECTING WHAT THEY NEED NOW--
SHOULD I KNOW WHAT THIS IS ABOUT? OR WHY WE'RE NOT JUST KILLING THE AVENGERS?
NOT FOR NOW. IT'S AN ENTIRELY DIFFERENT DEPARTMENT, SUPERIA...
AN ENTIRELY DIFFERENT TYPE OF EXPERIMENT.
THOUGH YOU WOULDN'T BE THE FIRST TO CONFUSE EVOLUTION AND ADAPTATION.
FINE. WHEN THEY'RE FINISHED, WE'LL NEED A REDIRECTION ON THE LURE, TO TRANSLOCATE US BACK TO--
A MACHINE? THAT'S WHAT YOU USE TO TELEPORT?
HOW ADORABLE.
IT'S EDEN FESI, MA'AM--MANIFOLD! HE'S THEIR TELEPORTER! HE'S--

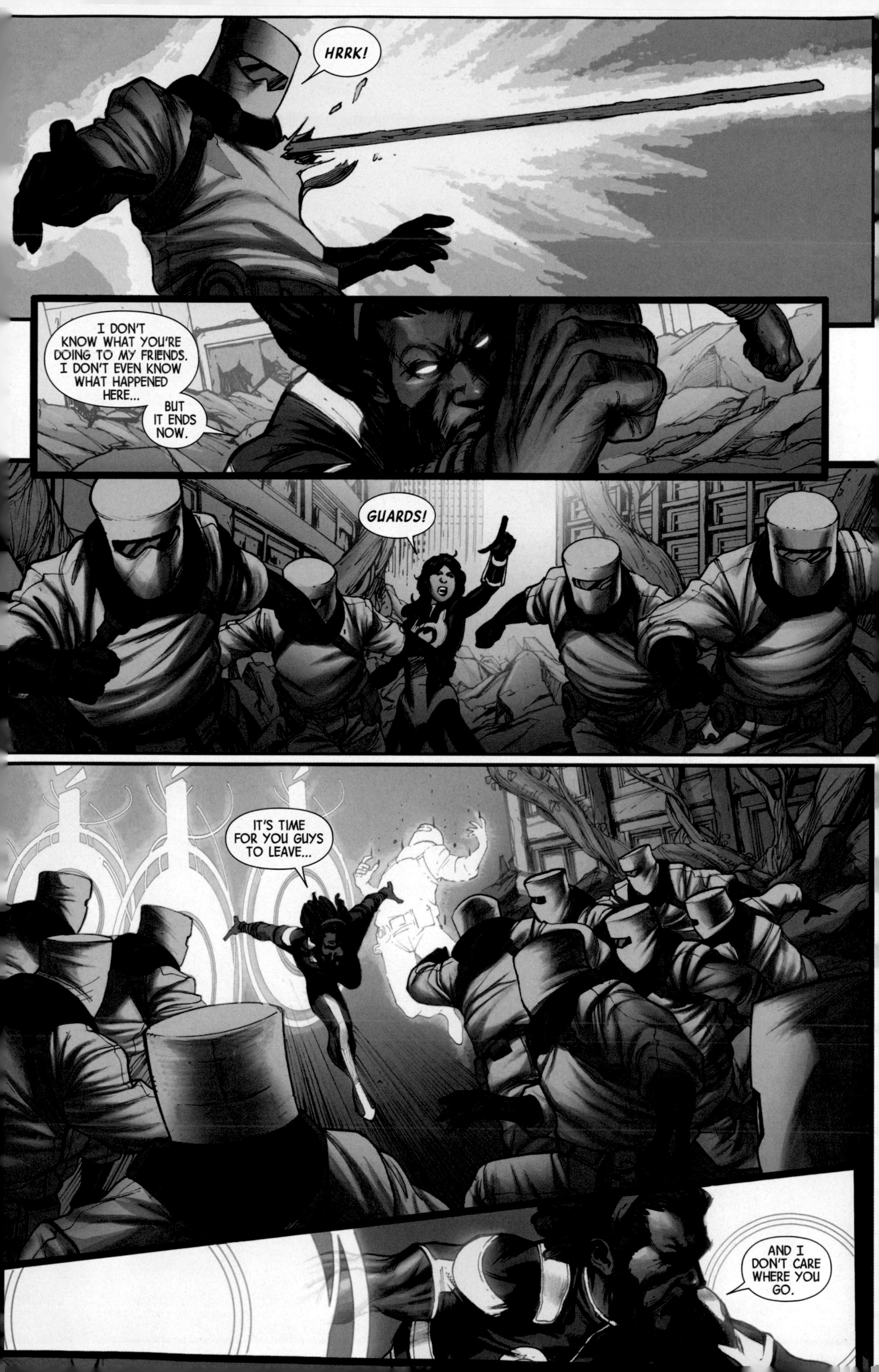
HRRK!
I DON'T KNOW WHAT YOU'RE DOING TO MY FRIENDS. I DON'T EVEN KNOW WHAT HAPPENED HERE...
BUT IT ENDS NOW.
GUARDS!
IT'S TIME FOR YOU GUYS TO LEAVE...
AND I DON'T CARE WHERE YOU GO.

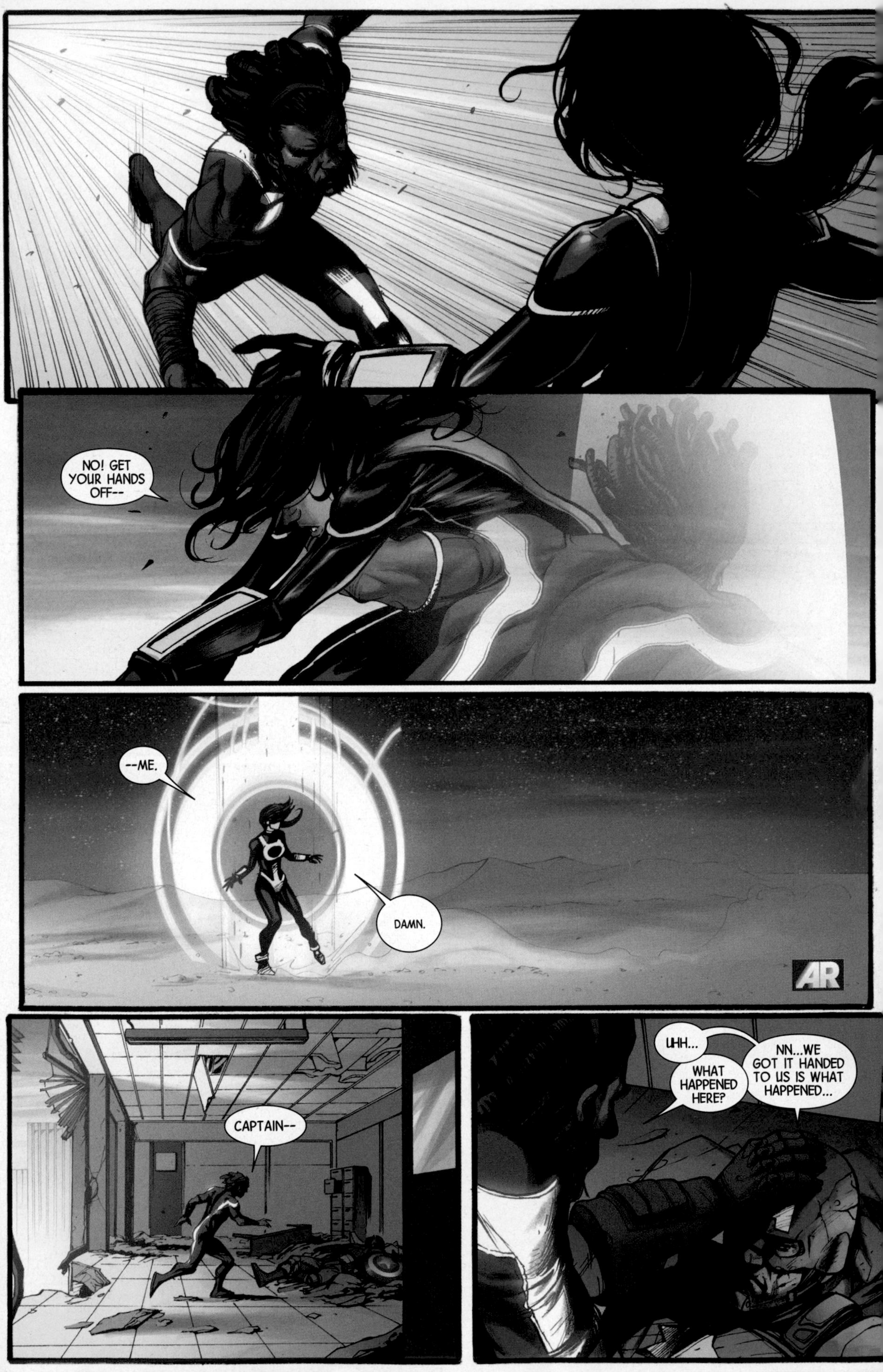
NO! GET YOUR HANDS OFF--
--ME.
DAMN.
AR
CAPTAIN--
UHH...
WHAT HAPPENED HERE?
NN...WE GOT IT HANDED TO US IS WHAT HAPPENED...

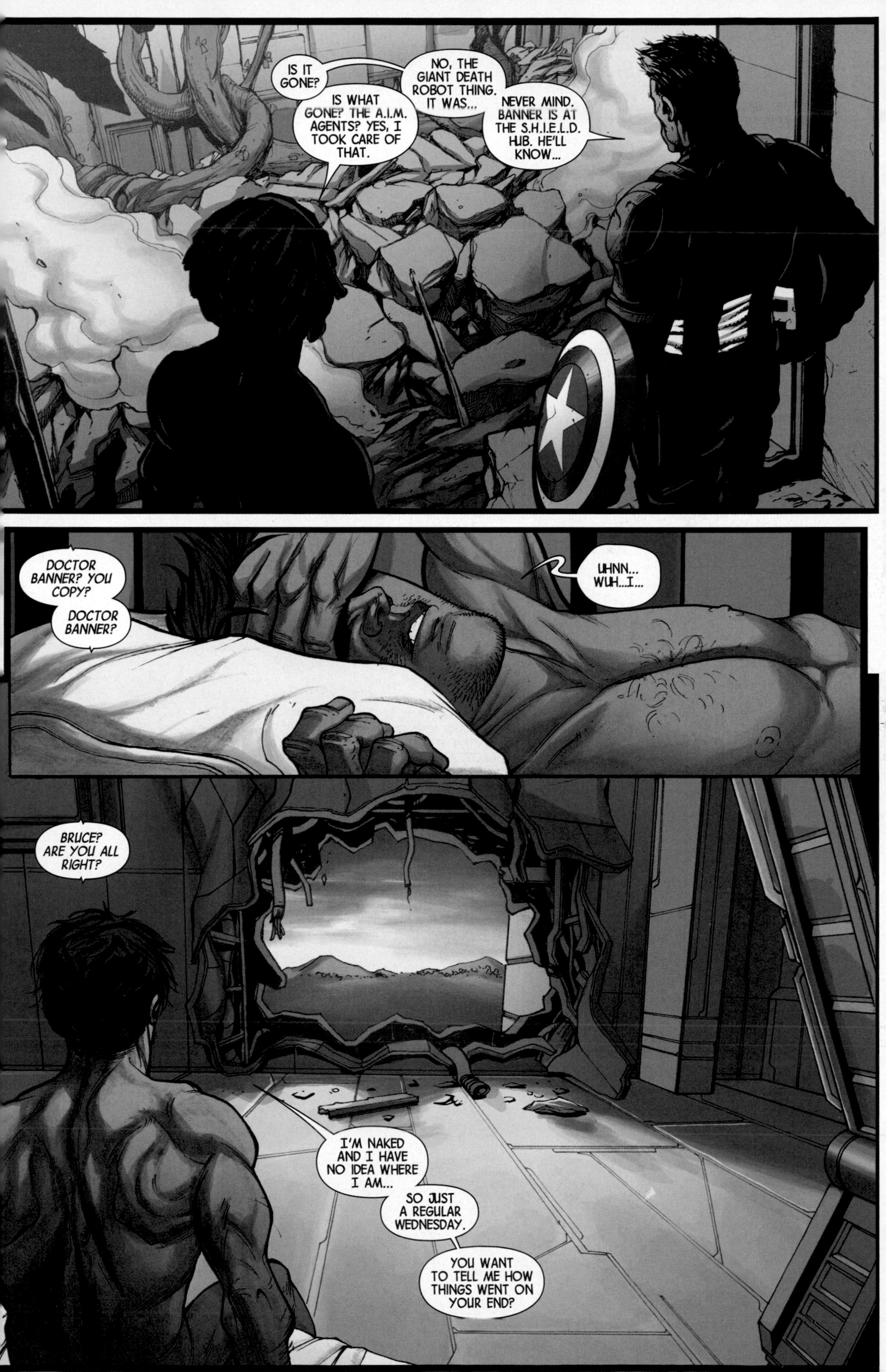
IS IT GONE?
IS WHAT GONE? THE A.I.M. AGENTS? YES, I TOOK CARE OF THAT.
NO, THE GIANT DEATH ROBOT THING. IT WAS...
NEVER MIND. BANNER IS AT THE S.H.I.E.L.D. HUB. HE'LL KNOW...
DOCTOR BANNER? YOU COPY?
DOCTOR BANNER?
UHNN... WUH...I...
BRUCE? ARE YOU ALL RIGHT?
I'M NAKED AND I HAVE NO IDEA WHERE I AM...
SO JUST A REGULAR WEDNESDAY.
YOU WANT TO TELL ME HOW THINGS WENT ON YOUR END?

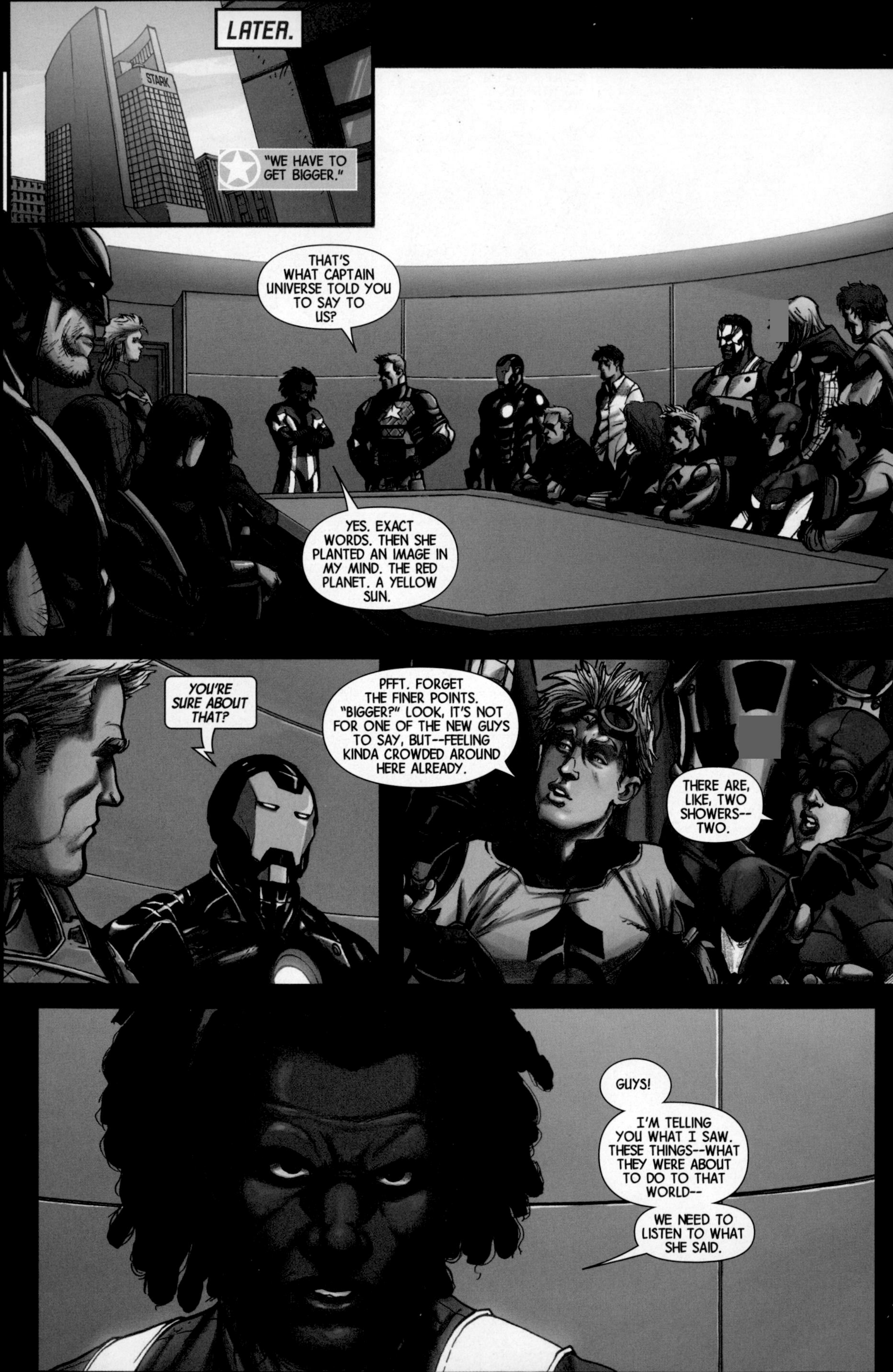
LATER.
"WE HAVE TO GET BIGGER."
THAT'S WHAT CAPTAIN UNIVERSE TOLD YOU TO SAY TO US?
YES. EXACT WORDS. THEN SHE PLANTED AN IMAGE IN MY MIND. THE RED PLANET. A YELLOW SUN.
YOU'RE SURE ABOUT THAT?
PFFT. FORGET THE FINER POINTS. "BIGGER?" LOOK, IT'S NOT FOR ONE OF THE NEW GUYS TO SAY, BUT--FEELING KINDA CROWDED AROUND HERE ALREADY.
THERE ARE, LIKE, TWO SHOWERS-- TWO.
GUYS!
I'M TELLING YOU WHAT I SAW. THESE THINGS--WHAT THEY WERE ABOUT TO DO TO THAT WORLD--
WE NEED TO LISTEN TO WHAT SHE SAID.

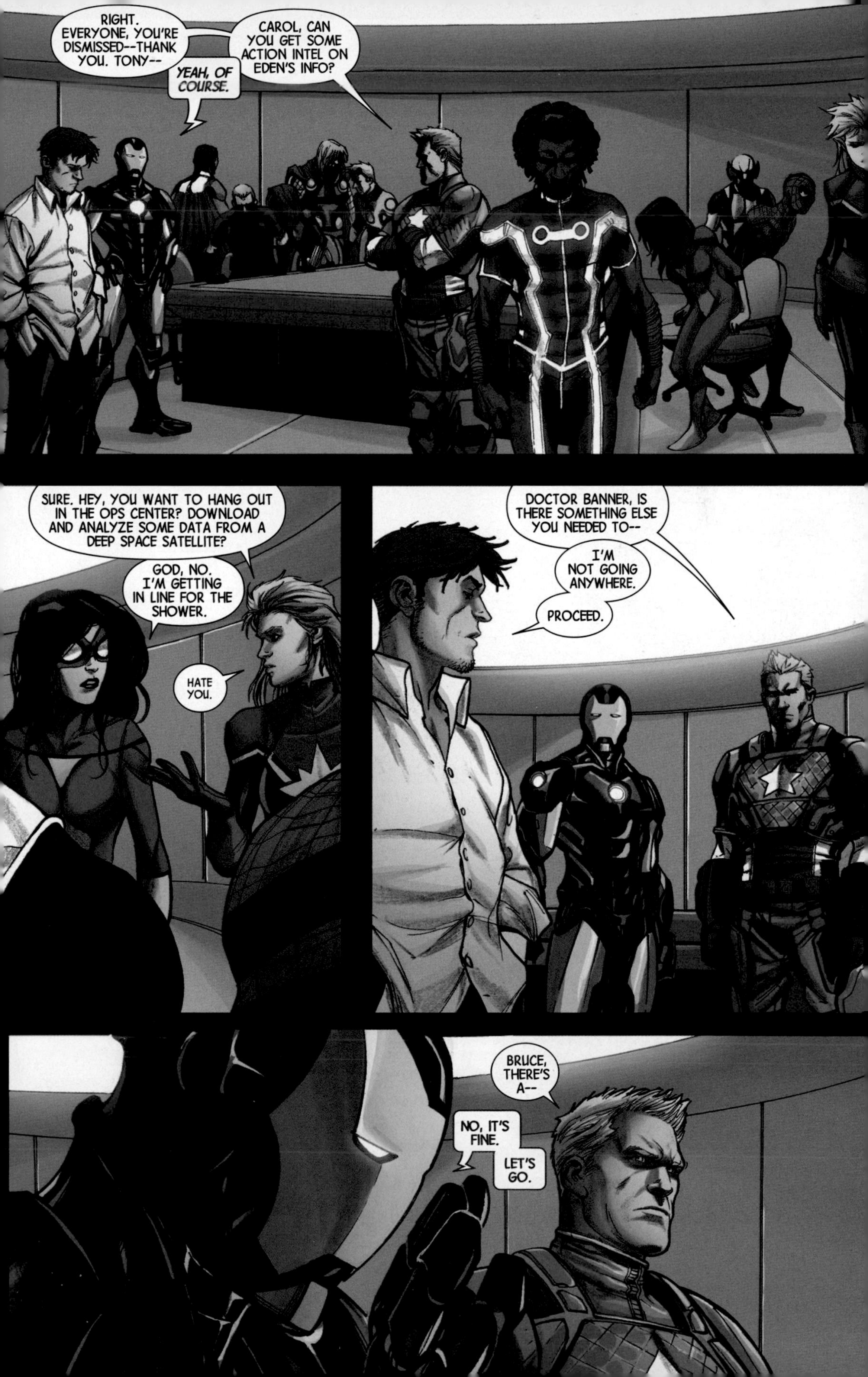
RIGHT. EVERYONE, YOU'RE DISMISSED--THANK YOU. TONY--
YEAH, OF COURSE.
CAROL, CAN YOU GET SOME ACTION INTEL ON EDEN'S INFO?
SURE. HEY, YOU WANT TO HANG OUT IN THE OPS CENTER? DOWNLOAD AND ANALYZE SOME DATA FROM A DEEP SPACE SATELLITE?
GOD, NO. I'M GETTING IN LINE FOR THE SHOWER.
HATE YOU.
DOCTOR BANNER, IS THERE SOMETHING ELSE YOU NEEDED TO--
I'M NOT GOING ANYWHERE.
PROCEED.
BRUCE, THERE'S A--
NO, IT'S FINE.
LET'S GO.

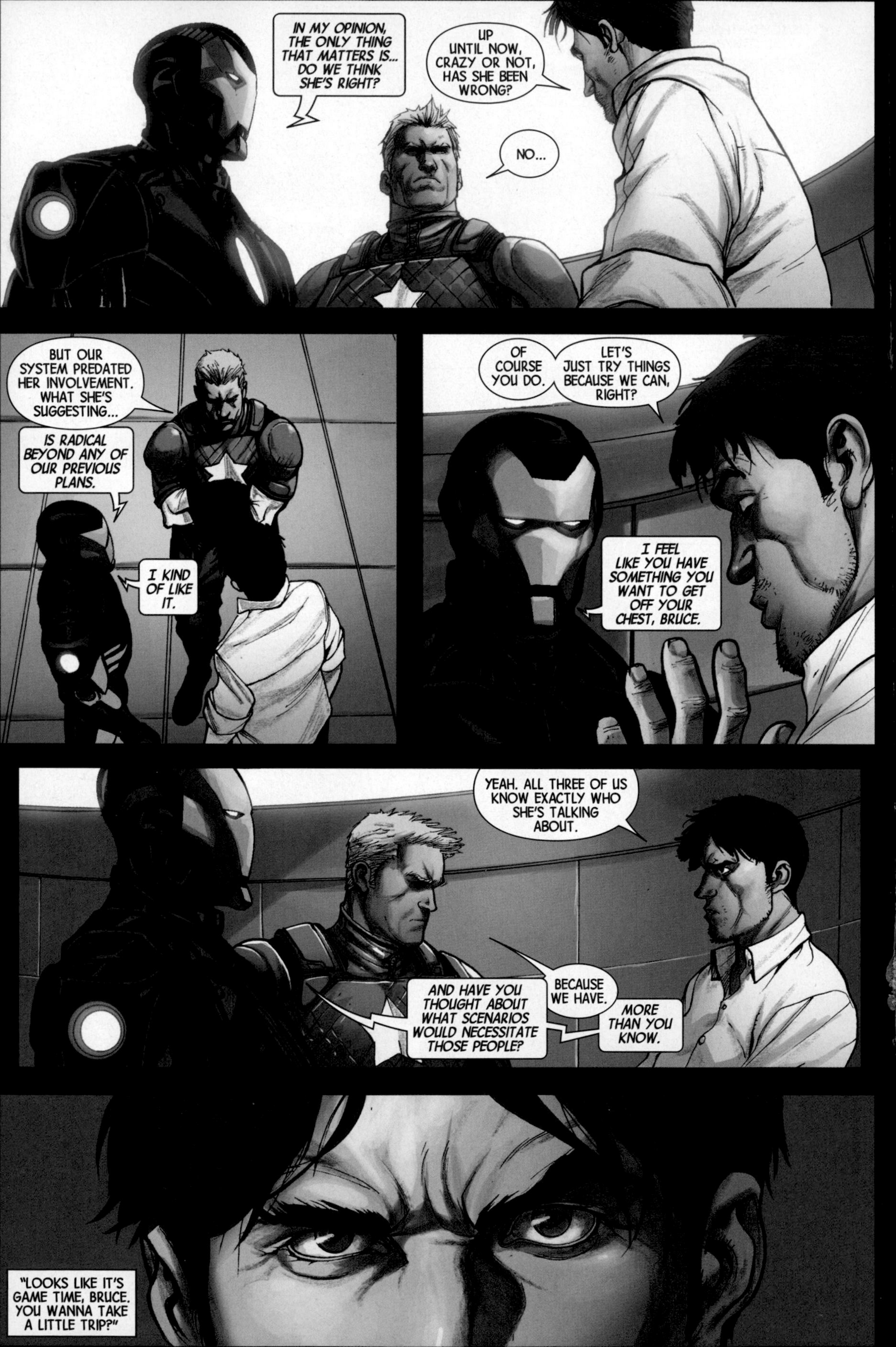
IN MY OPINION, THE ONLY THING THAT MATTERS IS... DO WE THINK SHE'S RIGHT?
UP UNTIL NOW, CRAZY OR NOT, HAS SHE BEEN WRONG?
NO...
BUT OUR SYSTEM PREDATED HER INVOLVEMENT. WHAT SHE'S SUGGESTING...
IS RADICAL BEYOND ANY OF OUR PREVIOUS PLANS.
I KIND OF LIKE IT.
OF COURSE YOU DO.
LET'S JUST TRY THINGS BECAUSE WE CAN, RIGHT?
I FEEL LIKE YOU HAVE SOMETHING YOU WANT TO GET OFF YOUR CHEST, BRUCE.
YEAH. ALL THREE OF US KNOW EXACTLY WHO SHE'S TALKING ABOUT.
AND HAVE YOU THOUGHT ABOUT WHAT SCENARIOS WOULD NECESSITATE THOSE PEOPLE?
BECAUSE WE HAVE.
MORE THAN YOU KNOW.
"LOOKS LIKE IT'S GAME TIME, BRUCE. YOU WANNA TAKE A LITTLE TRIP?"

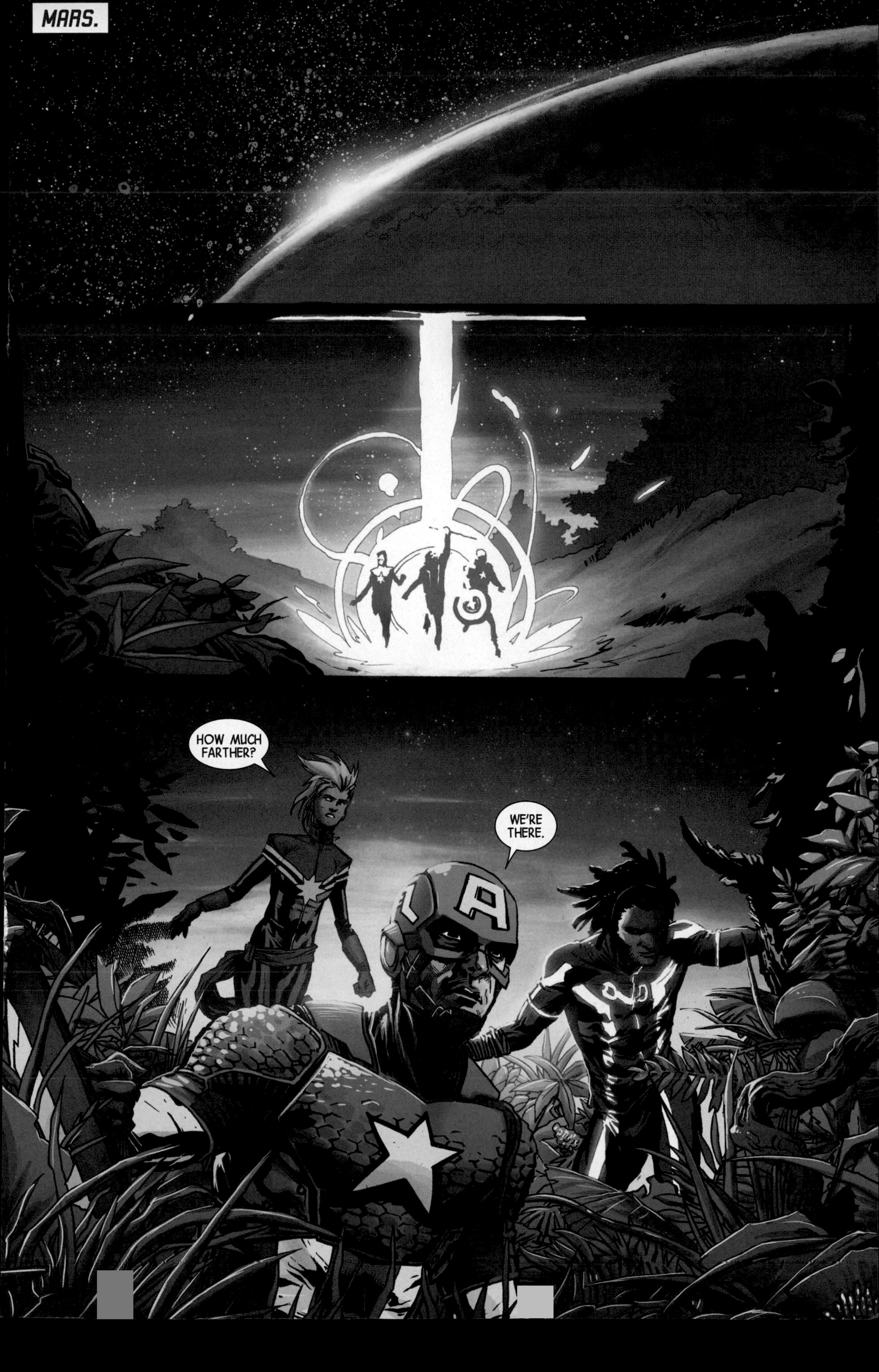
MARS.
HOW MUCH FARTHER?
WE'RE THERE.

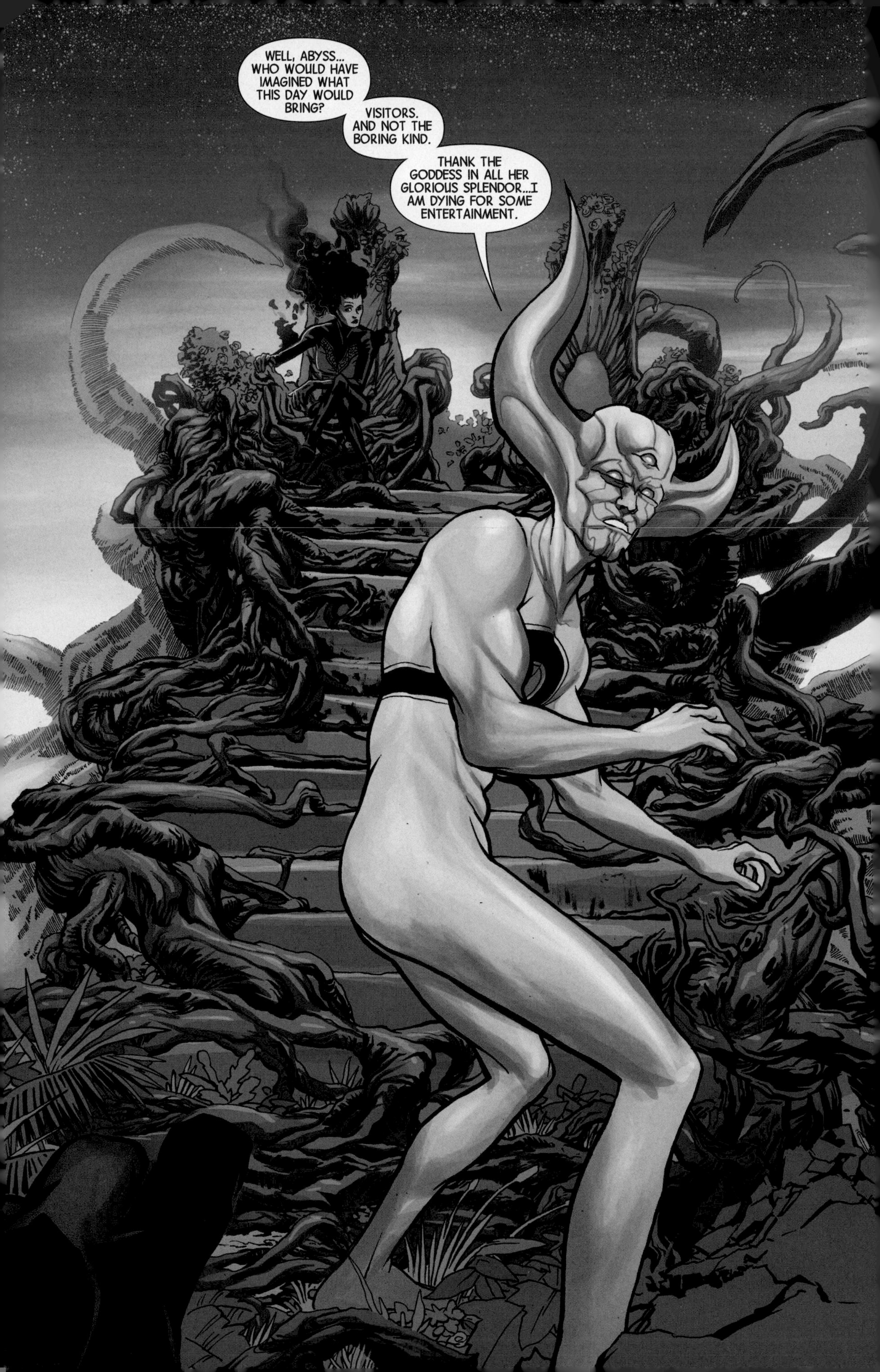
WELL, ABYSS... WHO WOULD HAVE IMAGINED WHAT THIS DAY WOULD BRING?
VISITORS. AND NOT THE BORING KIND.
THANK THE GODDESS IN ALL HER GLORIOUS SPLENDOR...I AM DYING FOR SOME ENTERTAINMENT.

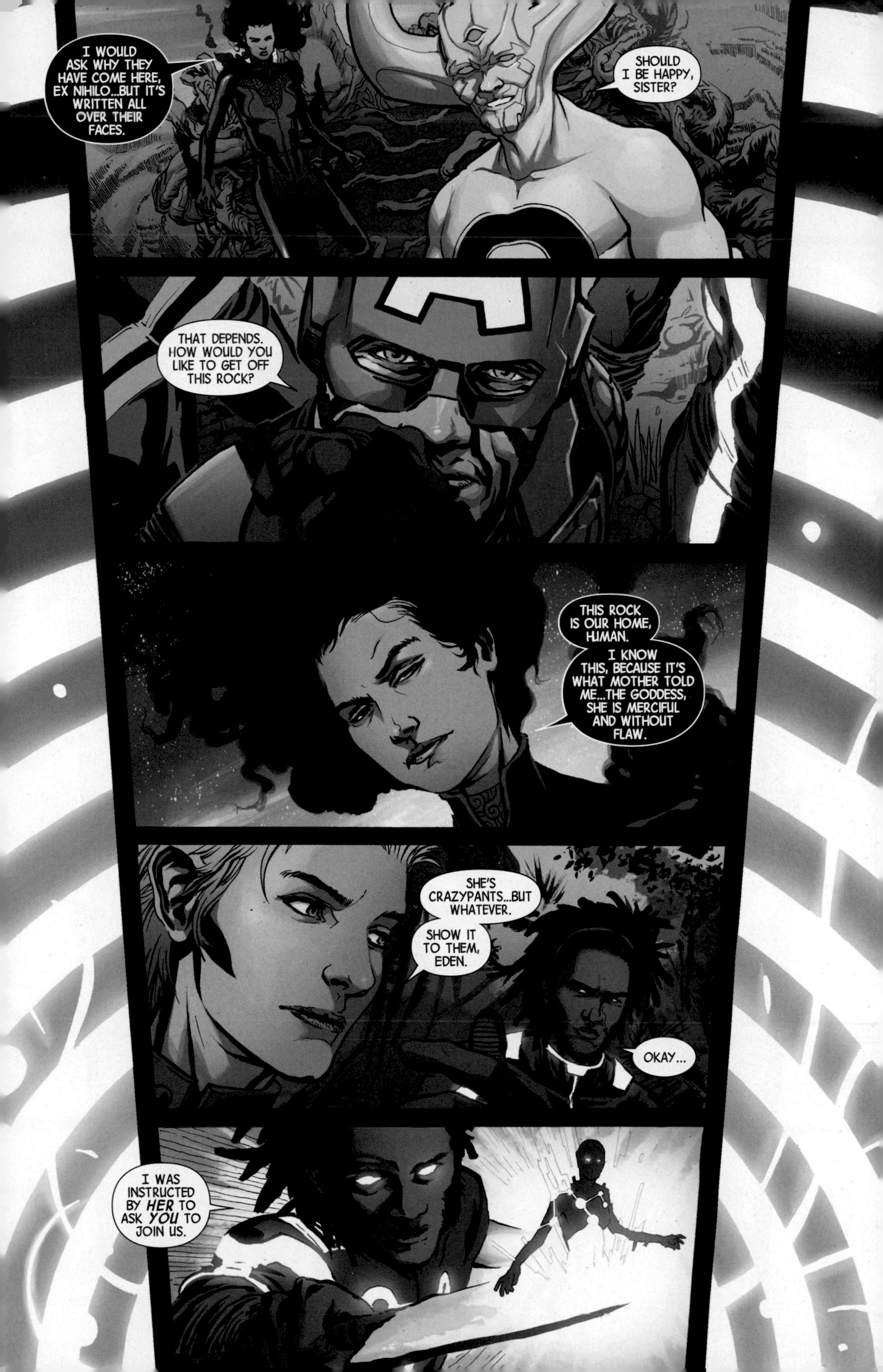
I WOULD ASK WHY THEY HAVE COME HERE, EX NIHILO...BUT IT'S WRITTEN ALL OVER THEIR FACES.
SHOULD I BE HAPPY, SISTER?
THAT DEPENDS. HOW WOULD YOU LIKE TO GET OFF THIS ROCK?
THIS ROCK IS OUR HOME, HUMAN.
I KNOW THIS, BECAUSE IT'S WHAT MOTHER TOLD ME...THE GODDESS, SHE IS MERCIFUL AND WITHOUT FLAW.
SHE'S CRAZYPANTS...BUT WHATEVER.
SHOW IT TO THEM, EDEN.
OKAY...
I WAS INSTRUCTED BY *HER* TO ASK *YOU* TO JOIN US.

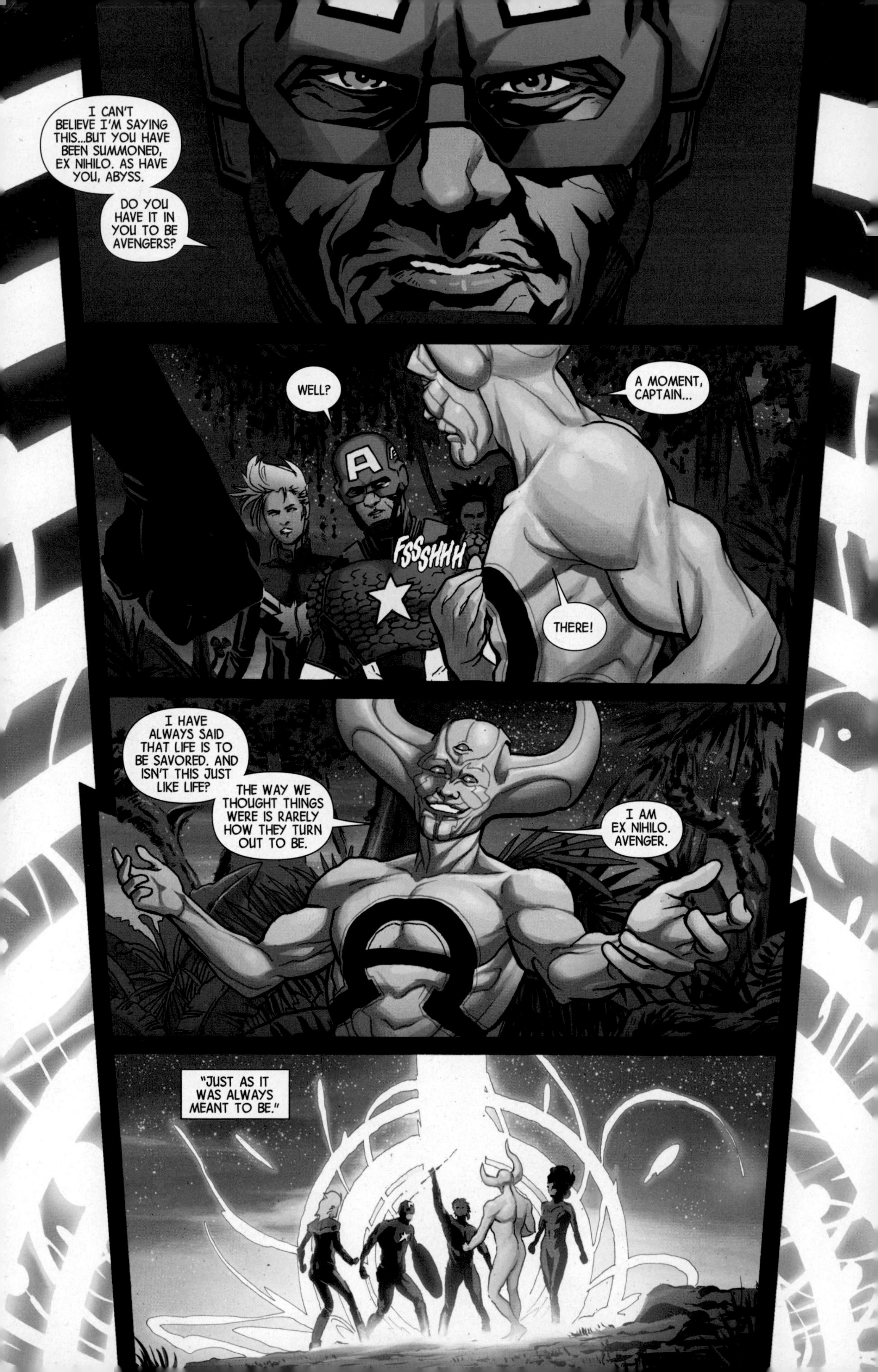

I CAN'T BELIEVE I'M SAYING THIS...BUT YOU HAVE BEEN SUMMONED, EX NIHILO. AS HAVE YOU, ABYSS.
DO YOU HAVE IT IN YOU TO BE AVENGERS?
WELL?
A MOMENT, CAPTAIN...
FSSSHHH
THERE!
I HAVE ALWAYS SAID THAT LIFE IS TO BE SAVORED. AND ISN'T THIS JUST LIKE LIFE?
THE WAY WE THOUGHT THINGS WERE IS RARELY HOW THEY TURN OUT TO BE.
I AM EX NIHILO. AVENGER.
"JUST AS IT WAS ALWAYS MEANT TO BE."

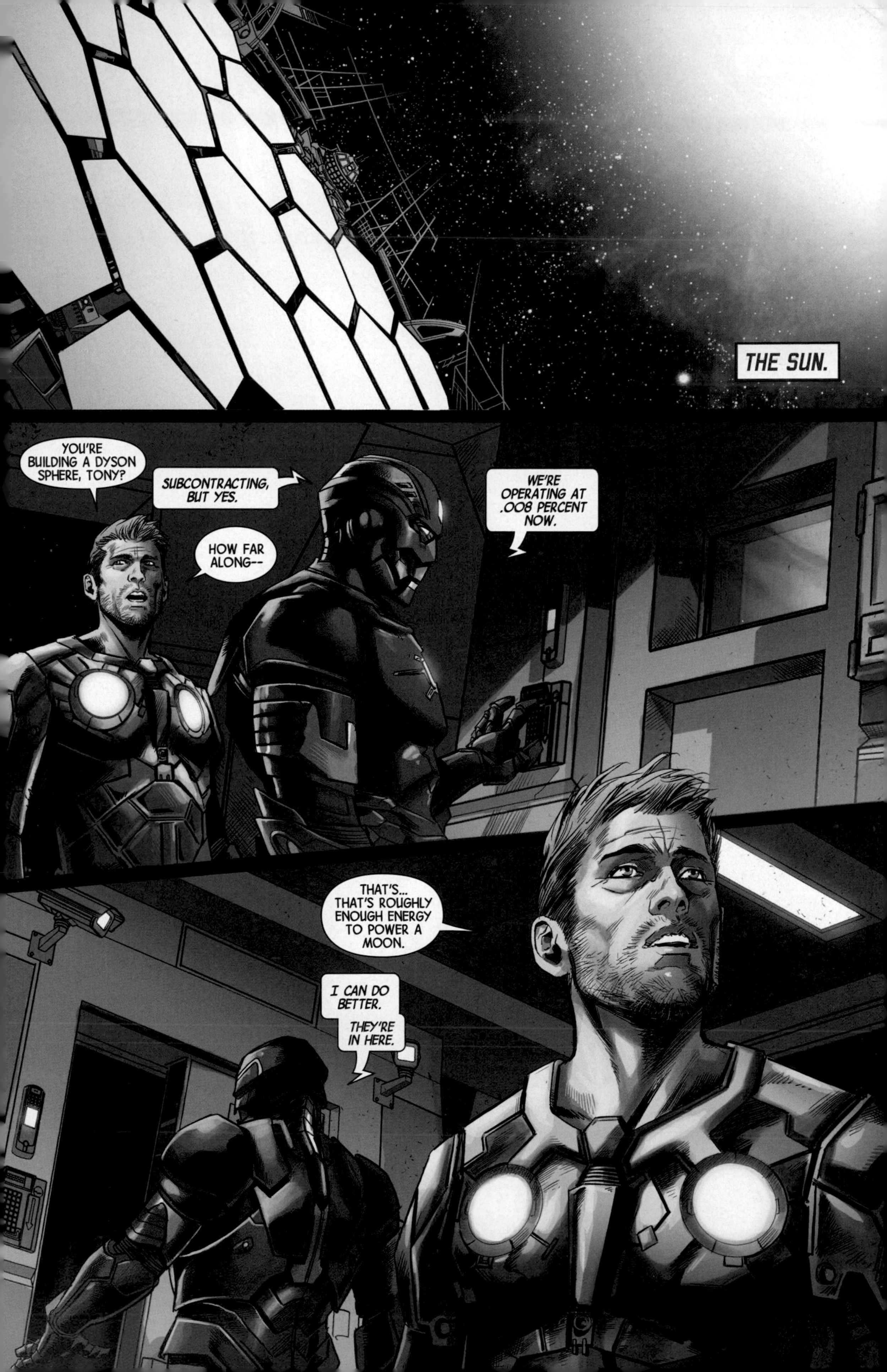
THE SUN.
YOU'RE BUILDING A DYSON SPHERE, TONY?
SUBCONTRACTING, BUT YES.
HOW FAR ALONG--
WE'RE OPERATING AT .008 PERCENT NOW.
THAT'S... THAT'S ROUGHLY ENOUGH ENERGY TO POWER A MOON.
I CAN DO BETTER.
THEY'RE IN HERE.

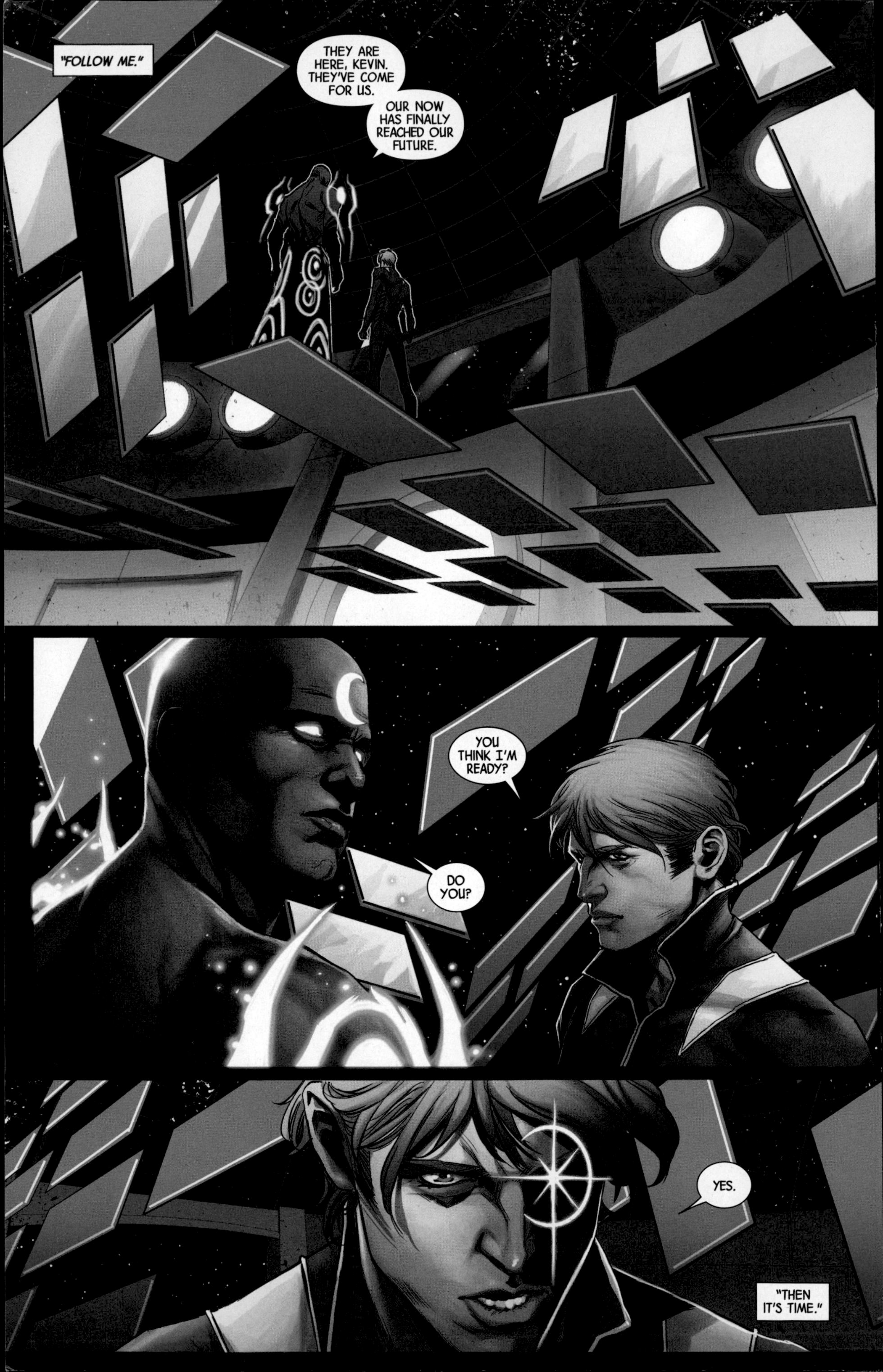
"FOLLOW ME."
THEY ARE HERE, KEVIN. THEY'VE COME FOR US.
OUR NOW HAS FINALLY REACHED OUR FUTURE.
YOU THINK I'M READY?
DO YOU?
YES.
"THEN IT'S TIME."

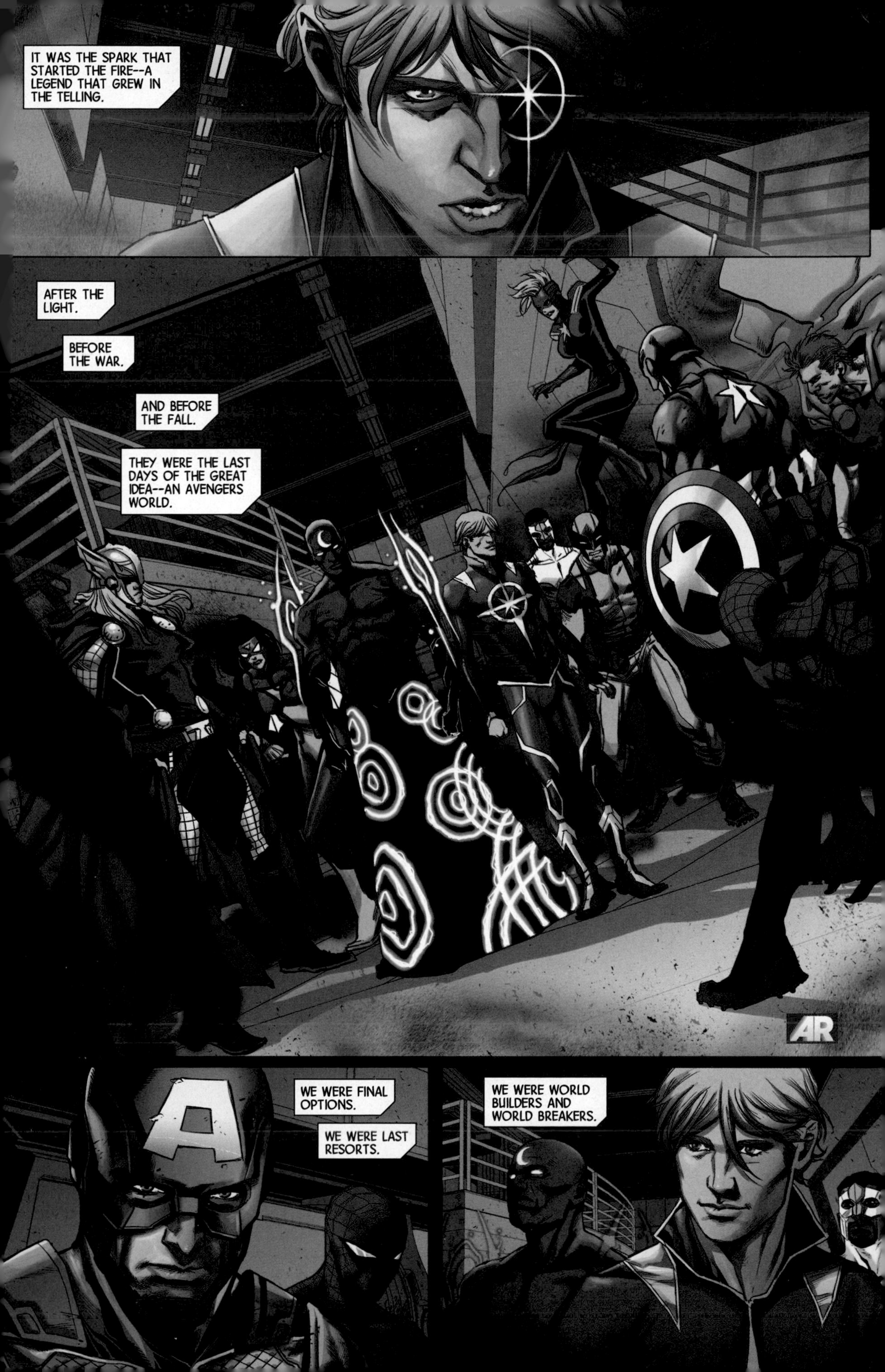

IT WAS THE SPARK THAT STARTED THE FIRE--A LEGEND THAT GREW IN THE TELLING.
AFTER THE LIGHT.
BEFORE THE WAR.
AND BEFORE THE FALL.
THEY WERE THE LAST DAYS OF THE GREAT IDEA--AN AVENGERS WORLD.
AR
WE WERE FINAL OPTIONS.
WE WERE LAST RESORTS.
WE WERE WORLD BUILDERS AND WORLD BREAKERS.

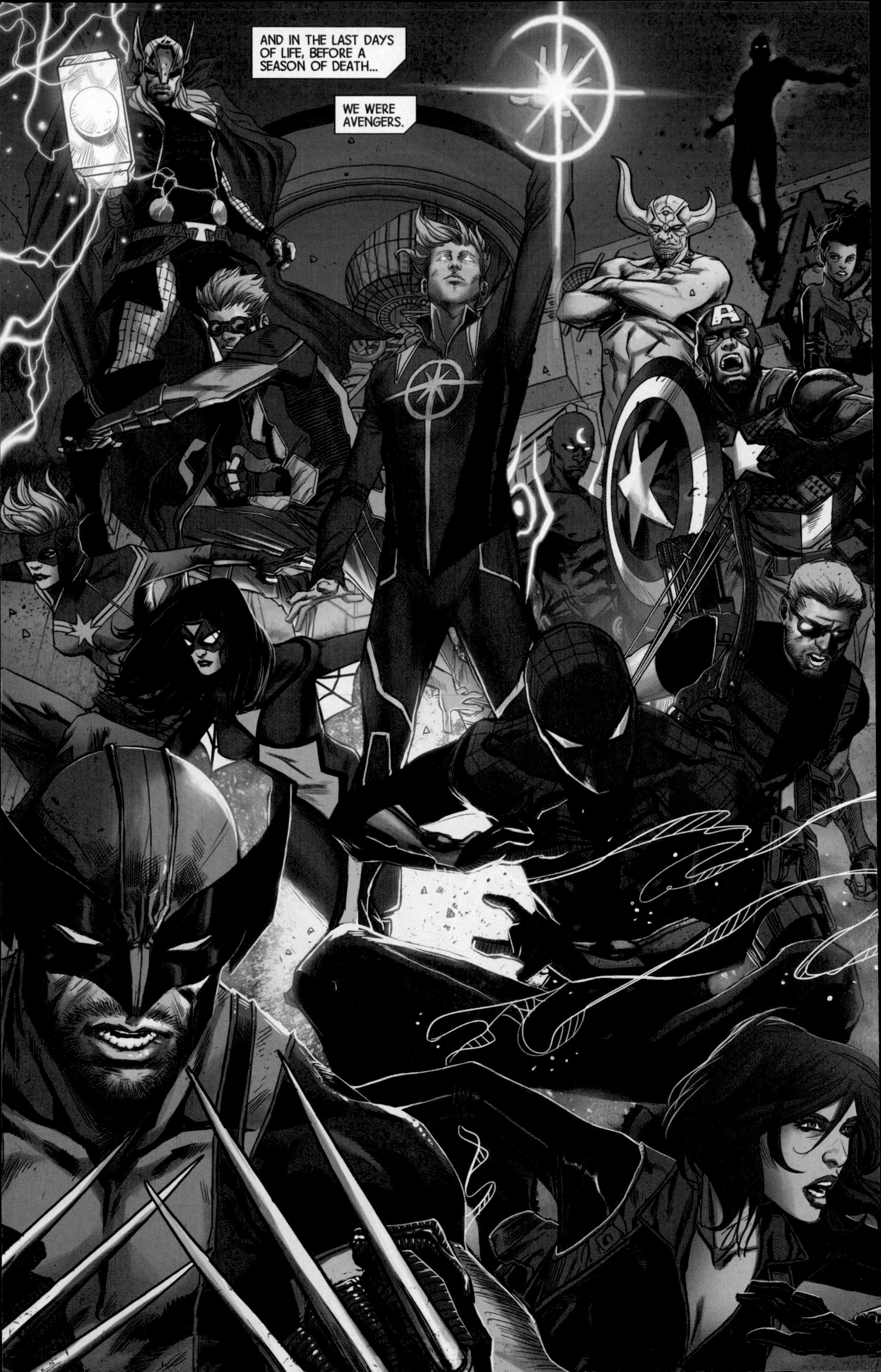
AND IN THE LAST DAYS OF LIFE, BEFORE A SEASON OF DEATH...
WE WERE AVENGERS.

END PRELUDE

COVER GALLERY

#12

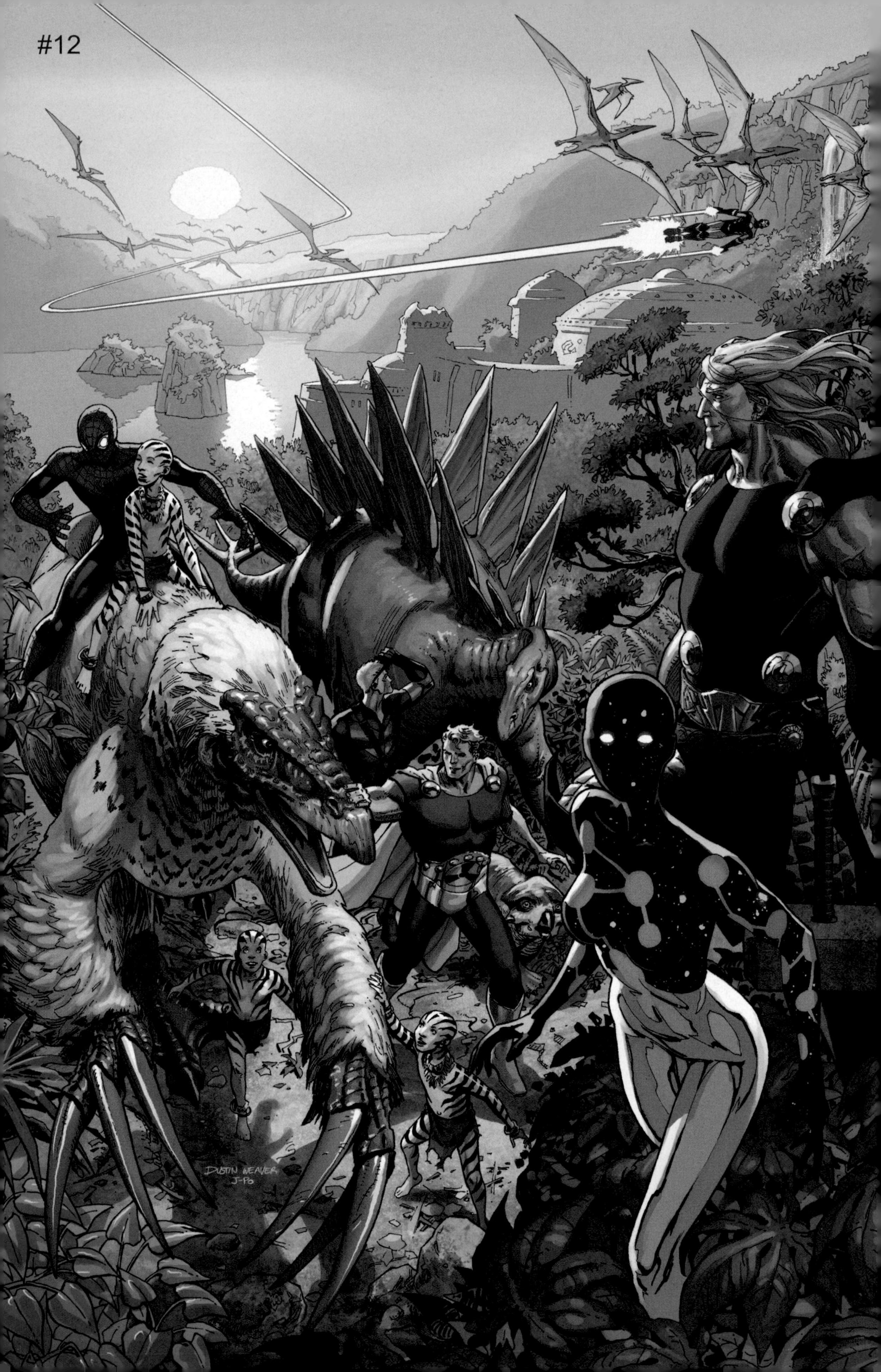
DUSTIN WEAVER
J-Po

#13

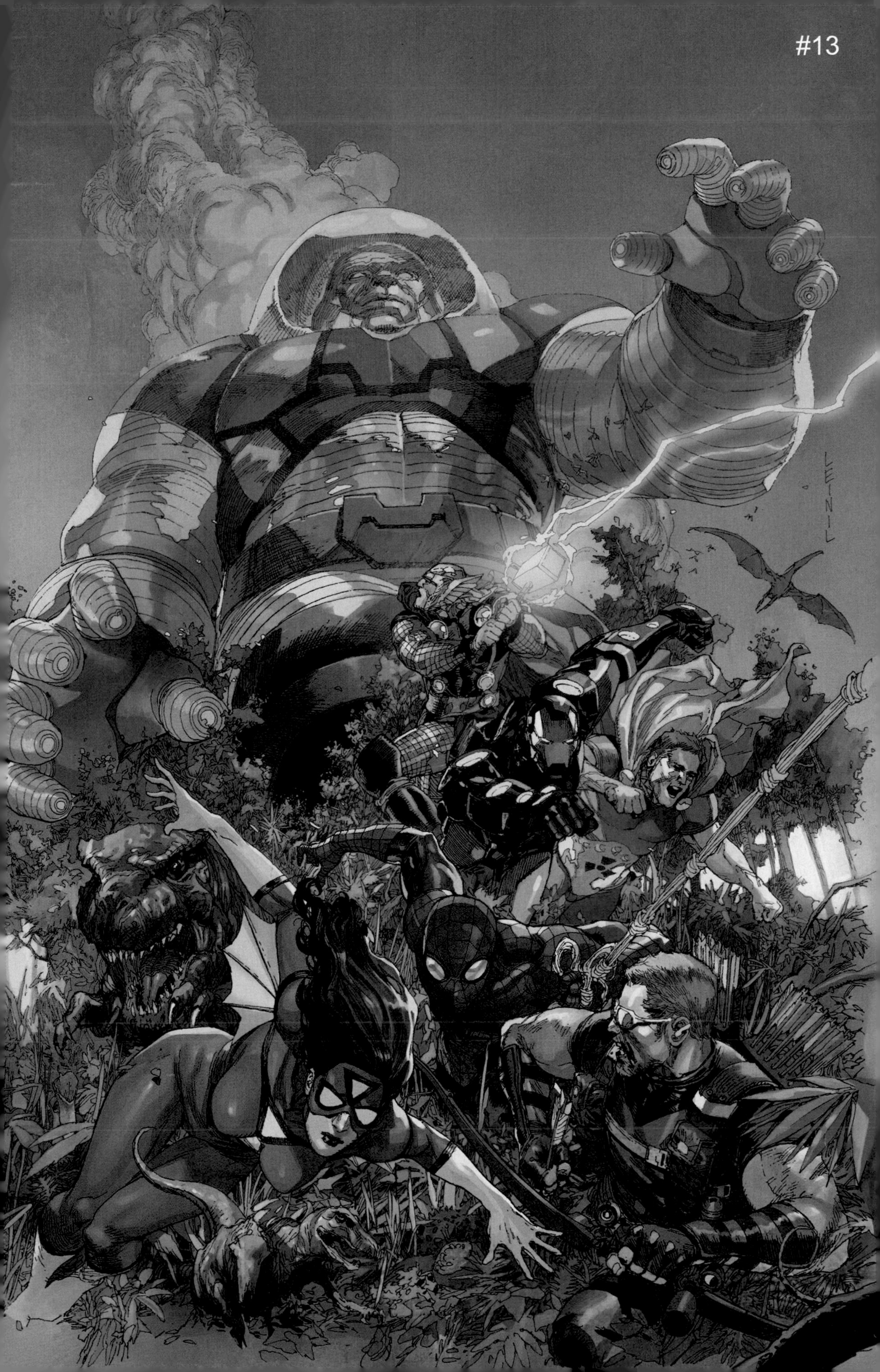
LEINIL

#14

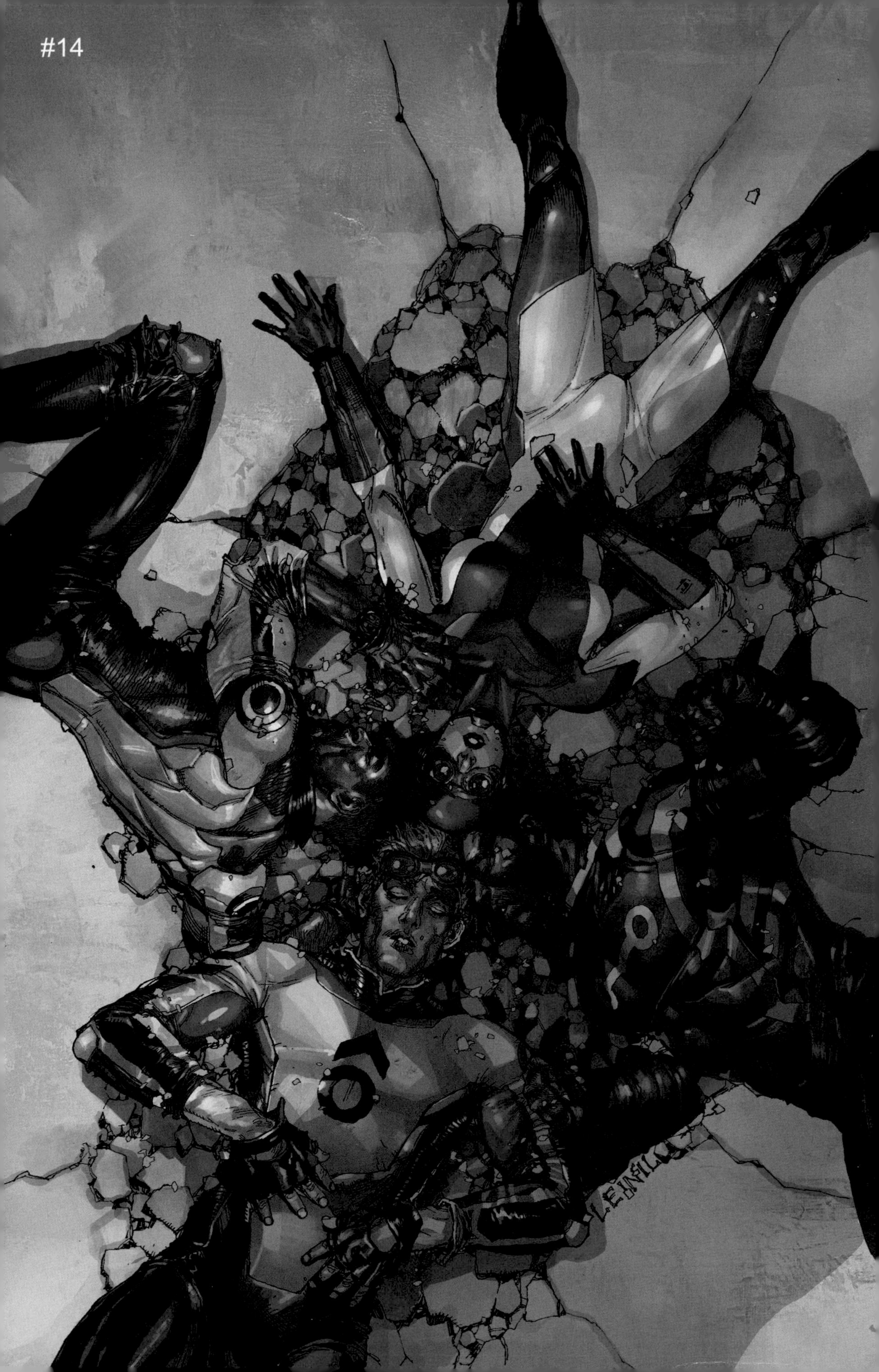

#15

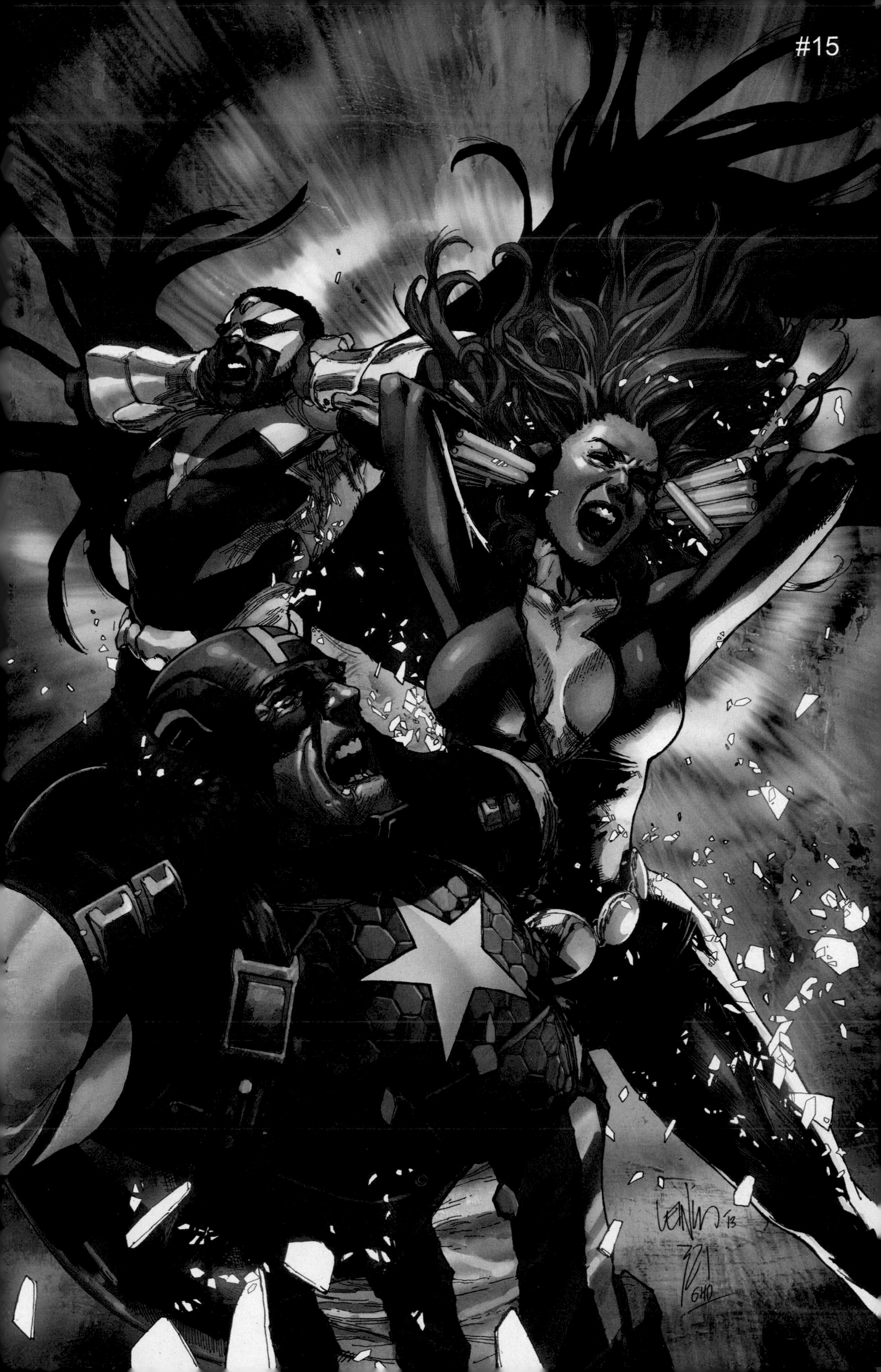

#16

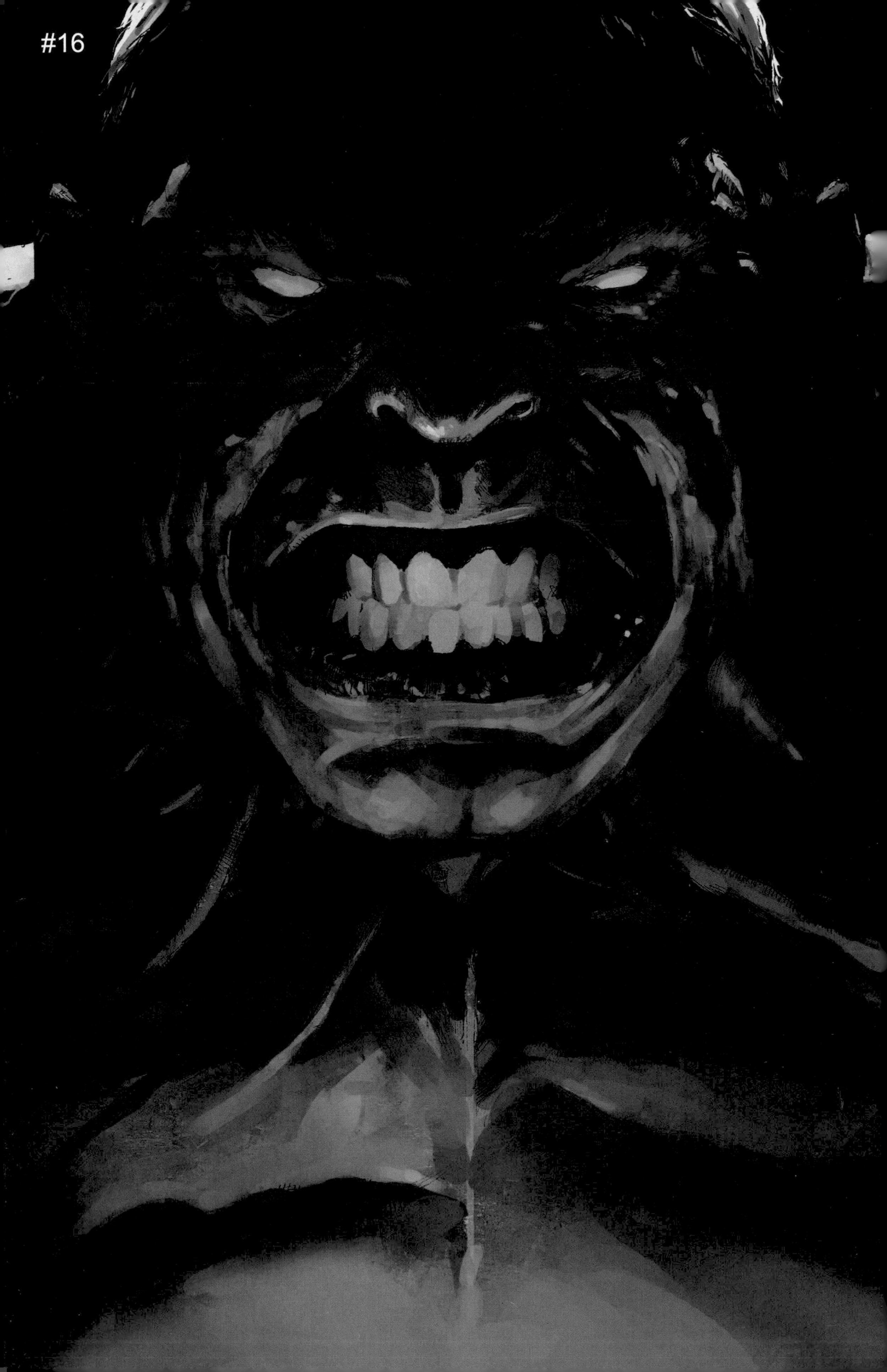

#17

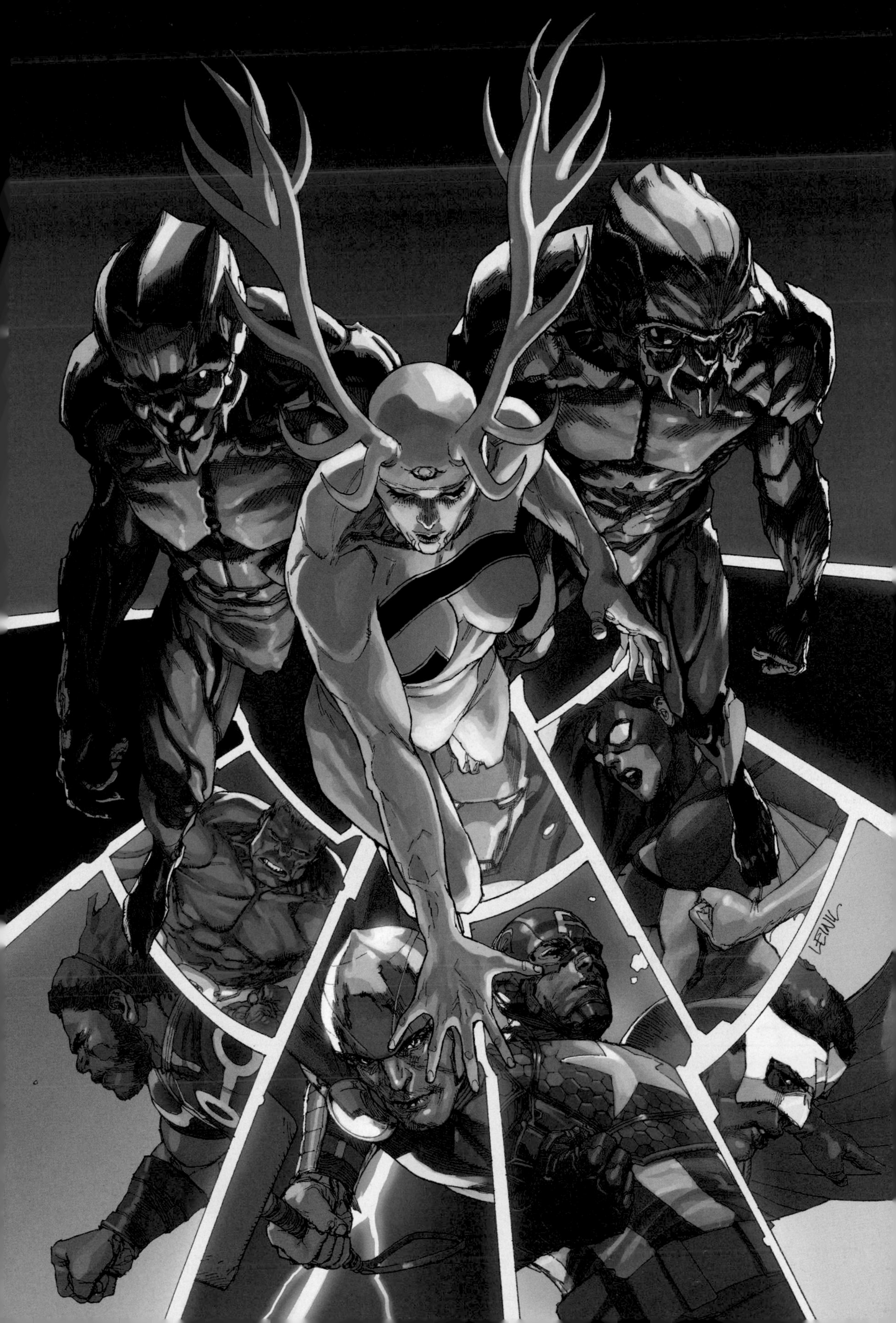

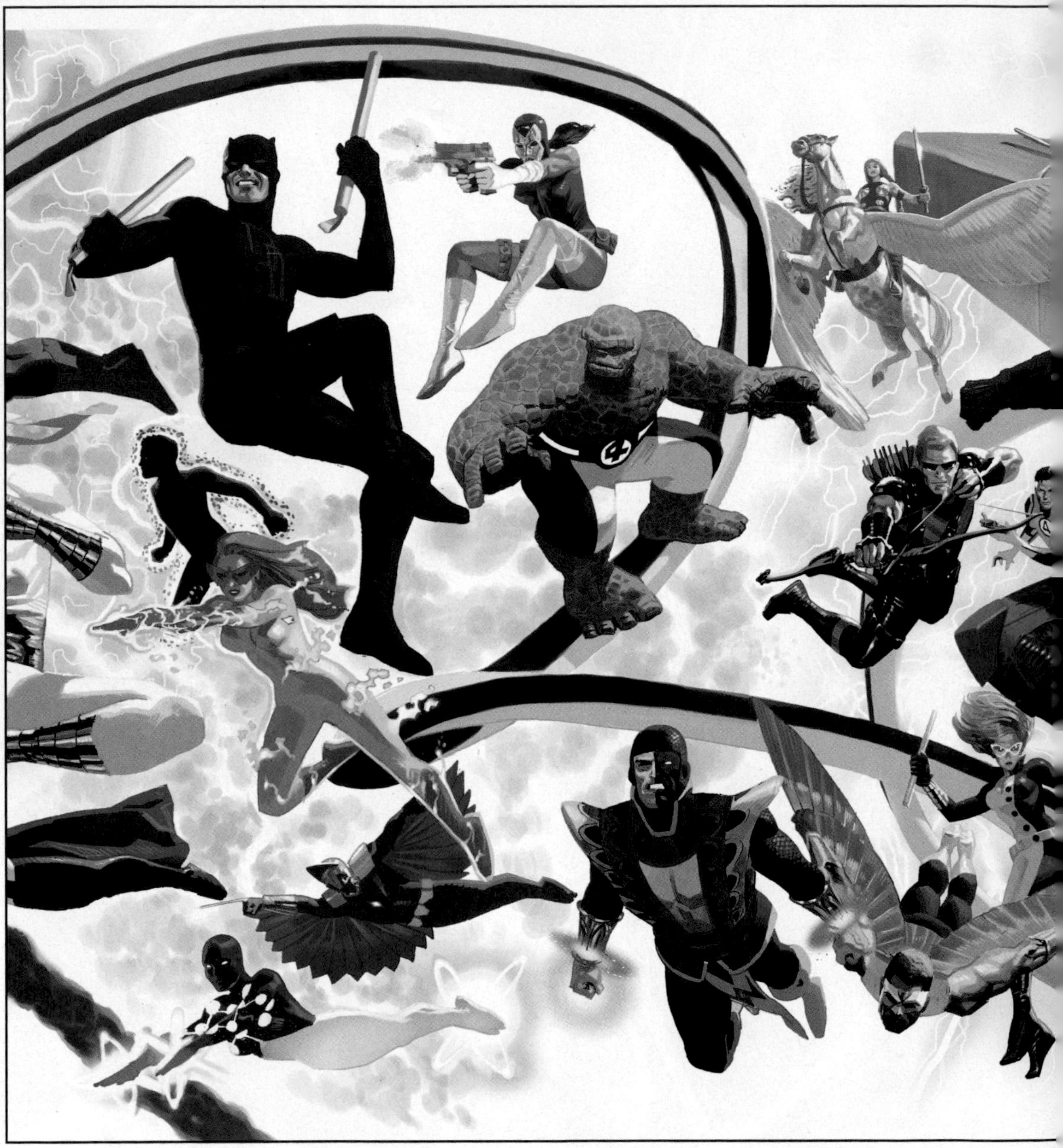

#12, #14 & #16 AVENGERS 50TH ANNIVERSARY VARIANTS:
DANIEL ACUÑA

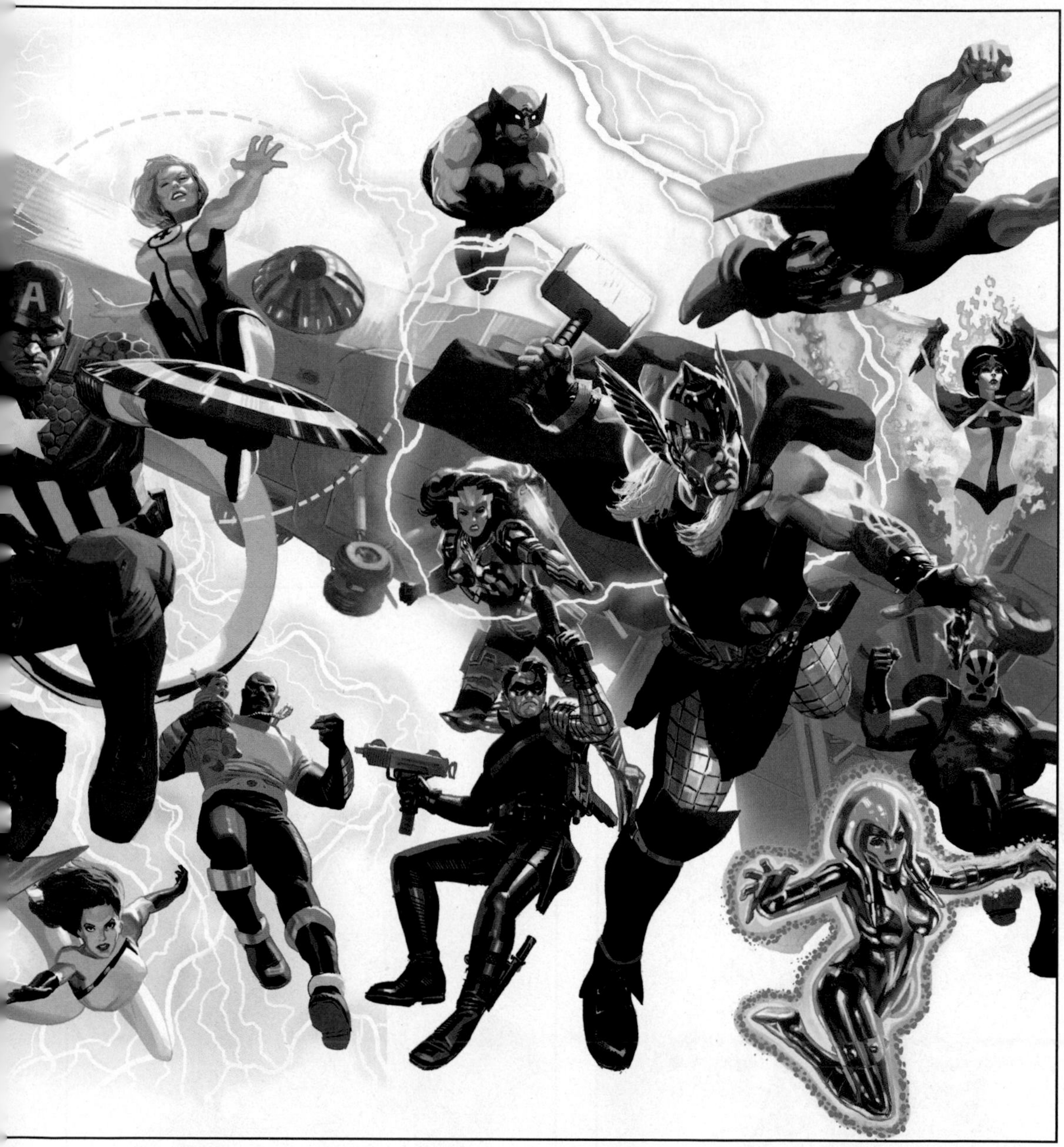

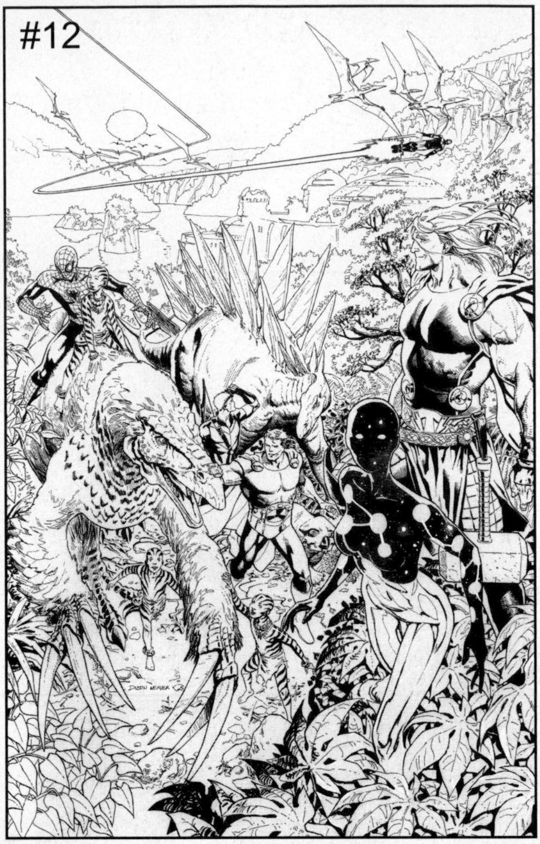
#12

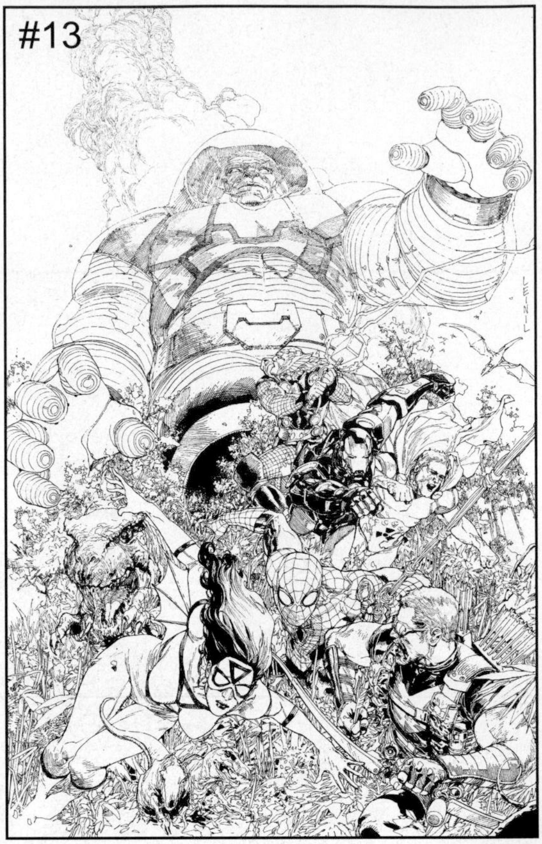
#13

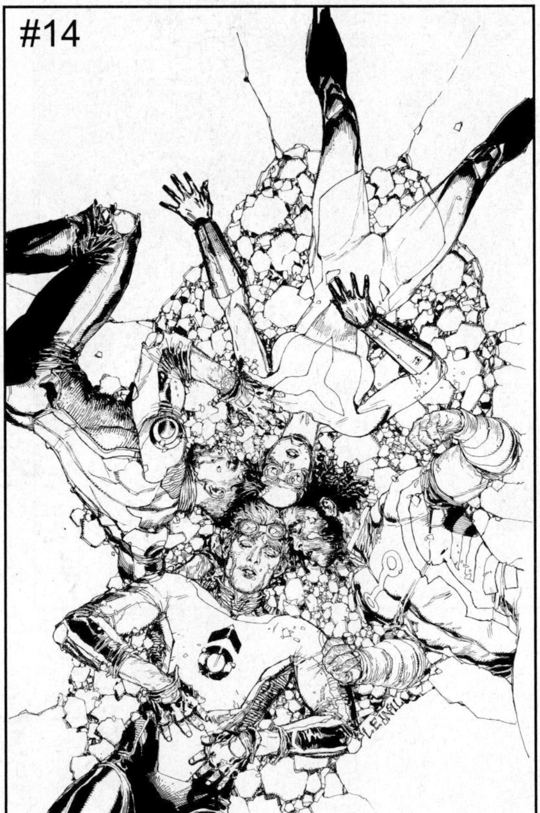
#14

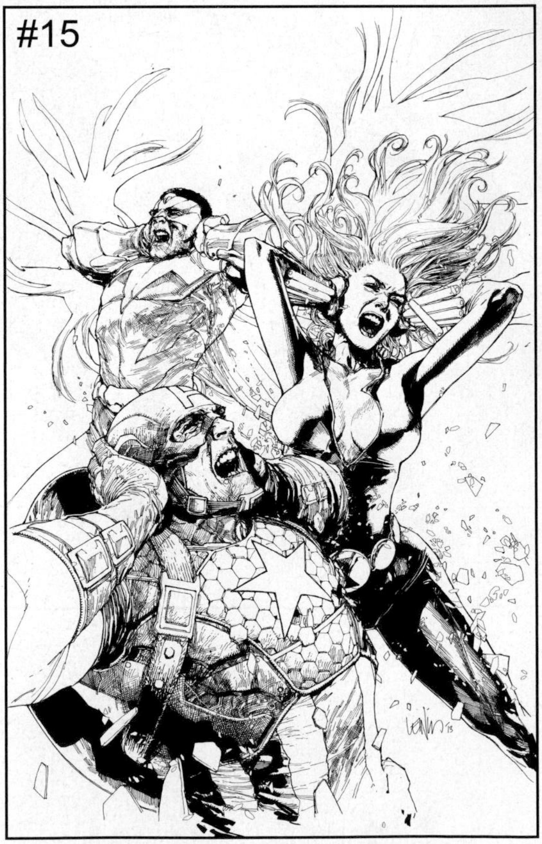
#15

COVER ART:

DUSTIN WEAVER (#12) & LEINIL YU (#13-15)

MARVEL AUGMENTED REALITY (AR) ENHANCES AND CHANGES THE WAY YOU EXPERIENCE COMICS!

TO ACCESS THE FREE MARVEL AR CONTENT IN THIS BOOK*:

1. Locate the **AR** logo within the comic.
2. Go to Marvel.com/AR in your web browser.
3. Search by series title to find the corresponding AR.
4. Enjoy Marvel AR!

*All AR content that appears in this book has been archived and will be available only at Marvel.com/AR — no longer in the Marvel AR App. Content subject to change and availability.

AVENGERS A.R INDEX